# AIRLINE PASIONADO

*Before, Braniff, and After*

Distributed by:

**Airlife Publishing Ltd**

**101 Longden Road, Shrewsbury SY3 9EB, England**

# AIRLINE PASIONADO

## *Before, Braniff, and After*

### Robert C. Booth

Paladwr Press

***Dedication***

*The decision to write this account came when Vanessa, my grand-daughter, said she wanted a copy of the Booth family tree, and this made me think how little I really knew about my own grandparents. So I am writing this for the grandchildren:  Shawnpaul, Vanessa, Nana, and Gandi.*

Published 1998 by Paladwr Press,
1906 Wilson Lane, Apt. 101, McLean, Virginia
22102-1957

Manufactured in the United States

Maps by R.E.G. Davies

Edited by R.E.G. Davies

Typesetting/Layout by Spot Color Incorporated

ISBN 1-888962-06-2

# Contents

# *Foreword*

In the early days of aviation, Latin America played a very important role with its diverse geography, long distances, and poor roads. Aviation was the perfect instrument for air transport development. Even though aviation continued to play a critical role in the region, it was not until recently that it became again a subject of great interest and involving major developments in the world. Bobby Booth has had much of the responsibility and can take much of the credit for putting Latin American aviation back in the headlines.

Bobby has been quite a visionary. He was advocating privatizations before the first one took place. He was preaching alliances before anybody even realized what they meant and he was predicting major management changes very early on.

There is no area of the world where the aviation business has evolved in recent times so quickly as in Latin America. In a period of ten years, all the airlines in the mainland continent have been privatized. There are more cross-equity alliances and partnerships than anywhere else in the world and the airlines have invested, grown, and succeeded to an extent that nobody thought possible. Bobby has been preaching these concepts day in and day out. The governments, leaders, and airlines have listened and the results are obvious.

No one knows the region from an airline marketing perspective better than Bobby and no one knows as many players in the Latin American aviation industry as he does. Bobby Booth has gained the friendship and trust of most of the airline chiefs and this has allowed him to influence developments in an unselfish manner, with the interest of both the airlines and the consumers at heart. We of the Latin American airline fraternity have much to thank him for.

*Federico Bloch*
*President & CEO*
*Grupo TACA*

# *Author's Preface*

This book of reminiscences started about 24 years ago as a work of fiction while I was commuting between my job at Braniff in Dallas and my family and home in Lima, Peru. I wrote about 100,000 words on a legal pad, on airplane rides (before laptops), mostly on Friday evenings: Dallas to Miami; the three- or four-hour layover in Miami; and Miami to Lima. Then on Sunday nights, the reverse process. The story line was about a guy who went to work for a major international airline in South America (fact), moved up in the ranks (fact), and then started his own airline called Air South America (fiction) which was the first multi-national Latin American airline before liberalization made it possible. He was a Bolivarian (fact) who believed in a united front, whether among airlines or, better still, among countries. This was before it all began to happen in NAFTA, the Andean Pact, Mercosur, and the Caricom in the Caribbean—after a fashion.

He was involved in a number of incidents, such as the Braniff hijack (fact) at El Alto in La Paz when Che Guevara tried to escape his destiny (fiction). He had played rugby (fact) against Che in Argentina (fiction) and when the hijack occurred, Che asked for his old rugby pal to negotiate (fiction). He was dedicated to the idea that people will rise to the occasion, given half a chance (fact) and established a management school in Lima called MAD-Management Arts Development (fiction) where he influenced some of the most important new breed managers and politicians. He was also involved in persuading South American nations to adopt a political union, called the Union of South America (fiction). This suggested the unlikely name of the book, "The Other USA." His other friends included the grandson of a President of Peru (fact), a communist member of Argentina's ERP (fact) and the first President of the Union of South America (fiction).

And then early in 1996 I decided, why write fiction when the truth is probably stranger, and may be, at least in the light of my lack of fiction-writing ability, more interesting. It also helps to be factual so that you are not confused with having to invent. So here it is: the story about the young guy who went to work for the dominant international airline in South America, Pan American World Airways, and then left to join Braniff, Pan Am's main rival. It is also about a personal passion with the airline business, with emphasis on the word business. Because in spite of a couple of extraneous interludes—my early experience as a cowboy, travel agent, and later as an advertising agency owner—the most fun and satisfaction have always come from working in and with airlines.

It is also a story about a passion for freedom and independence and being your own boss. And then it is a story about luck, because I have had incredibly good luck, in family and friends and the people I have worked with, for, and around. While I do not like apologies, either way, I believe that this might be a good time to make one: to all those people who are not included in this story but who contributed in so many ways to making the whole thing possible. If I listed every single person who either influenced, helped, or made a contribution one way or another, during close to 50 years of my professional life, this biography would fill several volumes. But I have not forgotten. If by any chance you read this story, please bear this in mind. In addition, I am sure that some of those mentioned may not agree exactly (or even entirely) with my view of the facts. Warts and all, this is my version of history with no apologies.

The story that follows is all based on personal experience. I have of course, checked other sources and people for accuracy, memory being what it is. It also tries to provide some insights into the people who had an impact on my own history and/or made the business so enjoyable. I have been lucky to meet many of the industry's most interesting personalities, not least of whom have been (at the risk of name-dropping) Tom Braniff, Lowell Yerex, Elmer ('Slim') Faucett, C.N. Shelton, Harding Lawrence, Ed Acker, Frank Lorenzo, Herb Kelleher, Howard Putnam, Bill Waltrip, Richard Branson, Sir Freddie Laker, Bob Crandall, and a host of others; also some presidents, dictators and revolutionaries who changed the course of history in Latin America, Rojas Pinilla, Alberto Lleras Camargo, and Guillermo Leon Valencia in Colombia; Galo Plaza in Ecuador; Fernando Belaunde Terry and Velasco Alvarado in Peru, and Che Guevara in Cuba.

The story is not finished yet, but I have brought it right up to the present, almost. It is about success, failure, and just plain survival. It might have been better in the reverse order. On the other hand, I like to tell young people that you need to fail sometimes just to enjoy life. I also believe in the British school upbringing (which is very un-American) that you have to be a good looser. Having tasted success early on, and then failure, survival seems all the sweeter. And what the hell, I may yet do the fiction version, which will have more sex, mayhem, and the way I would wish things to turn out. On the other hand, it might not necessarily be as rewarding or enjoyable as writing this.

Which, incidentally, is sort of the story of my life, enjoying what I do. I am certain that having fun has been an important ingredient of everything I have done. Another is that I have been incredibly lucky. I have a sign in my office which spells this out concisely and factually: "no amount of planning replaces dumb luck." This approach to life in general has carried me through periods of success and failure, and ultimately survival, in the corporate battle-grounds of a tumultuous industry.

While I have not written this as a management tract, it does serve, perhaps, to emphasize an underlying management approach which I suspect is worth mentioning. Good managers are people who love what they are doing and are less motivated by financial success than by personal satisfaction. Herb Kelleher, one of my heroes, says it best: "act like an owner." I also believe that getting things done through people, regardless of the job, can only be accomplished by being very, very people-oriented. I know many successful managers who are not, but they are smart enough to have surrounded themselves with those who are.

I have tried very hard to paint the picture as it happened and while I may have expressed strongly-held opinions, I have tried to support these with the facts. There are at least two sides to every story, but I have attempted wherever possible to verify and to confirm events with published reports and with the people themselves, many of whom have helped with suggestions and memory-jogging. However, I am sure that others who were involved have a different version, and that is all right. As I like to say, nobody's perfect.

*Robert C. Booth*
*Miami, 1998*

P.S. My word "Pasionado" in the title is a combination of "passion" and "Aficionado" which is clearly what I am all about.

RCB

# In the Beginning

Commercial aviation in Latin America, at least carrying passengers on a scheduled flight for hire on a sustained basis, began in Latin America about six years before the United States. Thus, as a South American-born aviation-bum, I feel it is only proper that I start out this personal history with a short account about the very early beginnings. With permission from R.E.G.Davies I am quoting (albeit edited, because the really interested reader should go to the original) from his book, published in 1983, *Airlines of Latin America since 1919* which has been, for many of us, the bible. I have used excerpts about some of the airlines that I knew or dealt with because some of these stories actually deserve a lot more attention than they have received. The following is the first of these, because I feel it might help to set the stage for my own story which follows:

## The Birth of SCADTA

*The oldest surviving airline in Latin America, indeed in all the Americas, is AVIANCA (née SCADTA) which was founded in Colombia in 1919. Several others were founded either just before or right after, but SCADTA/AVIANCA is the only one that has survived. Two days after the Colombian government had awarded airmail rights to C.C.N.A., a second airline was founded on 5 December 1919, the Sociedad Colombo-Alemana de Transportes Aereos (SCADTA). The group of eight founding fathers comprised five Colombian businessmen and three German residents. The heaviest investment was by Gieseking and Company, which nominated the chairman of the board, Alberto Tietjen. Prominent among the others were Ernesto Cortissoz, a Colombian banker, Cristobal Restrepo, and Werner Kaemmerer, a German engineer who was largely responsible for assembling the group....the capital was 100,000 pesos (equivalent at the time to the same in dollars)...On 20 September, 1920, SCADTA made its first survey flight from Barranquilla to Puerto Berrio (with two Junkers-F13 floatplanes). Dr. Peter Paul von Bauer, an Austrian industrialist was introduced to SCADTA in 1921 and he returned to Austria and sold his assets so as to invest in the enterprise. Scheduled services began between Barranquilla and Girardot, with an extension of some flights to Neiva on 19 September 1921. This date must be regarded as one of the most important in the whole calendar of events which comprises the world's history of commercial aviation*

# *Early Days*

I t all began in The Great War of 1914–1918 when my father, Edgar Booth—a native-born Brazilian whose father had come to the country as a ship's captain and settled there—left Brazil to join the Royal Flying Corps (R.F.C.), later the Royal Air Force (R.A.F.). In 1914 he had recently returned from nine years at Highgate, an upper-middle-class English Public School in north London. He was born in Porto Alegre in 1889 and had been sent to that boarding school at the age of seven or eight. After the war, my mother, Alice, joined him in England and he drove a London taxi—the only job he could find—for a couple of years before returning to Brazil. He went to work in his father's coastal shipping business, the Lamport & Holt steamship agency, which operated tug boats and barges which carried freight to and from the sea port at Rio Grande up the sea-lake to Porto Alegre and probably elsewhere.

During the war he flew Bristol Fighters in France. I do not know that much about his war experience nor if he shot down any Germans. With typically British reserve, he was not very talkative, about the war. But I used to have a picture (I have since lost it, damn) of him standing outside a hangar by his Bristol with its machine guns mounted right behind the propeller. I wondered at the time why he did not shoot the prop off when he pressed the trigger—he did tell me that this happened occasionally.

His father, Charles, had been a ship's captain in the sailing days. Born in Chester, he had run away to sea when he was 12 or 13 and then signed on and graduated from H.M.S. *Conway,* a British Navy training ship. Later on he became a captain with the Liverpool-based Lamport & Holt Line. He was

*My father, Edgar Booth.*

1

married to Jenny Adelina, who I think was born in Spain (which would explain my love-affair with bullfighting). Some of the Booths lived in Wales, one went to Natal, another was sheriff of Cheshire, and another was a Member of Parliament. I was never able to find out if we were related to John Wilkes Booth who shot Lincoln or the Booths of the Booth Line which sailed up the Amazon to Iquitos during the 19th century. Or, most unlikely, General Booth of the Salvation Army.

The following is summarized from the 1996 edition of "The South American Handbook":

> **Rio Grande do Sul, Brazil**—This is the distinctive land of the gaucho, or cowboy, of the flat black hat, of bombachas (the baggy trousers worn by the gaucho), of the poncho and ximarao (or mate without sugar), the indispensable drink of southern cattlemen. There are many millions of cattle, sheep, and pigs, and some 75% of all Brazilian wine comes from the state. Its population (who all call themselves gauchos) now number over 9 million. Rio Grande do Sul has the highest literacy index in Brazil.
>
> During the colonial period, wars with the Spaniards of Uruguay were frequent, and the Portuguese government introduced a number of military settlers from the Azores, and who inter-married with the Brazilian herdfolk in the area. The Jesuits built several settlements to acculturate the local Indians; relics of this process include the impressive ruins of the "Sete Povos das Missoes Orientais." At São Leopoldo, north of Porto Alegre, a group of Germans were settled in 1824 on their own small farms, and during the next 25 years, more than 20,000 more were brought into the area by the Brazilian Government.
>
> Porto Alegre, capital of Rio Grande do Sul, lies at the confluence of five rivers, which flow into the Rio Guaiba and thence into the great fresh-water lagoon, the Lagoa dos Patos, which runs into the sea, it is the most important Brazilian commercial centre south of São Paulo.

## *My Grandfather Invents a Job*

My grandfather had ended up in Rio Grande do Sul in the south of Brazil, which he liked and somehow talked the company, Lamport & Holt Line, into making him their agent and then started a tugboat and barge service between Rio Grande and Porto Alegre in the Lagoa dos Patos.

My mother, Alice, was also born in Porto Alegre, second generation Brazilian. Her grandfather, old man Hoffman, came from Hamburg. Her father was in banking, and may have helped to finance VARIG in its early days.

I was born in 1928 (the same year when several famous airlines were founded, such as Braniff Airways, Panagra, Faucett in Peru, and several others). My father was almost 40. My older brother, Ronald, was seven years older.

Dad was a terrific guy, he was just under six feet tall, and walked pigeon-toed, not unlike many soccer players I have known. He smoked and liked a drink and people loved him. He made friends with all kinds, from truck drivers to ambassadors. He was popular at all levels and I may have inherited some of this knack. My older brother, Ronald was the brainy one, I think from my mother's side. He wore glasses as long as I can remember, but was always the brother with the good looks; later in life people said he looked a little like Errol Flynn. He was also very good with engines and could fix anything, just like the old man.

## Soccer & Gambling

About the time I was born, Dad had some kind of major financial trouble. My grandfather had left the business to my father who was, according to all reports, something of a gambler. He was also a star soccer player, playing for *Gremio*, the leading professional team in Porto Alegre and also for Brazil in the 1920s. As Ronald told me years later, the old man gambled away the business and then lost his house on swanky Tristeza Beach (just outside town) in a poker game. My gambling had more to do with my jobs and career than with his kind of gambling.

Dad had to leave Brazil in something of a hurry (probably in the middle of the night, one step ahead of angry creditors) leaving my mother, brother, and myself with his wealthy brother-in-law, Arthur Bromberg, who was married to his sister, Dorothy. Interesting minor factor, while Dad was fighting the Germans in the air, his brother-in-law was an officer in the German crack cavalry regiment, 'The Death Heads Hussars.' The Brombergs then took us to Germany for a couple of years where I scared everyone that I was dumb because I did not speak until I was three or more. Later I developed the theory that anyone who grows up in a multilingual environment (in my case Portuguese, English, and then German) simply does not know which language to use, and is therefore reluctant to speak any of them. Somewhere around 1930, Dad had landed back on his feet with Shell Mex (as it was called in those days) as Depot Superintendent in Junin, Argentina, and he sent for the family.

Ronald stayed on as he was enrolled in some fancy private school. The Brombergs were supposedly "old" German money, and decided to leave in 1933 when Hitler came to power. Ronald had the edge on me in that he spoke fluent German for the rest of his life.

My early recollections are of Junin. I really cannot remember the German period or anything before that. Junin, incidentally, was Evita Duarte's birthplace. She became famous as Evita Peron, and more recently as plain Evita. Junin memories are of an English club at the town's waterworks, where there was a swimming pool and I remember my pal Fred Deakin sitting on an ant hill and getting bitten. He has had ants in his pants ever since.

In 1933 Dad was transferred to Paysandu in Uruguay where Ronald joined us for a short while before being sent to St. George's, Argentina's equivalent of an English public school. Paysandu was great, about 25,000 population at the time, the second largest city in the country, deep in cattle and grain country, on the Uruguay River, about 250 miles north of Montevideo, the capital. It was often called "The Heroic Paysandu", for its actions during the triple alliance war in the mid-1800s between Uruguay, Argentina, and Brazil on the one hand, and Paraguay on the other; or perhaps it had more to do with the early 19th Century rebellion against Brazil which had dominated most of Uruguay's history.

The city proper was on a hill overlooking the river and it had the second most important port in the country. It was across the river from Concepcion in Argentina. Paysandu was named after a Jesuit priest, Fray San (for saint) Du. Jose Gervasio Artigas, Uruguay's hero of the wars of independence with Spain, an interesting guy who had similar Bolivarian ideas about the need for a federation of independent states, also had a relationship with the city.

From the 1996 Edition of "The South American Handbook"

Uruguay is the smallest Hispanic country in South America, with the official name Republica Oriental del Uruguay. (See map).

The Spanish explorer, Juan Diaz de Solis, sailed up the Rio de la Plata in 1516 and landed east of the site of Montevideo, near what is now Maldonado. His second landing was in the present Department of Colonia, where he was killed by the Charrua Indians. With no gold or silver in Uruguay, only after about 1580 did the Spaniards show any interest in it. Military expeditions against the Indians were unsuccessful, but Jesuit and Franciscan missionaries, landing in 1624, founded a settlement on Vizcaino Island.

By 1680, the Portuguese in Brazil had pushed south to the Plata and founded Colonia as a rival to Buenos Aires, on the opposite shore. The Portuguese planned, but the Spaniards actually founded, the city of Montevideo in 1726. It changed hands several times and was also taken by the British in 1807, but after their failure to hold Buenos Aires, they withdrew altogether. In 1808 Montevideo declared its independence from Buenos Aires. The Argentines invaded again in 1812 and were able to enter Montevideo in June 1814. In January the following year the Orientales (Uruguayans) defeated the Argentines at Guayabos and regained Montevideo. The Portuguese then occupied all territory south of the Rio Negro except Montevideo and Colonia. The struggle continued from 1814 to 1820, but Artigas had to flee to Paraguay when Brazil took Montevideo in 1820. In 1825 General Juan Lavalleja, at the head of 33 patriots (the Treinta y Tres Orientales), crossed the river and returned to Uruguay, with Argentine aid, to harass the invaders. After the defeat of the Brazilians at Ituzaingo on 20 February 1827, Britain intervened. Both Argentina and Brazil relinquished their claims on the country, and independence was finally achieved in 1828.

Uruguay is a small country—less than 300 miles wide in any direction—but enjoys a thriving commercial economy, based mainly on its cattle ranching and beef exports.

## Growing Up and All That

The Shell Depot was on the outskirts of the city, by the river. It had its own pier and dock for the tankers which sailed up from Montevideo to fill the Depot tanks. At six or seven I was installed in the best Catholic school in town. But this did not last a year because I raised so much hell about catechism and Sunday school that my parents finally relented and enrolled me in Colegio Publico (not the equivalent of a British public school) Numero 8. Uruguay's public school system is one of the best in South America. It is also obligatory by law. If you do not attend a private school you must attend a 'Colegio Publico.'

Between seven and twelve I had a glorious life. In summer we would go to Santa Rita, the Campbell's 30,000-acre ranch just north of Quebracho river, about 35 miles from Paysandu. The British had several ranches ("estancias") in Uruguay and Santa Rita was one of the best. Arthur Campbell had a reputation for breeding the best Hereford cattle in the country and he was regularly invited to the Buenos Aires Palermo cattle show where he usually walked away with a grand prize. In Uruguay, he was called to judge cattle at the 'Prado' show in Montevideo every year.

## Playing Tom Sawyer

We spent a lot of time on the Uruguay River which separates Uruguay from Argentina and is about a mile and a half wide at this point. Dad had a small inboard motor/sail boat, about 18 feet long, called *Spoon Bait*, a replica of a lifeboat. We did a lot of trawling for dorado, a freshwater fish which fights like hell, with a spoon and line. Before I was nine or ten I would go out on the river on my own, with Dad's approval. He thought I should learn about boat handling and was not worried that I would get in to trouble.

One day, though, in a dead calm, the four-cylinder gasoline engine died on me. I drifted with the current, towards

*With my brother Ronald in* Spoon Bait, *October 1938.*

Fray Bentos, without oars. Fortunately a fisherman in a small boat agreed to tow me to the Shell jetty where we kept *Spoonbait* and I arrived home after dark. This created quite a stir as Dad had gone out looking for me in the club boat. Mum was cool but obviously very worried. I thought the whole thing was a great adventure.

The English expats—about five or six families—congregated at the Paysandu Golf Club which I think had been started by the railway for the expatriates who worked there. It had an 18-hole golf course and tennis courts. But the best part of it was hunting and shooting partridge, hare, pheasant, and duck at the *estancias* of my Dad's friends. I was a pretty good shot with a pair of 12-bore shotguns which I still have. They are lovely—double-barreled, old-fashioned hand-made (built in 1860). I also rode horses like a regular *peon,* straight-legged-long stirrups and all. A Mr. Gardner who had been in the Boer War, taught me to shoot and told me stories about the Boer War and the Boy Scouts, which was founded by a friend of his, Baden Powell. He also knew everything about sailing and taught me how to do knots, splice rope, and the names of all the sails on a full-rigged sailing ship.

## The Best Yorkshire Pudding in Paysandu

Mother was about ten years younger than my old man and very popular with everyone. The Booths entertained a lot and she was a great hostess. She cooked the best Yorkshire pudding and roast beef in Uruguay. Dad read to me almost every night from his favorites, which included everything from Mark Twain, *The Wind in the Willows* to Rudyard Kipling and Robert Louis Stevenson, G.A.Henty to the *William* books. Dad was an incredible mix of my three children, Valerie, Robbie, and Guy, or the other way around. He was mechanically oriented (Guy), a superb people-person (Robbie), and very thoughtful and literate (Valerie). I suspect he was quite artistic even though it never showed. Both Ronald and I could draw with considerable ease, while Valerie is a top-rate photographer.

## Off to School (and back)

When I was 12 my parents decided I should have an English education. They could not afford a second son at the expensive St. George's, even though my brother had left by this time and had somehow landed a job with Millington Drake, then Minister of Great Britain in Montevideo as a sort of secretary-cum-driver.

So I was sent to Montevideo to the British Schools to live with some old friends, the Deakins, who had moved there from Porto Alegre. Geoff Deakin had been in the Great War of 1914-18 and had ended up in Porto Alegre where he and Dad were good friends. He was with the British Embassy in Montevideo, and may have been in some kind of British intelligence service.

The Deakins had two sons, Freddie, who was my age (the ant-hill-sitter in Junin) and Francis a couple of years younger who were also enrolled at "The British" as it was known to every one. It was similar to schools in most of South America, and other parts of the world, subsidized by the British government which sent out English teachers to spread the word about "being British" to the sons, grandsons of British expats, and others who wanted to have an English public school-type education, play cricket, and generally learn to 'play the game', to be a good loser, and so on.

School was so-so. I did well in history and literature but failed everything else. I read everything I could find at the school library, from Hemingway to Shakespeare. Mr. Hobson was my favorite master, he loved books and we became pretty close, but I did not do too well in anything else. I could not stand cricket, but was on the boxing team and was lightweight champion of the school at 15.

## Sacked

Just before the end of the term, as the summer holidays were about to begin, and a year away from doing my school certificate exams which were sent to England for grading, the headmaster, a Scot named Ogston, suggested to my father that he was wasting his money keeping me in school. He called me in to his study to tell me about it: "Booth, you're not going to come back next year. I have talked to Mr. Booth, Senior, and he agreed that you would be better off doing some thing useful, like working, because you're not only wasting your time but also ours, here at the school."

He had been in the Great War in a Scottish regiment. He was a tough wiry guy with a military walk and mustache and short cropped hair going gray. When he spoke everyone listened, mostly because he scared the daylights out of you. I mumbled something and left his office as fast as I could.

## Post-graduate Education

I went back home for Christmas and Dad and Mum met me at the train station, and we all piled in to the Studebaker. "Bobby, what the hell do you want to do with yourself?" was his opening remark. I was 15 going on 16 and I really did not know the answer. But I thought I had better give it a shot: "I really don't want to go back to school, I feel that I should try to get a job somewhere and start earning a living."

Dad stopped the car, we were on the dirt road from the station to our house which bypassed the town of Paysandu, turned off the ignition and faced me, I knew something important was coming.

"Bobby, your Mum and I have been talking to Arthur Campbell about a job this summer at Santa Rita. Arthur said he'd love to have you but you are going to have to work like a regular peon. He's agreed that you can start the first of the year, so what do you think? It won't be like a holiday, you'll be expected to pull your weight just like everyone else."

I tried not to show my excitement, this was the best idea I had heard since Oggie called me in to his office to tell me that I was being sacked. At dinner we had roast leg of lamb which was my favorite (complete with freshly made mint sauce from Mum's garden) and Dad poured me a small whisky and water after dinner.

"Dad, I think it would be nice to work at Santa Rita; will I get paid?"

Dad said I would be getting the same as the peons, 2 pesos a day plus food and keep. I then asked: "What do you think, Dad, I'd rather work than spend the summer bumming around." He laughed and said: "I agree and if you don't want to stay at the end of March maybe I can convince Mr. Ogston to take you back for another chance."

I smiled to myself and wondered if that was the deal with Oggie. Maybe they thought I'd have second thoughts about school after a rough summer on the estancia.

So I spent Christmas at home, and Ronald was home for the holiday. He had been taking flying lessons in Montevideo and I knew he wanted to join up (this was 1943) even though his glasses would stop him from the Royal Air Force. Over the holidays he and I spent some time on *Spoonbait* fishing for dorado and talking about what he was going to do. He was 22 and wanted to fly and had found out that he could sign on with the Air Transport Command (A.T.C.) ferrying planes across the Atlantic, but he had not told our parents because Mum would be terrified. I told him that if the war lasted until 1946 I would join him.

We also spent a lot of time at the Paysandu Rowing Club. Ronald was a strong swimmer and the two of us participated in some competitions quite successfully. We were on the water polo team and we won several matches. I also took up sculling which was a national sport in Paysandu, which had produced some national champions. I decided then that if I had a chance I would do more of it.

Dad and Mum took both of us to the train station on New Year's Day. He was off to Montevideo and I to Quebracho, an hour's trip north of

Paysandu. Both trains left within thirty minutes of each other at about 9 a.m. The train was practically empty, at least mine was.

## Cow Punching

I arrived in Quebracho and Arthur Campbell's daughter, 21-year-old Helen, was there to meet me in the family model T Ford. She and I were pretty good friends in spite of the age difference. She had taught me to dance the fox-trot and tango last year when we spent the Christmas holidays at Santa Rita.

"Well Bobby, so you screwed up—huh?" was her welcome after a kiss on the cheek. I told her that I had it all figured out and just wanted to work on the estancia and marry her so I could inherit the place. She laughed: "You had better hurry up because I'm going to Rosario next week to marry Tommy Taylor, the dentist."

The next day I was re-introduced to Maldonado, the 'Capataz' (foreman) of the estancia, who knew me from before. About 50 years old, he had been at Santa Rita since he was a boy. He told me that I would have to be up by 5 o'clock in the morning to round up the men's horses in the nearby 'potrero.' He told me I would have my pick of four ponies which I then selected. These were mine for the duration and I would have to care for them, and see they were well fed and rubbed down at the end of each work day. The work was a lot of fun, sun-up to sun-down, except in winter when it was dark at 5 a.m.

The men were usually up about that time and sat around the 'kitchen' sipping *mate*. It became a practice that I would sip a couple with them before I rounded up the horses. There were seven or eight full-time peones on the estancia, ranging from a young fellow a year or so older than me to 'the old man', Raimundo who was about 60.

## A Different Kind of Life

Raimundo was the best 'domador' or horse breaker on the estancia and he taught me all the tricks of breaking in a horse. You start out on the ground with a 'lasso' around his neck and you walk him in circles and talk to him or her, and brush them down so they get used to human contact. Actual breaking in is plain riding the horse until it stops bucking and trying desperately to offload (which I found out later is also an airline term) the rider, including—sometimes if they are particularly wild—rolling over with the rider on top. I learned the trade pretty quickly and Raimundo said I was as good as he was, which was not true but made me feel good. I also learned to use the typical gaucho lasso made of braided leather. I could lasso a steer while flat out on my pony.

Life on the estancia could not have been better. We rode the range Monday through Saturday, looking for strays, and keeping an eye open for broken fences, and skinning cows, steers, or heifers when we found one that had died of natural causes. I became very good at it, in spite of the tricks the peones played on me: a lot of good nature "lets find out how much the gringo can take." One of their favorites was to locate a dead animal and then let it lie in some undergrowth for several days until one of them would "find it" for me and then tell me to go ahead and skin it. After several days in the summer heat, the animal would stink to high heaven and crawling with maggots. Skinning it was a major hardship but after the first couple of times I caught on and told the man who found it that I had to go back to the estancia because 'Capataz' had told me to be there at a certain time. The boys soon realized I had caught on and did not pull that one on me any more.

Rodeo time was great fun when we separated the young calves to have them castrated to become steers which were then sold for their beef. I learned to "separar" which was a trick, you had to ride in to the herd and work the young calves away from the cows and then lasso them and put them in a separate field. It was hard work but more like a game than work. I thoroughly enjoyed it. I also learned to castrate young sheep. The men did it with their teeth, but I did never reached that stage of proficiency.

On Saturday nights we rode over one of the neighboring estancias, for an asado or sometimes we entertained the men from the others. An asado was mainly barbecued beef, usually half a steer, cooked very slowly with the embers from the fire next to the grill. These became late night guitar-playing, meat-eating, and drinking 'caña' (sugar-distilled brandy, awful stuff) or 'grapa-miel' something made from grapes mixed with honey (which was even worse). Estancia peons love to play ballads, some of them handed down through generations, others made up on the spur of the moment. These went on for hours but they were real stories of the old days, the wars of independence, and civil wars in the country.

## Mabel

I lost my virginity in Quebracho at the local 'kilombo', at a fabulous whorehouse-cum-local- club where you danced, drank, and then proceeded to get laid. Her name was Mabel, which sounded English, and had green eyes, was probably in her twenties, but very sweet and tender. But a prostitute nonetheless. Which may be the reason I have always had a thing for 'ladies of the night.' Mabel actually picked me up as several of us sat at a table drinking beer and 'caña.' She asked me to dance a tango and before I knew what was happening we were in the back of the house in bed. It was a fantastic experience, and helped me to recover from Helen Campbell Taylor. I found out later that one of the men had arranged for the whole thing, including paying for it. After that first experience we would ride in to Quebracho about 25 miles every other Saturday night for a night of drinking and screwing Mabel. And back on Sunday morning in the daylight, terribly hung-over. But the ride did wonders.

## Back to Square One

I was 17 when the Second World War ended and the Campbells decided to sell the estancia, which left me jobless. I tried to get another estancia job and interviewed for a couple of openings but everyone was worried about the drop in prices for beef and grain and were cutting back. I spent a few months in Paysandu doing odd jobs, and worked for a while at the Marcenaro Boat Yard which was great fun, but the job did not have much future. I also did 'pony' duty at the Spring (Easter week) polo championships which meant bringing the ponies to the players between chukkas. I never actually played but I rode well and used to get to hit a ball now and then.

## I Miss the 1948 Olympics

I took up rowing and was Number 1 on a double sculls which did quite well. We won the Uruguay River international championship that summer, which brought in rowers from Argentina as well as from other cities in Uruguay. The coach was an international, he had been educated in England and gave me my first pipe (a Dunhill, no less) and a tin of St. Bruno Flake tobacco. He told me that as he knew I would smoke, a pipe was the lesser of the tobacco evils. He was a terrific coach and the stroke was a guy called William Jones, who spoke not a word of English, but went to Henley where he came in second behind

*Single-sculling in Paysandu.*

*A rare picture, autographed for my father, of PLUNA's 12-seat de Havilland D.H. 86B, acquired in 1938.*

Jack Kelly in the 1947 Diamond Sculls and went on to the 1948 Olympics. As for me, I have subsidized St. Bruno by chain-smoking the product ever since.

By this time I was into other things, girls and so on, and rowing was just too demanding on my free time. It involved being grounded for weeks at a time at the Paysandu Rowing Club, locked in for the night with a bunch of guys. At 18 this was not my style.

In the meantime, Ronald had spent two years with the Air Transport Command. During a couple of weeks in Paysandu I caught up on his war-time activities which involved ferrying aircraft across the Atlantic by way of Natal and Dakar. He said it was not like being in the war really. In spite of our age difference we very close, more like two friends, rather than brothers. I admired him tremendously. He had taken after Dad who could do anything with his hands, and they had built a three-wheeled motor-car when he was 15 back in the holidays when he was home from St. George's.

They had bought an F-N, (for Fabrique Nationale, I think) a Belgian built motorcycle of 1914–18 Great War vintage. It was a six cylinder (straight in line) powerful bike and they had bought the front end of a model T Ford and between them built the three-wheeled automobile which he drove all around the place. When he came back from the war he re-built the three-wheeler and let me use it for basic transport. Dad was a friend of all the cops in town so they looked the other way when I came along making a horrendous racket because it had a straight bell-shaped exhaust.

In 1948 Ronald became head of maintenance for PLUNA[1], the Uruguayan national carrier which operated DC-3s in domestic service. He had been offered the job by Roberto Langon, who was General Manager and another "Sanducero" (as they called people from Paysandu). Dad knew the Marquez Vaeza's, who had founded the airline before the war. The job was in Montevideo so I was anxious to get down there myself.

---

1. From R.E.G.Davies' "Airlines of Latin America since 1919": PLUNA, Primeras Lineas Uruguayas de Navegacion Aerea was formed by a group of Uruguayan financiers led by the importers Alberto and Jorge Marquez Vaeza, with some help from British associates, in September 1935...with a tiny fleet of two de Havilland D.H.90 Dragonflies-a scaled down version of the Dragon Rapide, with only three passenger seats...In 1943 the airline suspended service, but this was re-established on 15 September, 1945. The Government held 83.3% of the stock 1,000,000 pesos, or about U.S.$500,000, most of which went into the purchase of a small fleet of Douglas DC-2s and a C-47 to supplement the de Havilland machines.

*Author's note: in 1995 VARIG acquired 50% of the airline from the Government and today provides management as well as the DC10-30 service between Montevideo, Brazil, and Madrid. The airline has continued to lose money under the VARIG management, although at this writing, the airline appears to be on the right track. With MERCOSUR opening up regional routes, PLUNA is well positioned to take advantage of the new route authorities. Throughout its more than 60 years of scheduled operations, it has never had a fatal accident.*

# Pan American—
# Brief Encounter

One day in 1948 an old school friend, Joe Larrabee, called from Montevideo and told me that Pan American was hiring bilingual ticket agents. His father, Charlie, was the Pan Am director so I called him and he told me to get my ass down to Montevideo. I stayed with another school chum, Martin Macadam, whose mother had decided to take in boarders and went to see Mr. Larrabee the day after I arrived. He hired me on the spot. I had to report to the station manager, Billy Fernandez, who was a couple of years older than I was, on the first of the month, two weeks away. The job did not pay a whole lot but it sounded interesting and it had to do with airplanes.

I joined The Montevideo Cricket Club (for the rugby team) and spent time at The Old Boys Club which had a couple of squash courts and a bar downtown in the port area and was a good place to meet friends. I played squash three or four times a week and rugby on Saturdays. I was completely fit, having spent the last two years riding, and most recently rowing, and living a generally healthy outdoor life (except for the occasional Saturday night bash).

## First Airline Job

Being an airport ticket agent at Pan American was somewhat boring but at least I was around airplanes. The job consisted in meeting the DC-4 flights which arrived from the north (with stops in Rio, São Paulo, and Porto Alegre), loading the mail and checking it against the manifest, and then driving it to the port of Montevideo to put it and any other company mail, freight, and sometimes lost baggage on the river boat over to Buenos Aires. At the time there was some kind of a problem involving operating and traffic rights (which was resolved after a few months) and Pan American did not fly between Montevideo and Buenos Aires.

The river boat, *Vapor de la Carrera*, which had been built in Liverpool as a sort of ferry-boat, left the docks at 10 p.m. every night and I had to be there about 8:30 three or four times a week and then again the next morning at 7 a.m.

to pick up the inbound mail, cargo, and baggage and greet the passengers who were connecting to Pan American. The driver of the Pan American truck and I would convene at the Ancla Bar in the port after the river boat had left, and many times we stayed all night partying with the "girls" who hung out around the port and would pick us up, or vice versa after their last "paying" customer had gone home. As we had to meet the 7 a.m. arrival this was not hard to do, but it made us pretty tired, no to say hung over, during the day.

At Pan American I made some lasting friends, in particular Herbert Buencristiano, known as "El Gordo", who was the city ticket office manager downtown. He was a couple of years older and he took me under his wing. One day, I was in trouble for failing to show up for work after a particularly rough night at the Ancla, and he went to bat for me and saved my job. Pan American had recently moved over to what is now Carrasco Airport when they substituted the 'milk-run' DC-3 for the larger—and at that time, very impressive, four engine-DC-4.

## Motorbikes, Rugby, and Juan Manuel Fangio

Shortly after I started work I bought my first second-hand motorcycle, a 350 c.c. British Velocette KSS, winner of the Isle of Man Tourist Trophy and a great bike. I actually bought it with Malcolm Henderson, who played full-back for the M.V.C.C. and Uruguay. I used his name to race so that my parents would not have a heart attack when they read about me in the paper. That worked until I had a road-race in Paysandu, which I won handily. Dad was in the crowd and thought it was terrific, and we then broke the news to Mum. Who took it very well.

I was playing rugby for the Old Boys Club every Saturday and racing motorcycles on Sundays. Most of the races were at the 2 1/2 mile dirt track at the Barra de Santa Lucia, about half an hour's drive from Pocitos where I was living. Martin Macadam, with whom I shared digs along with several other bachelors, would drive his father's Morris car and I would ride the bike to the races. I won my first race and was invited to join Chiquito Costa and Masseratto, the 500 c.c. champs in their 'scuderia' which meant that I had some professional help and access to their mechanic, one of the best in Uruguay. Chiquito was quite a bit older and he and Masseratto sort of 'adopted' me. We would go to the races together and had a ball.

Other hot riders at the time were Jose Carlos Garcia, who had won several South American championships, along with the Rosich brothers, Evaristo and 'Nene.' Bike races were held around the country, on city streets or at horse race-tracks, and at a brand new racing track built outside Piriapolis, the beach resort. This track was the first special road-race venue in Uruguay and I inaugurated the track, winning my 350 c.c. race, with Juan Manuel Fangio winning the 1,300 c.c. automobile race the same day. I met Fangio, one of the nicest, unassuming professional guys in the world, in spite of having won the first of his five Formula One championships. Fangio, called 'El Chueco' by all, was very friendly and he invited me drive around the track in his car after the races. We had a couple of beers later that evening at the hotel.

Shortly afterwards I graduated to the 500 c.c. class with another second-hand English bike, a 1948 Norton Manx, probably the hottest machine of its time, long before the Italians and Japanese took over the sport.

## Dating Martha

About this time I began dating Martha, Nelly del Campo's cousin. Nelly and I had been in the same class at the 'British School.' She and Nelly played tennis at the Cricket Club where the Old Boys played rugby on Saturdays. I suspect that Nelly had talked Martha into switching boyfriends from Johnny Boyle, a nice guy in the American embassy. I took her riding on the bike which impressed her, I guess. Her parents, the Oses, were very conservative Uruguayans who thoroughly disapproved of me. We went out behind their backs for about a year before she finally convinced them I was okay, at which point they reluctantly accepted me.

Martha was very pretty and very popular. She and I became a fixture and all my friends welcomed her as my official girl friend. We went to parties

*Dating Martha at Punta del Este.*

and had a great time together. One day on the #121 bus, on our way from Pocitos, where we both lived, to the train station and the Cricket Club, I told her that I was going to be very successful, except I did not quite know how. She laughed and told me she did not care that much about success. Which I guess sealed our future together.

## Punta del Este

After less than a year Maitland Moore-Davie called me out of the blue. He was another Anglo who ran the American Express correspondent agency, Viajes y Transportes (Travel & Transport) in Montevideo. I had met him at the airport several times as he met VIPs on Pan American and we both belonged to the Cricket Club where he would occasionally buy me a drink or two. He was a neat guy, single, and probably in his early fifties. He had gone to school in England and loved rugby. As I was now playing for Uruguay (no big deal, there were only five clubs in the Uruguayan Rugby Union) he was one of my fans. I played third-row forward and he told me that was his position when he played for Dulwich, one of the best rugby schools in England. He invited me to have lunch at the English Club, the downtown businessmen's club which I had recently joined, along with Martin Macadam and several other Old Boys.

The club was a men-only, teak wood-typical, cigar-and-pipe-smoking enclave. I found replicas all over South America in later years, watering holes for British expats. Snooker tables in the back room, where we all honed our skills to take on all comers. Maitland was 'one of the boys', the younger brother of Dick Moore-Davie who owned the company and had married into one of the wealthier families. Maitland was about 5 ft 10 in, kind of stocky with a ruddy complexion (probably because he drank a lot) and grayish hair. He smoked about three packs a day and his nicotine stained fingers showed it. I enjoyed being with him because, even though he was in his early fifties, he treated me like an equal.

"Bobby, how about spending the summer in Punta del Este, all expenses paid?" was his opening gambit right after the first g & t (gin and tonic) at the bar. I was intrigued, it was my day off so I was in no rush to go anywhere. Punta, as it is generally known, is the swank summer resort 75 miles east of Montevideo on the Atlantic. It has fabulous beaches on both sides of a penin-sula which sticks out into the ocean, surrounded by expensive homes and pine forests. I had been to Punta several times on the motorbike with friends and loved the place.

I asked him to explain, which he did. Viajes y Transportes was opening an office in Punta this summer, mainly to meet the boat train from Montevideo which brought in the high income Argentine tourists who used the Buenos Aires office of Villalonga-American Express to handle their baggage and belongings door-to-door. The Punta office would have a full time-driver and truck which would meet the boat train every day and I was to be responsible for meeting the customers, having their baggage checked, and making sure the driver delivered the stuff to their rented or owned homes.

I could go to the beach in the afternoons, after spending a few hours in the office before midday and perhaps a couple of hours late in the afternoon to check the incoming messages from the B.A. office which would send me the next day's list of customers with their addresses so that I could organize the delivery.

At the end of the season we would reverse the process, arrange to pick up and deliver to the train for the afternoon departure. The pay was about the same as Pan American's but the idea of an all-expense 'temporada' in Punta sounded pretty good to me. I asked him about the winter months and he said I would be responsible for supervising and organizing American Express FIT's (foreign independent tours) meet-and-transfer and local sightseeing. Maitland explained that they had just acquired the American Express representation and he was not sure how much was involved but I could help him to organize things. It sounded like a pretty good deal.

## Have Some Fun—Then Quit

I gave notice to Billy Fernandez at Pan American who seemed relieved that I was leaving, probably because he felt (incorrectly) that I had some kind of inside track with Charlie Larrabee, his boss downtown. I started work in December and after two weeks in the office I moved out to Punta, motorcycle and all. The only problem with the job was that it was a seven-day business and I would not be able to keep up with my racing schedule. Rugby was off for the summer so it did not bother me that much. The important bike races were between April and November anyway.

Punta was terrific. Martha was staying at Solis, about 35 miles away, and I could reach there in half an hour on the Velocette whenever I could get away, and she spent some weekends with her family in Punta. I had kept the Velo as my means of transport, the Manx for racing. I would drive the company truck to deliver wealthy Argentine's baggage and household effects off the boat train to their posh homes. Most of the time I was invited in to have a gin & tonic with the owners and even dated a couple of rich (and pretty) daughters. I drove a truck by day and lived the life of a rich playboy at night.

After the summer I was installed in the downtown office and organized sightseeing tours and handled the correspondence with Amexco in New York.

One of the most enjoyable parts of the job was organizing shore excursions off the Moore-McCormack Lines combination cargo/passenger ships, the s.s. *Argentina, Brazil,* and *Uruguay,* which docked every Monday in Montevideo. I had 'invented' the idea of doing a deal with the pursers on all three ships. They would offer shore excursions for a commission. As soon as the ship docked, at about 7:30 in the morning, I would run on board to the purser's office and he gave me the list of customers. I became good friends with several of them and I enjoyed going on board at the end of the day for drinks with the purser before the ship sailed at 22:00. In addition, we were picking up considerable revenue business which Maitland thought was great, because no one had thought of the idea before.

I stayed at *Viajes* for two years and learned something about the travel business from the ground up. But I did not think it was something I wanted to do for the long pull.

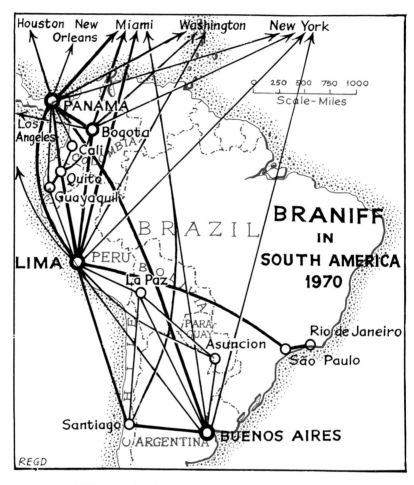

*By 1950, Braniff had established an international network that
reached all the major cities in South America.*

# *Daily Service to the United States*

In 1950 I heard about a new airline, Braniff Airways, which had recently inaugurated service from Dallas to both Buenos Aires and Rio de Janeiro. The flights stopped at Lima where its DC-4s fed each other to Ecuador, Panama, and Havana en route to Dallas via Houston in the north, and La Paz and Asuncion to B.A. in the south and Rio to the east.

I decided to do some research on the airline, partly from Charlie Larrabee, who knew Tom Braniff and told me quite a bit, and actually offered to be a reference, which helped later. Some of it was from the local public library which, amazingly, had quite a lot of information on the airline industry, at least the very early days. I also talked to Ronald who had his own sources.

## *Braniff*

*Braniff Airways was founded in Oklahoma City, in May 1928 (I liked that, I was senior by a month) by Paul Braniff, who had flown in WWI. His brother Tom was the first vice president. They started out as an airline, flying school, parts distributor, and air taxi operator—the archetype multi-modal company. The first schedule was between Oklahoma City and Tulsa, all of 116 miles. It operated single-engine Lockheed Vegas and gradually expanded until in 1935 the airline was operating between Dallas/Fort Worth, Oklahoma City, Waco, Austin, San Antonio, Houston, and north to Wichita Fallas and Amarillo. It was one of the first airlines to serve meals and provide hostesses. It added DC-2s and 3s to the fleet and during the Second World War it operated domestic and military air transport routes between Texas, Mexico, Central America and the Canal Zone in Panama. During the war Paul left the airline to serve in some government capacity, and his older brother, Tom, took over the airline. In 1945 and 1946 it operated a Mexican subsidiary, Aerovias*

*Braniff, and in 1946 was awarded its South American route au-*
*thority which it took up in 1948 with DC-4s and new pressurized*
*DC-6s. In 1949 it inaugurated Lima-Rio, at the time the longest*
*nonstop segment in the world.*

## The Selling Proposition

I managed to find a schedule which told me that the four flights to Buenos
Aires were on alternate dates to the three flights to Rio, providing daily
service north of Lima. I came up with the idea of daily service to the United
States from Montevideo by offering alternate connecting flights to Rio and
B.A. I did some elementary figuring that while the Pan American/Panagra
group had fewer than daily flights from either by Panagra from Buenos
Aires up the west coast, or by Pan American up the east, I could offer daily
service. I wrote to Mr. Tom Braniff, president of the airline in Dallas,
suggesting that I could generate an estimated $150,000 worth of business if
he would appoint me as the Braniff agent in Uruguay. At the time I was still
working for Viajes y Transportes, but was not getting anywhere in a hurry
and at age 22 I felt the need to do something else. About two weeks after
mailing the letter, I received a call from a John Long who announced
himself as the Braniff 'country manager' in Buenos Aires and invited me to
come across for a job interview.

I parlayed myself a ticket on the Montevideo "shuttle" (operated by
CAUSA with converted wartime Sunderland flying boats) and made my way
to the Braniff office in B.A. on Calle Viamonte. John Long turned out to be
an affable Texan who introduced me around as the new Braniff 'general
agent' in Uruguay, even before we had discussed details. After he shut the
door and invited me to sit down, he told me that Mr. Brack (pronounced
Brock) has instructed him to hire me. He said that Dallas felt $150,000 was
probably way out of line, but they would be happy with $100,000 out of
Montevideo if I would accept a commission deal. We agreed on 5%, plus
office rent, communications, and other incidental expenses. $5,000 annually,
(5% of $100,000) was a lot more than I had made to date, so I jumped at it. I
was convinced, based on my own research, that I could do at least $150,000,
probably more. The maximum salary I had earned was $225 per month at
Viajes y Transportes and $100 at Pan American. So if I could make my own
goal of $150,000 I could be making $600 or better. Mr. Long gave me a
prepared letter outlining the deal and suggested that I take it home and then
return the original if I agreed. I smiled, and said: "I'll sign it now, I want to
start in two weeks, and I need to give notice."

We talked about office rents and other expenses, telephone, and a secretary (which was part of his proposal). I said I would get back to him on these items within 48 hours and shook hands and left his office. On the way out I ran into Bill Allen, an old rugby friend from the Carrasco Polo Club. He worked in reservations and showed me around the office. He then took me next door to the local bar and pumped me about what I was doing. He thought it sounded great and offered to help if I needed to clear space for some one. We had a couple of beers and I took a taxi back to the docks to catch the 6 p.m. CAUSA flying boat to Monte.

The next couple of weeks were hectic. I gave notice to Maitland Moore, my boss at Viajes y Transportes, and he told me he was sorry to see me go but wished me luck and offered any help I might need. He and I remained good friends until several years later he walked in front of a Central Railways locomotive just outside Sayago, the Montevideo Cricket Club station. After Maldonado, at the Santa Rita estancia, Maitland had been my mentor and I was very fond of him. There was a certain sadness about him that always worried me.I found out later he had been drinking. His death, suicide or accident, made me think a lot about life. I was quite depressed for a while.

## My Own Boss—At Last

Now aged 23 I was in business for myself. I have come to realize, many years later that this has always been my greatest motivation: a need for independence, to be an entrepreneur, and to be my own boss.

I arranged to rent a small suite of offices, one for the reception area and one private office at Edificio Artigas, in the old part of town. The building had just been opened with the New York City Bank on the ground floor, and it was owned by the Brown family from Texas. When they heard I was leasing space for Texas-based Braniff they could not have been more helpful. I then hired my old school friend, Nelly del Campo, at $100 salary, with travel privileges, which she thought was fine. We opened the office two weeks from the day I accepted the deal. It took a couple more weeks to install telephones and a SITA connection for the teletype machine.

I quickly called on the U.S. embassy, where the ambassador introduced me around to the staff, every travel agent in the city, and the 15 or 16 U.S. companies whose staff traveled back and forth to the United States. I had produced a two-fold handout which showed connecting schedules to Rio and Buenos Aires under the headline "The Only Daily Service to the United States" plus the Braniff 'special': a free overnight in Rio or Lima. I had negotiated this with John Long after I arrived back to Montevideo—it had been an afterthought which turned out to be the real clincher. Because B.A. connections were easy in the same day, I offered a free night at the Bolivar Hotel in Lima in lieu of the free overnight in Rio which was necessary because the flights did not connect. I did a deal with K.L.M., B.O.A.C., and S.A.S. which between them had four flights a week which stopped in Rio, en route to Europe. They agreed to a special pro-rate for the Montevideo-Rio de Janeiro sector, which gave Braniff a better net on the through fare from Montevideo which was established by the International Airline Traffic Association (I.A.T.A.) and which we had to abide by. In other words, the Montevideo-Dallas fare was the same for Braniff, Pan Am or Panagra, thus when we transported the passenger from Rio de Janeiro, Braniff ended up receiving a higher pro-rata portion of the total fare than it did for a Rio de Janeiro-Dallas ticket sold in Rio.

Travel agents loved us because the Pan American monopoly had been broken. Pan Am had never bothered to call on travel agents because they did not need to. I made the rounds every day, offering to make reservations and generally answering questions. Many times I ended up actually helping an agent close a sale with a customer at the ticket counter. The embassy decided to split its business between Pan American and Braniff. This alone was something of a sales coup, as Braniff was not even on-line, i.e. its aircraft did not land in Montevideo. I had more or less established Braniff as an on-line carrier. That first year Braniff sales in Montevideo broke $250,000, and I made slightly more than $1,000 per month in gross income—a princely sum compared with my $200 per month at *Viajes y Transportes*.

## Marriage and So On

In March 1953 Martha and I were married. We spent the first couple of nights, after a great wedding party, at our favorite, *El Chaja* in Solis and from there took K.L.M. to Europe—on a free pass compliments of Bob Crawford, K.L.M.'s manager in Montevideo. We spent a week on the island of Capri, compliments of one of our travel agent friends, a few days in Rome, and stopped at Estoril in Portugal on the way home. Bob Crawford, a Dutchman with a British last name, eventually left K.L.M. and lived in Panama where he consulted for COPA. We recently met again in Montevideo when the SKAL Club celebrated its 40th anniversary.

Some time later that year Tom Braniff and a team of senior executives, including John Long's replacement, Don Grefe (who became my boss and long time friend), visited Montevideo on a quick trip through the region. Don had first joined P.I.A. (Peruvian International Airways) which had a short career right after the war and flew DC-4s between New York and Lima. After

*Wedding picture.*

*Sitting on the sidewalk at Carrasco Airport in Montevideo, Tom Braniff accepts a light from off-line sales agent Booth.*

it failed he had joined Braniff in Panama. John Long went on to Asuncion, Paraguay, as country manager.

## Braniff, Brack, and Bytes

Tom Braniff was truly one of the pioneers in the business. He had both a vision for the airline and a real feeling for the importance of people in the airline business. Unfortunately, he was killed in a small airplane accident in New Orleans on a fishing trip in 1954. Also on the trip to Montevideo was Reginald K. Brack, with whom I had corresponded. Rex, as he was known by all, was a 'U.S.-born son of a Russian immigrant and had been a successful businessman before joining Braniff as the head of sales. We hit it off very well and over the years he became more or less my mentor at Braniff. His son, Reginald Jr., became the publisher of *Time* magazine. I later met his family and established a long time relationship. Rex was one of the most effective sales people I ever met and I tried very hard, over the years, to pick up his common-sense approach to sales. He once told me: "Answer your own 'phone calls as often as possible, you'll be amazed at how much business you can pick up. And when you get a call from the media, you'll find out that they are looking for a quote and by just being available, you'll get your name in the paper."

This was before sound bytes, but it has served me extremely well over the years and I appreciate the advice, early on.

## First Time in the U.S.

Also in 1953, I made my first trip to the United States, stopping off for 24 hours in Lima. I wanted to investigate the potential for additional stopover incentives for Braniff passengers. I stayed at the Bolivar and introduced myself to Bill Wilson, a Chilean-born Anglo and now the Braniff District Sales Manager whose office was round the corner. I asked him about local travel agencies who provided sightseeing and the like and he directed me to All Transport, just off the Plaza de Armas. There I met Eduardo (Eddie) Arrarte, about two or three years older than me, my height, six feet or so, only dark and good looking. He gave me an all-inclusive price for in/out transfers, a half day city tour.

We established a relationship which lasted for the next 45 years. With his wife, Toti, Eddie started Lima Tours about a year or so later. They became the lead travel agency and tour operator in Peru. A few years later, when I was in Dallas, I was able to help them to obtain their IATA appointment because Panagra, which, for all practical purposes, ran the local AIB (Agency Investigation Board) which approved new IATA travel agency appointments, did not want to approve them. In order to obtain appointment, a travel agent needed two sponsoring airlines, and Panagra dominated the local Board. I had called Bill Wilson, in Lima and told him that Braniff wanted to see some competition among the travel agencies in Lima. He was able to convince a couple of European airline representatives on the Board in order to over-ride Panagra's objections. At the time I think there were only five IATA-appointed agencies in Lima, and they were all beholden to Panagra. So Braniff sponsored Lima Tours and they were appointed.

In Dallas I met several Braniff executives at the General Office at Love Field in a converted war-time hangar. I was impressed with the overall business-like, cost-saving culture. I immediately liked some of the middle management people, with whom I would deal later on, and with whom I developed a strong relationship, in many cases until I left the airline some 20 years later. I was impressed by the treasurer, Lloyd Eden, one of the most sales-oriented financial people I ever met. He was credited with having invented "Ticket-by-Mail" (TBM) which was a neat way to deliver tickets to a customer based on a 'phoned-in order. It was way ahead of electronic ticketing and Braniff at the time even accepted personal checks, as long as the customer was listed in the telephone directory. They would actually mail the ticket before they received the customer's check. Lloyd Eden told me it was a terrific way to get to know the customer direct and it also by-passed the travel agent. He told me that Braniff's experience with bad checks was negligible.

Bobby Cairncross the District Sales Manager from Buenos Aires, was there at the same time. He was a few years older than me, an Anglo-Argentine and had been in the war. We had originally met in Uruguay when he worked for B.O.A.C. We returned to Miami together and spent a night in a bar near the airport where we proceeded to get drunk and disorderly and just managed to get on the flight which left in the morning. Bobby and I became close friends and we worked closely together on a number of deals until some time later he left Argentina for Australia.

## Salesman of the Year

The second year in Montevideo, I hired a sales representative, Alex, and paid him out of my own commission. Alex was a Hungarian immigrant and a great salesman, although he had no prior airline experience. This allowed me to spend more time on sales in the interior where I set up sub-agents at a commission rate of 3% of their sales. A school friend of mine, Walter Fernandez, had joined the Uruguayan Navy straight out of school and was now an officer. He called me one day to tell me that Uruguay had just bought three U.S. ex-WW2 destroyers and was going to take 150 Uruguayan navy personnel to Norfolk, Virginia, by commercial airline. I found a Buenos Aires-Norfolk fare which undercut the Montevideo fare because the latter was based on an add-on to the B.A. level fare. By offering one in 15 free (the original 'tour conductor' discount for groups) I undercut PanAm by about $25 per passenger. On 150 that came to a $3,750 saving on top of the free overnight. The sale was worth $100,000 net on-line to Braniff. That year we broke $300,000 in sales and I was invited to Dallas to receive the annual Braniff 'Salesman of the Year' award.

## *Punta del Este Film Festival*

I sold a charter from Los Angeles to Montevideo for the Film Festival in Punta del Este, the first such event in South America. Mauricio Litman, a major Argentine promoter who had contributed to "inventing" Punta del Este, had developed the San Rafael Country Club as a very successful real estate project. He liked me and gave me an inside tip on what PanAm and Panagra had quoted so that I could win the bid by a few bucks. Braniff in Dallas was delighted, the publicity alone was going to be worth millions. Rex Brack insisted that I fly to L.A. and travel with the group on the specially configured DC-6. Danny Lewellyn Jones, Don Fraser, and Maruja Salazar, the Lima-based Braniff cabin crew assigned to the flight, did a fine job as we arranged sleeper berths for everyone on the 36-hour flight, with stops in Houston, Panama, and Lima, where we had airport press conferences which generated massive free publicity for Braniff.

I spent two weeks in Punta with the 50 movie stars, producers, wives, and husbands and others, and made friends with the movie people who included Walter Pidgeon; John Swopes, a famous still photographer, and his wife, Dorothy McGuire; Wayne Morris; and Pat O'Brien, who drank like a fish all the way down and while there. Martha joined the flight in Panama with Nelly del Campo who had been in Washington, D.C., and we made friends, particularly with the Swopes.

My major objective during the film festival was to fight off the competition from Pan Am and its associated Panagra. The charter package had included open return flights on regularly scheduled services to allow the movie stars a choice on their return. Panagra had sent Jack Regan, from Lima, to solicit their return trips. Because of the personal relationships we had established I was able to keep 100% of the group on-line with Braniff—which did no harm to my reputation in Dallas. In spite of this, Jack Regan and I became good friends and I was able to persuade him to join Braniff several years later in Dallas.

*(Top) With Dorothy McGuire and John Swopes;*

*(center) with Mr. and Mrs. Jack O'Brien;*

*(bottom) with Wayne Morris— at a time when Havana was still on the tourist map.*

Unrelated to the film festival, we also entertained other celebrities who came through Montevideo. Among these were Debbie Reynolds and Pier Angeli who were on some kind of a promotional tour, I forget the specifics—but we made lasting friends in many of these instances. At the same time I was having a lot of fun. My school pals were all doing their own things, Martin Macadam had taken over his father's bookstore in the old part of town. John Linn was working for his father's company, Linn & Compañía, which imported Studebaker automobiles among other things. Tommy Morton had joined a wool firm. Freddy Deakin, the 'ants in his pants' guy, was working for a travel agency, but was supposedly doing some confidential work for the CIA, although we did not find out about it until many years later. We were all very close and spent most weekends together—one way or another—playing rugby, or going to the beach, or partying, when I was not racing.

John Linn's brother, Arturo, was our hero. He was a few years older than us and had flown in the Battle of Britain and later in Mosquito fighter bombers and had been awarded the D.F.C. He came back after the war and everyone wanted to be with him. But he was somewhat reserved and (he reminded me of Dad) did not really want to talk about it.

## *Corporate Animal*

The bad news was that Braniff decided that, under its newly-acquired membership in IATA, it was illegal to pay me a commission. They proposed a salary deal based on $350 a month but they would pay Alex, plus all expenses and give me a generous, almost unlimited, expense account. All I had to do was submit bills, bar checks included. As we did a lot of entertaining (I was one of the big spenders in my group) it made sense, and so I accepted because I was now paying Alex $200 a month and with other expenses I was not really netting that much more under the previous arrangement.

I was racing my Velocette—I had sold the Norton Manx—on road racing and

*In the days when British motorbikes were all the rage, my choice was a Velocette.*

*Our rugby team (oddly from the Montevideo Cricket Club) was champion of Uruguay in 1953. I am fourth from the left, standing.*

off road events—I was Uruguay's 350 c.c. champion and raced in Buenos Aires as well as in a number of interior cities. I played rugby for The Old Boys Club (third row forward) and for the Uruguayan selection against Chile, Brazil, and Argentina. We were always licked by Argentina, which had the best rugby in Latin America (or the Americas, if there had been a championship), but we consistently beat Brazil and Chile. Between the job and my extra-curricular activities, I was kept busy and well content.

## Los Angeles

In December 1953 Valerie was born. A few months later in 1954, Canadian Pacific's VP for Latin America, Peter Baronas, invited Martha and me to dinner at the Bertie Dodero's in Carrasco. Bertie was married to an Uruguayan and his family had owned FAMA, the Argentine flag carrier which eventually became the main component of Aerolineas Argentinas when all the airlines were nationalized into one under the Peron regime. They were also very influential and had been General Sales Agents for Braniff in Argentina before the airline's start of service and now represented Canadian Pacific. The Doderos also owned the Dodero steamship line, which similarly became the Flota Mercante del Estado under Peron.

Peter wanted me to come to Buenos Aires as Sales Manager for Canadian Pacific. I was now 26 and it seemed like a major opportunity. Bob Phinney, Agency & Interline Manager for Braniff in Dallas, arrived in Monte about that time and I told him I was thinking about a career change. He insisted that I should not make a rash decision and asked me to wait a few weeks. Bob and Maggie, his wife, became very good friends of ours over the years.

*Martha and I take the K.L.M. connecting flight, a DC-6B, en route to Los Angeles.*

That was when Rex Brack came down on a special trip. I met him at the airport in Montevideo and I drove to the Victoria Plaza, the brand new Pan American-Intercontinental Hotel where I had booked the presidential suite for him through my friend Jack Dutton-Jones, the manager. After a couple of drinks he told me why he was in town. He proposed that I accept the position of DSM (District Sales Manager) for Braniff in Los Angeles at the princely salary of $450 a month plus expense account and an automobile. This sounded pretty terrific, and in mid-1955 I made the move.

By that time Robbie was on the way so Martha agreed to stay with my parents who had moved to the *Chacra* (a really lovely farm-house) just outside Montevideo. I found a place to live in West Hollywood with Rodolfo Vallarino, a Uruguayan playboy with whom I spent about six months as a bachelor. Through Bertie Talbot, one of my pals in Monte, I met his cousin Malcolm Middleton, an Anglo-Argentine. Malcolm and his family took me under their wing and I spent most of my off-work time with them. Malcolm had a business cleaning swimming pools and I would sometimes accompany him on Saturdays on his pool-cleaning chores. We cleaned several pools for movie stars and were invited in for gin and tonics every now and then.

About this time I met Peter Ueberroth who had recently started Travel Consultants International, T.C.I., a travel representation firm which was very successful representing clients such as Hawaiian Airlines in California. Peter had started out as a sales rep with one of the charter airlines and later became famous as the organizer of the L.A. Olympics, and later still as Baseball Commissioner. After that I helped him when he tried to buy Eastern Airlines

*This picture of a Braniff DC-6B at Carrasco Airport, Montevideo, offers a touch of true nostalgia to Latin American airline veterans. Braniff never served Montevideo on a regularly scheduled basis. This picture was taken during the Film Festival charter flight.*

from Frank Lorenzo. We became close friends, and later on he invited Martha and me to use his weekend home in Laguna Beach, which we did, several times, kids and all.

The job was off-line. Braniff did not fly to Los Angeles but had an interchange service with T.W.A. which connected at St. Louis with Braniff which then connected over Dallas to South America. The job involved calling on travel agents and other airlines in the west, from San Diego to mid-California and Arizona. I would take off on Monday morning in the 1954 second-hand convertible Mercury I had bought through a connection at Hertz, calling on travel agents on the road. My predecessor, Norm Kidd, had left me a rollerdeck with travel agent names and addresses and a history of sales for Braniff. The office was over the Statler Hilton in downtown L.A. and staffed by one secretary, Dottie, and myself. She was one of those incredible ladies who had worked for Braniff for 25 years and taught me everything I needed to know about the agents and airlines in the area. She was about 50-something and handled the office single-handed, did my expense reports and kept me on schedule. I would call in once a day from wherever I might be, say Bakersfield or Tucson, and she'd say: "Bobby, don't forget to ask Bill (so and so) at (such and such agency) about his 'fam trip' to Argentina on Braniff."

## The Old Man and the Sea

I also called on a handful of major corporate accounts, among which were a couple of the larger studios where (Dottie had given me the names) I would make contact with the Production Manager's office which handled transportation for movies on location. I actually lucked out on one of those calls when I discovered that Spencer Tracy was to shoot a good part of *The Old Man and the Sea* (which I had read during my 'Hemingway' period at school in Montevideo) off Cabo Blanco in Peru and Salinas in Ecuador. I made arrangements for the entire production team with Spencer Tracy and a couple of other movie stars to fly on Braniff with a bunch of equipment. This was a major sale with lots of publicity shots in L.A. and on arrival. Dallas was very happy about this deal and I was congratulated by C.E. ('Chuck') Beard, who was now president and C.E.O. of the airline, after Tom Braniff's death in 1953. Fastidious and elegant he had joined Braniff right after the war. He was dedicated to the Braniff culture of 'people first.'

As soon as Martha arrived in L.A. with baby Robbie and 2 year-old-Valerie, we moved into a house in West Hollywood and the Swopes gave us a 'welcome to L.A.' party where we met Henry Fonda and other notables, including the director John Frankenheimer who was just beginning his long career. Enjoyable, but we were not really into the Hollywood scene. Martha had a school friend who was married and living somewhere between L.A. and San Diego and we spent some time at their beach-front home on the weekends.

About six months later, before the end of 1955, Dallas beckoned (I thought I was in trouble over expense accounts which my immediate boss had thought excessive) to learn that I was being offered a promotion as Country Manager in Panama. Braniff had instituted the Country Manager concept when it started its South American service. The Country Manager was responsible for everything in his assigned country and reported directly to Rex Brack, Senior Vice President-Traffic & Sales and second-in-line to Chuck Beard, who was President and CEO.

## *Panama*

*From Cadogan Guides—"Central America" published in 1993.*

*A slither of land strung between Colombia and Costa Rica, the tiny Republic of Panama is something of a misfit. Largely ignored by international tourism, it is famous for just three things: a canal, a hat and an infamous military leader. Typically none of these are entirely Panamanian: the hats are made in Ecuador, the canal belongs to the United States and the general is now buried so deep beneath a Miami courtroom that his cell is referred to as "the submarine." P.J.O'Rourke once described the country as "a put-up job, sleazed into existence by Teddy Roosevelt so he'd have somewhere to put the Big Ditch."*

*The nation is riddled with complexities—from its murky beginnings to the broad racial mix, which includes Chinese, Russians, Indians, Spanish and French. Bound together in an uneasy partnership these elements have produced one of the most contradictory and cosmopolitan nations in all of Latin America. The Panamanians were slow to focus on the independence issue. In the end Los Santos pre-empted Panama City by declaring its independence in November 1821, closely followed by the rest of the country. Panama then joined Ecuador, Peru, Venezuela, Bolivia, and Colombia to form the vast Republic of Gran Colombia. Five years later Simon Bolivar held a congress in Panama to discuss the future of the Americas and proposed a great union of American states. A hopeless lack of agreement soon led to the break-up of Gran Colombia and prompted a disillusioned Bolivar to declare that "Those who serve the revolution, plow the sea.'*

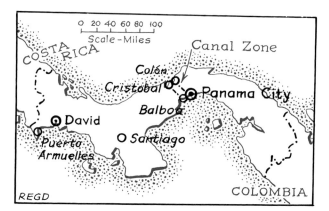

*Panama is the only city on the entire American land mass where you can see the sun rise over the Pacific Ocean.*

*While other Republics broke away, Panama remained part of Colombia. By the turn of the century the U.S. government had become increasingly interested in building a canal of its own. The greatest stumbling block was the Colombian government, which wanted to be cut in on the deal. but in 1903, by a stroke of good fortune and with the support of U.S. troops, a revolutionary junta took control of Panama. Within days a treaty was signed guaranteeing the U.S. the right to build a canal and exercise all rights of sovereignty in exchange for $10 million and an annual payment of $250,000.*

## Not Just a Canal

Early in 1956 we moved down to replace Mel Doolittle who was going to Buenos Aires. I was Braniff's first non-U.S.-citizen Country Manager. This eventually became customary, but at that time was quite revolutionary. Some of them (along with other expats) did not even speak the language. Panama was very different, both as a country and the job. I had total responsibility for everything, sales, operations, and administration of about 120 people who worked for the airline. We had an off-line office on the Atlantic side at Colon which I found very interesting. It was the headquarters for the Free Zone which was a major cargo center. A lot of goods came in from the Pacific through the Panama Canal by ship and was then packaged for air cargo to South America. Much of it went to Asuncion, Paraguay, mostly contraband destined to Argentina, Brazil, and other countries. I would drive across the isthmus and spend the day calling on local accounts with our manager. This was the my first so called 'on-line' job and I spent a lot of time at Tocumen Airport where flights came through in both directions (north and south) in the wee hours of the morning. I enjoyed talking to the captains and crew and generally being very visible to our regular local passengers, many of whom I came to know.

## King of the Upgrade

One of my favorite ploys was upgrading local VIPs who were booked in Tourist Class (Economy to those of you too young to remember when we called it Tourist) to First Class without their knowing it until boarding time. The country manager was the only one who could authorize upgrades and waive excess baggage charges. PanAm and Panagra's country directors (as they were called) rarely went to the airport, and they did not do as much of this as Braniff during my administration. The clients loved me for it and I consolidated a number of accounts as a result and made a lot of Braniff-friends. I justified it to Dallas by saying it was "product-sampling" and these people might like First Class so much they would buy First Class next time. But the real reason was that we were converting a lot of frequent flyers (before the term was invented) to Braniff from Pan American and Panagra, which had 'owned' Panama for 25 years. Braniff's airport staff also liked it because they felt (correctly) that I was paying a lot of attention to the airport operation. Which is where the action is in the airline business. They did not realize that for the past three or four years I had never seen an airplane in the line of duty.

Camilo and Berta Fabrega were good friends and helped to introduce us around in Panama. Camilo was a Braniff sales rep and had recently been promoted to DSM. He was related to half of Panama and knew everyone that was worth knowing. Through him we met people like Alberto Motta, who practically owned the Colon Free Zone and did a lot of business with his company and established a long time friendship. Alberto eventually bought COPA, one of PanAm's local subsidiaries, and survives as a thriving airline to this day.

The Panama Canal Company, which operated the Canal, was a major client with something like 30,000 expatriate Americans living in the 'Zone' as was the military. I spent a lot of time there, calling on the administration's travel (they called it 'traffic') department, something that neither of my predecessors nor colleagues at PanAm and Panagra did. The people there liked this and I suspect that as a result I won more than our proportionate share of business which was supposed to be evenly divided among the three U.S. carriers. My counterparts never left their offices except to play golf and go to 'the club' at Fort Amador. They sent a sales representative to call on the accounts and travel agents in Panama proper. But I enjoyed getting out of the office and seeing customers. And it was obviously working because more and more passengers were flying Braniff out of Panama.

Our social life was also pretty hectic. There seemed to be an embassy cocktail party every night of the week, what with some twenty Latin America countries represented, in addition to the U.S., Canadian, and Europeans; and we were on every one's list—the word had spread that I was king of the upgrade. The local 'society' had also taken us in as their own, as the combination of my being Braniff's senior person and, with Martha, being a South American couple, and bilingual: all this seemed to be very attractive for some reason. And three or four times a week I would drop Martha off and drive to the airport, so I did not get very much sleep and probably drank more than necessary (the story of my life). But I was young and fit (I was swimming a lot on the weekends). We were also members of the Fort Amador country club which was the meeting place for high society, both Zonians (as they were called) and Panamanians. It had a private beach with a shark fence—Martha never became used to the idea that a shark might find a way inside the fence, so she refused to go swimming very much. But the kids liked the beach.

## *Teddy Roosevelt Slept Here*

We had a company driver, a Jamaican, Warren Sealey, one of the nicest guys you could want to know. He took me under his wing and introduced me around. We became more like friends and his wife came to cook for us. We had moved in to a fabulous old 'landmark' 1890s-vintage home in the El Carmen suburb shortly after arriving in Panama. It was a wooden three-story house with verandahs all round and lots of grounds. The house belonged to the Arias, one of the '14 families' and they had entertained Theodore Roosevelt there during the early days of independence and the Canal construction. And when we were not going out to a party we entertained at home, inviting travel agents and other airline managers (all the Europeans and several South American carriers had offices in Panama) and the employees of Braniff and their families. Again, this was not customary for a Braniff country manager. But we made a lot of friends which did no harm to the business, and helped employee morale.

Our stay in Panama was marred when Mum called us to tell us that Dad was in the hospital with lung cancer. We made a quick trip to Montevideo and managed to see him briefly before he died. He was barely 60 and he missed enjoying his grandchildren. We convinced Mum to come and stay with us in Panama which she did. She was a great help with the children.

## Side Trip to Bogota

The territory included "off-line" Colombia which I covered with periodic visits to Bogota and Medellin, then the second largest city, and both were potential 'feeder' markets for Braniff. Early in 1957, Rex Brack called me from Dallas, and told me that a Braniff delegation was coming through Panama, on its way to Bogota on the company DC-3, with president Chuck Beard; head of operations, R.V. Carleton; our public relations chief, Walter Henshel; and others. Braniff had just been awarded the right to serve the Colombian capital, the first U.S. carrier to do so, and he wanted me to join them and travel to Bogota for a week of meetings, in preparation for the beginning of service some time in March. He did not say anything else so I figured that he wanted someone who could speak Spanish and act as translator because no one else in Dallas spoke Spanish. Martha was pregnant and I did not like to leave her alone with our cook but Warren agreed to move in while I was out of town. It was a sort of 'command performance' and I liked Bogota anyway which was very cosmopolitan, and at 8,400 feet above sea level boasting a cooler climate that was a relief from Panama's heat and humidity.

I met the airplane at Tocumen Airport and boarded after a 60-minute stopover during which I arranged for Mr. Beard to meet the employees at the airport VIP room. The flight to Bogota was a lot of fun. R.V. Carleton sat in the left hand seat and flew the airplane. About half way to Bogota, he opened the door to the cabin and tossed an empty bottle of Johnny Walker Black Label down the aisle. It was his idea of a joke. Chuck Beard was at first taken aback and then burst out laughing. People were in a great mood.

In Bogota we were met by Braniff's lawyer, Eduardo Zuleta Angel who had been Colombia's first General Secretary of the United Nations. We were whisked through customs and immigration and driven to the Hotel Tequendama, another PanAm/InterContinental property.

## General Rojas Pinilla

During our stay we called on the U.S. Ambassador, a cousin of Henry Cabot Lodge, either a Cabot or a Lodge, or both; the head of Colombia's civil aviation, a colonel; the president of Avianca, Juan Pablo Ortega, a visionary who was the first to try to form a united front among airlines in the region, unsuccessfully; and president Rojas Pinilla, the dictator. He was not exactly pro-U.S., but he was polite and receptive, at least on the surface. I found out later that the reason was not so much that he disliked *gringo* companies, it was our choice of attorney that bothered him the most. I later got to know Juan Pablo

Ortega and admired him tremendously. He tried very hard to convince the airlines of the Andean countries to form an association so as to compete more effectively with the gringos: Braniff and Pan Am. He was ahead of his time. Most, if not all, of the other airlines in the region were government-owned and managed by nationalistic air force-appointed generals who probably killed the idea before it ever got off the ground.

We also held a reception for the travel agent community and I was able to introduce several of the leaders because I had met them on my monthly sales trips. Jaime and Jorge Correal of TMA, the lead travel agent, were good friends. In fact, Jaime, the older brother, was married to a Panamanian and both Martha and I had entertained them in Panama. This impressed Rex Brack no end because he knew that the Correals were among the most influential. By the end of the week, the night before we were returning, Chuck Beard had a small party for the Braniff group, including Eduardo Zuleta, his young partner, Carlos Urdaneta, and two or three guests. At the end of the evening, Rex Brack asked me to stay over for a conversation with Mr. Beard after everyone else had left.

"Bobby, we want you to move to Bogota" Mr. Beard said as Rex Brack poured me a scotch and water once I had sat down. I almost spilled the drink because we had been in Panama less than ten months and another move seemed pretty painful, particularly with Martha expecting next month. I mentioned this but they did not seem to accept this as an excuse. Apparently the proposed Country Manager, an American who had been pre-selected, had not done very well during the visit. His Spanish was only so-so, and he was not very couth (to use Rex's remark). Bogota was very formal and European. My British-ness and fluent Spanish had impressed some of the officials we had met during the week. Chuck Beard said: "Look, Bobby, Bogota is going to be far more important than Panama, this is also the first time an American airline has been authorized to serve the capital of Colombia and we think you will do a terrific job. Rex is going to discuss salary and so on when we get back to Dallas. But I want you to accept."

On the way back to Panama Rex Brack told me that Braniff would make special allowances for Martha to have the baby in Uruguay if that was what she wanted. I realized that I really had no choice, and I kind of liked the idea of starting an operation from scratch. I convinced Rex to give Camilo Fabrega, my sales manager, the chance to replace me. I told Rex that this would send a great signal because we were promoting a Panamanian, something that no other U.S. carrier had done in the past, and he agreed. The American candidate was to be assigned to Ecuador, so everyone was happy.

## Bogota, the Athens of South America

From the 1996 edition of "The South American Handbook" (there will be no test):

> *Colombia is the fourth largest country in South America. It has coast lines upon both the Caribbean and the Pacific. Nearly 55% of the area is almost uninhabited with only 4% of the population; the other 96% are concentrated in the remaining 45%, living for the most part in narrow valleys or isolated basins, or in the broad Caribbean lowlands.*
>
> *The Spaniards sailed along the northern coast as far as Panama as early as 1500. Cartagena was founded in 1533. In 1536, Gonzalo Jimenez de Quesada pushed up the Magdalena river to discover its source; mounting the Eastern Cordillera in 1536, he discovered the Chibchas, conquered them, and founded Santa Fe de Bogota in 1538. In the meantime, Pizarro's lieutenant, Sebastian de Belcazar, had pushed down the Cauca valley from Ecuador and founded Pasto, Popayan and Cali in 1536.*
>
> *The movement towards independence from Spain was set going in 1794 by a translation into Spanish by the criollo Antonio Nariño of the French Declaration of the Rights of Man. Late in 1812 the young Bolivar, driven out of Venezuela, landed at Cartagena, in a brilliant campaign in 1813 he pushed up the Magdalena to Ocaña, and from there to Cúcuta, and obtained permission from the Junta at Tunja to advance into Venezuela. In 90 days he marched the 1,200 kilometres to Caracas, over mountain country fighting six battles, but he was unable to hold Caracas and withdrew to Cartagena in 1814. Napoleon fell in 1815, and the Spanish Government immediately set about reconquering, with some success, Venezuela and New Granada. Bolivar had now assembled an army of Llaneros, fortified by a British legion recruited from ex-servicemen of the Peninsula wars, in Venezuela and Angostura, or Ciudad Bolivar as it is called today. In the face of incredible difficulties he made a forced march across the Andes in 1819. After joining with Francisco de Paula Santander's Nueva Granada army, he defeated the royalists at the Battle of the Swamps of Vargas in July and again at Boyaca on 7 August. He entered Bogota three days later.*

*Until the advent of air transport, Colombia's capital city, Bogota, was commercially inaccessible, except via the River Magdalena, followed by a tortuous rail or road connection.*

## Four Musketeers

In 1957 when I arrived there, Bogota was known as "The Athens of South America." It was cultured, the people civilized, and had oodles of history. This is where Simon Bolivar lived with Manuelita Saenz after the wars of independence. They lived at the Quinta Bolivar, now a museum, before leaving for Santa Marta, on the north coast, where he died. The city probably has more museums and historic buildings than any other in Latin America. When I arrived the population was something like two million (it is now about five million).

Late in February I packed Martha, Valerie, and Robbie off to Montevideo where Martha would have Guy—due in March, and I then proceeded to pack our stuff and move to Bogota where I arranged to live at the Tequendama while Martha was in Montevideo. I did most of it wrong, I left certain important items like the water heater in the house but packed all of Valerie's precious crayons.

When we were there in January, we had agreed to headquarter Braniff at the Hotel Tequendama, where there was ideal space for a ticket office at the rear of the hotel, with administrative offices just overhead. Living there would make it easy to spend a lot of time on the job.

Among the first people we hired was Percy Welton as the station manager. He was an Anglo-Colombian who had had airline experience with Avianca. He became my personal assistant in the job of recruiting, selecting, and hiring about 75 employees for sales, administration, and the airport. Carlos Urdaneta, Dr. Zuleta's young partner—about two years older than myself—quickly became a staunch friend, and also helped with introductions, including acceptance to the Gun Club, the prestigious downtown business lunch club, and the San Andres Golf Club. His father, Roberto Urdaneta, had been a former president of Colombia, which did not hurt.

Carlos introduced me to Alvaro Castellanos, an advertising agent, and I hired him to handle our account. This was a wise choice, and Alvaro became a close friend and very good at his job. We also hired Guillermo ('El Maestro') Payan to handle public relations, another lucky break because he became invaluable. El Maestro was a journalist friend of Alvaro's and some-time poet and published author. We used the media to very good effect, publicizing the airline before startup and getting some great editorial coverage. He was a real friend and supporter. I was incredibly lucky in assembling a team which included a number of others, all of them very loyal and dedicated.

Through Jaime Correal, I met Ian North, the British B.O.A.C. manager, who had lived in Peru and South America since after the war, and Juan Ucros, the General Traffic & Sales Manager of Avianca—I had met him in Panama. We became inseparable and had a very social, if somewhat pissy time. Colombians all drank like crazy. Ian and I, not to be outdone, did likewise. Ian had been in the war, had joined the British army straight out of school, and had spent time in India. His mother was Spanish and he had that incredible mixture of being very British but with a dark Spanish-kind of swarthiness. He had a terrific sense of humor and was always laughing and telling stories. One of his favorites was how he put down some kind of Indian mutiny somewhere on the Ganges River and was sent back to England in disgrace, having ordered his men to fire at the Indians which was a no-no. He was married to a Peruvian, Rosita Pestaña. He had met and married her in Lima.

Juan Ucros and Jeanne, his American wife, were lovely people. Juan was Mr. Avianca in Colombia and in spite of our being competitors, we spent a lot of time together and became close friends. Juan eventually left the airline to run the helicopter subsidiary, HELICOL, and later on I lured him away to become Country Manager for Braniff in Colombia. He remained with Braniff and then Eastern Air Lines until he retired a few years ago. Juan was one of the true gentlemen in the business and I miss him sorely. He passed away in 1995.

Jaime, Ian, Juan, and myself became known in Bogota as the four musketeers, we were always partying together, playing golf or something, including out-of-town trips to Cartagena and other parts. The fact that Jaime was probably the number one travel agent, while Ian and I represented foreign carriers, both in direct competition with Juan's AVIANCA, made the friendship even stranger. It was probably a sign of the times, competition was very much a gentleman's sport, a sort of country club atmosphere pervaded the business at the time. Not that we didn't compete, just that it was done in a Marquess of Queensbury rules environment. The fact was that we were close personal friends—we enjoyed the same things, and our wives and children got along as well.

## The Colonel Calls

We were scheduled to start service on 1 April 1957, and life was hectic. About three weeks from startup, I received a call from the Air Force Colonel who was head of civil aviation, to come and meet him at his office near the airport. I decided to take Percy with me as he was in charge of the airport, but when we were announced to the Colonel, we were advised that I was to go in to his office alone. Inside, the Colonel was in full uniform, with a huge 45 caliber automatic that he took off his belt and placed on the desk. After shaking hands rather coldly, and without a smile, said: "Sr. Booth (he pronounced it more like Booze), I have to tell you that my government is very unhappy with your legal representative in Colombia, Dr. Zuleta Angel. For your information, he has been conspiring against president General Rojas Pinilla and I have to advise you that as long as he is your 'apoderado' (legal representative)—Braniff will not be allowed to land in Bogota, or any other Colombian airport."

I thanked him for the information formally and advised him that I would notify Dallas, and left his office rather smartly. In the cab I told Percy about the message and headed for the U.S. embassy. We were met by the U.S. Ambassador, who told me that this was a dictatorship and his recommenda-

*With Bob Burck, Braniff VP, I share pleasantries with the Colonel who, on this occasion, was amiability itself.*

tion was that we switch lawyers. This would be a lot easier than trying to get the State Department to lodge a complaint. I asked him why and he said: "Bobby, look, Rojas Pinilla may not last, it is true that Zuleta is involved with the liberal and conservative coalition which is trying to get Rojas to resign. While Rojas won't resign easily, the U.S. is supporting this and we aren't going to complicate matters by fighting over your lawyer. And anyway, I'm sure there are a number of perfectly acceptable lawyers."

He was pretty emphatic and asked if I wanted him to call Chuck Beard himself. I said no, I could handle that and would pass on his recommendations.

At the Tequendama I placed a call to Dallas and spoke to Rex Brack, my direct boss. After telling him about the Colonel and then the U.S. Ambassador, Rex asked me for my recommendation. I said I would personally gamble that the Colonel was bluffing. That if we changed Zuleta we would look like a bunch of ninnies in Bogota society because it could not be kept secret. And, what the hell, I said: "Rojas Pinilla isn't going to live for ever, and I suggest we call the Colonel's bluff and go ahead as planned."

Rex chuckled over the phone and told me to stand by the 'phone, he would talk to Chuck Beard and get back to me within the hour. In the meantime I had called my pals Carlos Urdaneta, Alvaro Castellanos, and Maestro Payan to join Percy and me in the suite. They arrived within ten minutes of my conversation with Rex Brack and we opened the bar. Percy told the others about the Colonel and the ambassador. Carlos Urdaneta was shocked and wanted to call Dr. Zuleta but I told him not to do so until we heard back. The call took longer to come, almost two hours. By that time we were all well on our way to getting smashed. When the call came it was Chuck Beard and not Rex on the line: "Bobby, you still want to hang tough and keep Eduardo?"

I replied in the affirmative, even though I was beginning to wonder. I heard Chuck actually laugh and he said: "Go ahead, Bobby, tell Eduardo Zuleta that no colonel nor general is going to choose who represents us or works for us. And you can tell the ambassador the same thing."

At that point we all proceeded to get drunk and Carlos put his arm around me and said he was proud of me and Braniff. Alvaro, who knew the colonel personally, said we should not do anything and just wait, after all we still have three weeks for the inaugural flight. "In the meantime we are going to launch the advertising campaign starting this Sunday with a double truck ad in 'El Tiempo', and that should tell the colonel we aren't going to play his game."

Maestro was even more positive. He obviously knew about the liberal-conservative coalition which was in the making. He only added: "Let's hope these guys move quicker, rather than slower."

## *No Amount of Planning Replaces Dumb Luck*

The next day, 10 March, Rojas Pinilla stepped down under pressure from the coalition and the United States. He left on an Avianca flight to Madrid and a temporary government was set up pending elections. And Braniff inaugurated service on 1 April. Flights were full, not least because the word had spread that we had supported Zuleta Angel and he was part of the coalition which had ousted the dictator. And I became something of a celebrity, which was not bad going for a 29-year-old high school drop out.

Martha arrived some time in April with the three children and we moved in to a lovely English-looking house in Calle 84 in 'el Norte', the most fashionable suburb on the side of the mountain surrounding the Bogota 'sabana.' Again we entertained like mad, we were somewhat the 'toast of the town', partly because of the Rojas Pinilla incident, partly because Martha was very pretty and everyone liked her, and partly because as the Braniff Country Manager, I was able to do a lot of favors.

We spent three years in Bogota and it was a pretty fabulous time. Mum spent quite a bit of time with us, commuting back to Montevideo for a few weeks at a time and also to Porto Alegre to visit her sisters. We made dozens of friends and traveled the country to the major cities, especially Cali, Medellin, and Barranquilla. We particularly liked Cartagena where we spent time on the Rosario Islands just off the coast. We had made friends with 'Conejo' Lemaitre, a local 'big-wig' in the famous walled city (his great-grandfather was reported to have been a famous pirate) who owned one of the islands and had built a terrific house on the beach there. The reef off the islands had some of the best spear-fishing I have ever encountered.

To some extent Braniff had become the fashionable way to fly to the U.S., because Avianca had had a monopoly for too long and had become somewhat sloppy, and also because our Bogota-based airport staff and flight attendants were society girls who knew all the passengers and did a terrific job. In addition, the fact that we had recruited all the employees from the somewhat snobby Bogota society was very good for sales. The Braniff schedule, which had our flight arriving in the morning and departing at 1730 back to Panama and Miami was very popular. Because of the long turn-around we were able to maintain a very high on-time record, which AVIANCA was not able to match. We became The On-Time Airline and the frequent flyers loved it.

One night we were invited to a dinner at the Zuleta Angels where we were introduced to Alberto Lleras Camargo, a former and later president of Colombia. In fact, Martha was very impressed because there were four ex-presidents at the party. Roberto Urdaneta, Carlos's father, Alberto Lleras, and at least two others. On the way home from the party she told me she had been introduced to four presidents! We were too young to know that ex-presidents are always addressed as "Mr. President."

## Luis Miguel and Antonio, Olé

In Bogota, we discovered bull fighting and were lucky enough to meet Luis Miguel Dominguin and Antonio Ordoñez, the bull fighters who were made famous by Ernest Hemingway later on. I still believe they were among the best, ever. Antonio was actually married to Luis Miguel's sister. We never missed a bullfight during the season at the famous Bogota 'plaza' across the street from the Tequendama. I also did some bull-fighting myself, at a farm outside Bogota where they organized "tientas" for tourists. I didn't fight real bulls, just young steers and heifers. The feeling was great, particularly when the young steer charged the cape and you kept your two feet still as if in cement and you felt it swish by you. I knew how real bullfighters felt and loved it. Except one time when we were entertaining travel agents from all over Latin America during the annual COTAL (Latin American Travel Agents Federation) convention. I had too many 'aguardientes' before stepping out in the plaza and the young heifer gored me and cracked two ribs. Very painful and nothing much you can do about it. It took about two months to mend, but travel agents from all over would congratulate me for years afterwards.

*This picture was taken at José Maria Plaza's ranch in Ecuador, during a travel agents' convention. A short time later, I was gored, with two cracked ribs. I should have stuck to my Velocette.*

Later I tried, unsuccessfully, to organize a Braniff-sponsored "mano-a-mano" between Ordoñez and 'El Cordobes', this would have been a major event because of their different styles. Ordoñez was the classical, while 'El Cordobes' was the 'new wave', a lot of showmanship. We met 'El Cordobes' in Quito, Ecuador, on a trip there later for the December Feria de Quito, a five-day bullfight 'extravaganza.' We also met Galo Plaza, another former president (of Ecuador), and secretary general of the Organization of American States, one of the most interesting people ever. He invited us to his farm where his brother, Jose Maria, bred bulls.

I also discovered Simon Bolivar. Bogota was second only to Caracas as custodian-caretaker of Bolivar memorabilia and historical places. The 'Quinta Bolivar', a few blocks from the Tequendama, was one of my favorite tourist sites and I started reading everything I could find that was written about him. Bolivar seemed to me to have had it right, and this began my life-time fascination with this half-breed Venezuelan who fought the wars of inde-pendence from Caracas to Lima, and wanted to create a Federation of Spanish-speaking states from Venezuela to Bolivia. Bolivar's writings from exile in Jamaica and his letters from Lima, Quito, and Bogota: all these show the vision he had about the future of the region. After living in Lima with his Quito-born mistress, Manuelita Saenz (who was divorced from a boring Englishman, by the name of Thorne) he returned to Bogota. One of his lines, which I have used hundreds of times, regarding his efforts to unify South America, was that it was "Like plowing in the sea." He died in Santa Marta, Colombia, at the age of 44.

We made a lot of friends, including Philip Tibble, a Brit married to a Colombian and head of Phoenix Insurance. We made Ian North godfather of Guy, along with Sonha Correal, Jaime's wife, the godmother. We had a hectic social life but we were young and were able to keep up with the pace. I took up golf although I did not have the patience to play the game very well. We joined the local golf club, San Andres, which was not in the same class as the "Country Club," which we also joined; but I enjoyed the crowd at San Andres much more.

## Cartagena de Indias

One of my favorite places in Colombia, which drew me like a magnet, was Cartagena, primarily because of its history. It was a fort city on the Atlantic ocean, founded in 1533, and one of the oldest cities in the Americas. It had been attacked by Sir Francis Drake among others—and it was Bolivar's starting point for his campaign in Colombia in 1811. Through Maestro Payan and his buddy Alvaro Castellanos, I made friends with another "cartagenero", 'Bebe' Martelo, another fascinating character who became president of the Colombian Tourism Corporation.

In addition to Bebe, we established a lasting friendship with Luis Zalamea, a bright young Colombian writer and journalist who had been with the United Nations in New York, and through Luis I met Guillermo Leon Valencia, the President of Colombia, who was also a poet, like most people born in Popayan. He also liked to drink and was a great party-goer. With his help we organized the first Caribbean Tourism Organization (C.T.O.) Conference in Colombia and arranged for Colombia to join the organization. During the conference I met Abe Issa, of Jamaica, probably one of the smartest tourism promoters in the world. He ran the Jamaican Tourism Board and was a successful hotelier. He liked to tell the story about how Jamaica's Cabinet approved his tourism budget: He would tell the Cabinet that it cost $8 to bring a single visitor to the island, and then asked "How many visitors do you want next year? That's the budget!"

We also engineered some very effective public relations ploys with the help of Maestro Payan who was loved by the media. One of Bogota's perennial (to this day) problems was children on the street. These poor *gamines*, many of them orphans, roved the streets and back alleys and stole anything they could lay their hands on, because of the extreme poverty. We hired one of these, Elmer by name, and arranged for his education and he would work in the office after school as a messenger. He became a big favorite and was a terrific kid, but could not hire several hundred, which we would have liked to. But it was—I almost hate to admit it because it sounds exploitative—great public relations.

## Into the Corporate Jungle

Some time in 1959 I was beckoned to Dallas where I was offered a promotion to become System Manager-Sales Development, a newly-created job in the sales department. Rex Brack, who by this time had become something of a mentor, wanted me to back up Bob Burck who had been recently made head of sales. Bob was a Texan from Austin and a long-time Braniff veteran. Rex had been made Executive Vice President—Traffic & Sales and was effectively, along with R.V. Carleton, Chuck Beard's second-in-command. Burck was a strong sales executive but he did not have much of a feel for Latin America or international sales. My role was going to be to bring some internationalism and creativity to the organization.

The Latin American Division (although at the time still not a separate entity) was beginning to be the most profitable part of the airline. Rex told me that we were going to receive jet aircraft within the year and we needed to expand the market to handle the additional capacity which the larger and faster jets would generate. Braniff had ordered the Lockheed Electra in the mid-1950s and was late in introducing jet aircraft, as other airlines had done and were already introducing in 1959, so we were running behind the pack, especially in Latin America where Panagra and Pan American were starting jet service. The Braniff Boeing 707 would be delivered some time late in 1960 and would increase system capacity by at least 25 per cent. The 707s ordered by Braniff were a unique with a shorter fuselage than standard, with upgraded engines which would make it 'The Fastest Jet in the World', and, more important, enable it to land and take off with full payloads from airports at Bogota (8,400 feet above sea level), Quito (10,000 feet), and La Paz (13,400 feet).

# The Corporate Jungle

We arrived in Dallas in July 1959 after a round of farewell parties that left us exhausted. Martha took the children to visit in Montevideo and then came back with Mother who had sold or given away most of her belongings in Uruguay. Many people in Dallas helped us to settle in, especially Dwight and Alice Chiles. Dwight and I had become friends in the earlier days, when he had taken over as Agency & Interline Manager from Bob Phinney, who had been transferred to London as Off Line Manager for Europe. Dwight and I traveled a lot together because most of what I was trying to do overlapped his responsibilities and vice versa. Dwight had a Texan's low key sense of humor and we had some great times together. We became known as 'The Terrible Two-some.'

Dwight, about four years my senior, had been a B-25 pilot in the Second World War, had been shot down over Germany, and had been a prisoner-of-war. He and Alice took us under their wing. They had three children a little older than Valerie, Robbie, and Guy, and we spent a lot of time together.

Early on I set up a New York-based South American Sales Group with a Manager and three 'ethnic' sales representatives recruited from other airlines and within Braniff. The Group was designed to develop South American sales from the northeastern region, including Washington, D.C. It did a great job and started to show positive results very quickly. This effort gave my position a boost as we

*The Terrible Two-some.*

introduced the Boeing 707 in South American service and the Eastern Air Lines interchange from New York to Miami which gave us a through flight from northeastern U.S.A. to the west coast of South America and onward to Buenos Aires and Brazil.

## The World's first Code-Share Agreement

In São Paulo we were obliged to serve the new international airport at Viracopos, which is at least an hour's drive from downtown. We arranged with Omar Fontana, president of Sadia, at that time a small regional airline, to provide what was probably one of the first 'Code Share' flights, to connect our passengers between Viracopos and the downtown Congonhas airport. This was a huge success. We actually called it a 'change-of-gauge' flight, the term 'code share' not having yet been invented. But the impact was the same.

Omar was a large man with huge hands and fingers like sausages, but this did not inhibit his ability to play classical piano at the drop of a hat. We were never close friends but I always had a special feeling for him as a real aviation entrepreneur. He had started his airline in 1955 with one DC-3 hauling meat from Concordia, his father's meat packing factory, to São Paulo and other markets. In 1963 he replaced the DC-3 with two British Handley Page Heralds and later on he changed the name of the airline to TransBrasil. At this writing he operates a fleet of large jets and serves the United States, Europe, and Argentina.

## The Panama Incentive Travel Program

Late in 1959 I heard from one of my contacts in Panama's Tourism Board (the IPAT, Instituto Panameño de Turismo) that a certain Bill Conley was coming to Panama to investigate the potential for a major travel incentive program. Conley was the President of Gibson Refrigerator which was headquartered somewhere in Michigan. I did some quick checking and finally telephoned his assistant. They had not set their travel plans so I suggested that they should use Braniff and that I would meet them—without any prior commitment. I pitched the fact that I had been Braniff's Country Manager in Panama and that I knew the place and all the key people there. After a while Bill Conley called me himself and agreed that a team of five people would be traveling and that they would book themselves on Braniff.

I met them in Miami and we flew down together. As a result we sold the largest travel incentive program ever, some 30 round trips from all over the United States for 5,000 Gibson dealers and sales people. The program was a terrific success and Braniff received a lot of publicity on top of a valuable

*The world's first code-share. In 1963, on the same ticket, passengers on Braniff DC-8 (center) could switch to Sadia's Handley Page Herald (bottom) at São Paulo's international airport, to connect to the downtown airport. Sadia was led by the remarkable Dr. Omar Fontana (top).*

chunk of business. Later Braniff sold Gibson again, this time to Honolulu in another massive incentive program.

In Dallas Bob Burck was a tough boss. In fact he was probably one of the toughest yet in a sense he was very good for me. He would send back my memoranda, correcting my grammar with a red pencil and tightening them up. He believed in 'short is sweet.' He was also a terror on expense reports and gave me a hard time as I had been used to a liberal allowance when reporting to Rex Brack who always approved everything without question. Bob also arranged for me to go to the AMA (American Management Association), in New York for a management course on MBO (Management By Objective) which had just come into its own. I picked up on it pretty quickly and became the company's greatest proponent, implementing it in the sales department. And it worked. He also had me go to a speech trainer at SMU (Southern Methodist University) which was also useful, but did little for my public speaking. He told me not worry about this as long as I believed in the subject matter. I still have a real hard time with nerves and sweaty palms every time I have to speak in public—according to the speech trainer: "If you aren't nervous in front of a bunch of people, you shouldn't be there." Which I keep in mind every time I have to do it to this day. According to him, Winston Churchill had a bad case of the nerves every time he had to speak in public. Not a bad endorsement.

## El Ché

I traveled a lot, most of the time with Dwight Chiles. We used to attend the ASTA (American Society of Travel Agents) conventions, the premier annual travel bash—usually in some exotic locale such as Hawaii or Havana. In 1959 I attended the ASTA Convention in Havana right after Castro came to power and had to sit through a four-hour opening ceremony speech by Fidel who was trying to 'make friends and influence' the U.S. travel agency community.

The Convention was held in October 1959 and Castro had taken over on the first day of the year. At the time he was still a hero to most people, including many in the United States. A travel agent friend of mine from Buenos Aires, Edgardo Nicholson, was there and at the opening reception he asked me if I would like to meet his cousin, Ernesto 'Ché' Guevara. Nicholson's mother and Ché's were cousins, I think. I know that Ché's father was a Lynch, (I wondered later if she and 'La Lynch' of Paraguay fame were related?) on his mother's side and there was obviously a connection there. I jumped at it because I had read a lot about Ché and knew about his motor-cycle-trip through Latin America in 1952. Edgardo told me to stand by and that we would be going to the Palace at 11 p.m. to say hello.

*The charismatic revolutionary (and Norton motorcyclist) Ché Guevara, circa 1960.*

It was an unforgettable meeting. We drank Courvoisier brandies while he talked about South America generally and his experiences in Bolivia, Peru, and Ecuador; and later in Guatemala and Mexico City, where he met Fidel. He hated the *gringos.*, and probably accepted me because he thought of me as a fellow South American, with some anglo blood in common (we talked about the Irish and the Welsh at one point) rather than the representative of an 'Imperialistic' American company. Later I found out that much of his anger at the United States came from his experiences as he traveled through Peru and Central America where he felt U.S. corporations in mining and other enterprises were "exploiting his Latin American brothers." He was also influenced by the Guatemalan experience during the early 1950s when the CIA masterminded the Arbenz downfall.

He was my age and looked just like the famous posters, beard and fatigues and all. The Palace office was huge, and we sat in comfortable leather settees by his desk. After the introductions, he came around his desk and sat with us. He chain-smoked cigars while I puffed on my pipe. When Edgardo told him I had raced motorcycles he was immediately interested. We both had ridden Norton 500 c.c. bikes. He had used one to travel through South America in his early twenties. I mentioned the fact that he had called it "La Poderosa" (the powerful one), and he laughed. I told him mine was a 1948 model, a replica of the motorcycle that had won the famous Manx Tourist Trophy in 1946. He recognized that my Manxman was far superior to his 1937 model. He was a fascinating guy and I know how he must have charmed Fidel and the other revolutionary Cubans.

We talked about rugby (he had played scrum half to my wingforward, and we had several mutual friends), and we talked about Simon Bolivar and

San Martin and their famous meeting in Guayaquil. We speculated on what happened at the meeting. We agreed that San Martin had simply decided that he could not, or would not, share the limelight with Bolivar and had returned to Argentina. I knew at the time that he was a Marxist communist, and that he hated the United States. On the other hand, I could tell from our conversation that he also had a deep commitment to Latin America, something that Bolivar had in a far greater degree than San Martin who was far more of a European.

He had a twinkle in his eye and was very charismatic, with a great sense of humor, rather self- deprecating. After the opening four-hour speech from Fidel I thought Ché was far more interesting. Thinking about the meeting later I thought that he was a Simon Bolivar to Fidel's San Martin—although my Argentine friends would never agree. Actually, Ché went on to fight other revolutionary wars, unsuccessfully, in Africa and finally in Bolivia. We agreed to meet again some time in the future, but that never happened. Edgardo and I returned to our hotel in the wee hours, pretty sloshed but delighted at having spent as much time with Ché as we did.

I later read the story of how he became head of Cuba's Central Bank, which is supposed to be the gospel truth. At a cabinet meeting Fidel asked for an 'economista' to be appointed head of the bank and Ché raised his hand and said "Yo soy." After the appointment, Ché told someone: he thought Fidel had said 'comunista.' True or false it's a helluva good story and reflects his sense of humor. Whatever one thinks of him, he died for his beliefs, right or wrong, in Bolivia in 1967 at the age of 39. At the time I was living in Peru as a Vice President of 'imperialistic' Braniff. Much later I read his "Motorcycle diaries" which were published posthumously by his father, as well as several biographies. To this day I am fascinated by the man. We shared a deep seated commitment to the region as a whole, even though I do not subscribe to his approach.

## Formation of SATO

At that convention in Havana, the first 'South American Suite' was organized by a group of South American tour operators to try to form a unified tourism promotional program, which included my old pal, Jaime Marquez of Turisport (he had taken over the American Express representation from Maitland Moore-Davie after his death) in Montevideo; Bobby Begg of City Service in Buenos Aires; Eddie Arrarte, Eduardo Proaño of Metropolitan in Quito; and a bunch of other chaps I knew. This led to a lot of close work with the 'Suite' guys who invited me to make a presentation on the subject of tourism marketing, at The Interamerican Travel Seminar which was a Mac Seligman invention. Russian-born Mac, after a stint in B-25s during the war in the Pacific (where he had been a prisoner-of-war) had been a newspaper man in Haiti, and then joined Hertz as its Latin American Sales Director. He organized the Seminars as a means of bringing all the travel interests together. He and I were old friends and remain so to this day. He is probably one of the best public relations practitioners in the country.

I taped a bunch of interviews with tour operators, travel agents, and consumers (I spent a lot of time at airports and asked questions about where they were going, and why not to South America). The tapes demonstrated the need for a major educational-promotional program. Even highly respected tour operators were totally ignorant about South America (many still are!). I edited the tapes from seven or eight hours down to about 25 minutes, highlighting the need for promotion and played them at the Seminar which was held in Miami at The Columbus hotel. The response was terrific from airlines and travel industry representatives, and we organized a small steering committee to come up with what became the South American Travel Organization (SATO).

SATO kicked off the first cooperative tourism development program with participation by both the public and the private sector. We had received a lot of help from Gordon McCoun of Panagra, and from Juan Homs and Jim Woodman of Pan American. It was a real cooperative effort because we all recognized the potential for increasing air travel in that most elastic sector of the airline business, the leisure market. Because I had played a very active role in the development of SATO I was elected as its first (non-paid) president. Braniff gained much credit for our involvement and we made many friends in high places as a result. It also won us an inside track with government tourism boards and others in the governments of the time. In the first year we were able to invest close to $400,000 in the United States in trade advertising and other promotions. The funds were generated through membership and direct contributions from airlines, tour operators, hotels and the governments. We had a totally voluntary staff in the beginning which meant that 100% of the moneys collected was invested in marketing and sales rather than in administration.

Meanwhile I was having trouble with Bob Burck because he felt I was spending too much time on the international end of the business. He did not like South America or anything outside Texas. We had a number of arguments about where I was spending most of my time and effort and it was becoming difficult. The relationship was not untenable, but there was constant tension between us. He also resented, I suspect, my personal relationship with Rex Brack, his boss. The problem was that to a certain extent, Bob was right. I found the international side of the airline business far more dynamic and interesting and as a result I probably was spending more time on it than I should have. The November 1963 Kennedy assassination in Dallas had also had a profound effect on my feelings about Dallas. Quite unfair, but a fact nonetheless. Both Martha and I were tremendous Kennedy "fans." I was beginning to question whether we wanted to stay in Dallas indefinitely.

## If it ain't Fun— Invent a New Job

Early in 1964 I called Rex Brack at his home one Saturday afternoon. I said: "Rex, I want to talk about an idea regarding Latin America." He told me to come over. The region had grown to a six-airplane operation and was beginning to have some problems because of the increased competition from South American airlines which had acquired jets and were beginning to make inroads. Aerolineas Argentinas, as an example, had introduced the British Comet as early as 1959 and was doing extremely well competing against the U.S. and European airlines in the region. I felt that Braniff needed better direction and supervision in the region.

"What have you got in mind, Bobby?" Rex asked. I told him I wanted to run Latin America, preferably from Lima. "Rex, there's no one around here who knows more about it, I've run two countries and I've spent the last five years here in the G.O. I know the people and I know the competition. I have

*This is how I looked behind a desk, which was not bad, but not my idea of an airline life. At least I had my pipe.*

the contacts in the government because of my SATO involvement. I can build a cohesive organization. Just give me the chance. The reason for basing myself in Lima is that I will have to travel a whole lot and it will save a lot of wear and tear because it is centrally located."

Rex was thoughtful. We were sitting in the front porch of his rambling house. He asked me to walk inside and said: "Lets have a drink on it. I think you're right but I have to tell you that you've got competition. Charlie South has been talking to Chuck about the same thing. Let me figure things out over the weekend and I'll talk to Chuck. Okay?"

I was flabbergasted. Charlie South had been Country Manager in Brazil and for the past several years had been Braniff's vice president in Washington in charge of government affairs. We were friends, but not close. I had first met him when he was Country Manager in Rio and I was in Montevideo. He was very likable and a scratch golfer. His wife was sweet and she and Martha became friends. He was about ten years older than me, and had joined Braniff very early on in Panama, after starting out with Pan American. I knew he was close to Beard but I felt that I was more qualified for the top Latin American job. I went home worried, because I did not want to report to him, I knew our relationship would not be the same. In a sense we were competing for the same job which I had 'invented.' On the other hand, Charlie probably thought that he had too.

On Monday Rex called me up to his office on the 10th floor and then walked me across to Chuck Beard's office. Chuck was all smiles when he said: "Okay Bobby, I think we have the perfect arrangement. Charlie South is going to move to Dallas and will be Vice President in charge of Latin America, you will move to Lima as Staff Vice President-Sales reporting to Charlie. What do you think?"

This was not what I had in mind when I broached the idea but it was not all bad. I could work for Charlie, even though it was not the ideal situation. But I wanted to be out of Dallas and this would do it. The corporate life was not my idea of fun. While I had enjoyed my five years and had learned an awful lot, I really did not want to be a corporate animal. So some time later we moved to Peru.

From the 1996 "The Handbook of South America":

*Peru is the third largest South American country (twice the size of France) but presents formidable difficulties to human habitation. The whole of its western seaboard with the Pacific is desert on which rain seldom falls. From this coastal shelf the Andes rise*

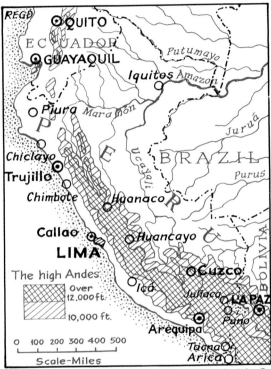

*Peru is the largest country in South America. Until the end of the Second World War, Lima was the only Peruvian city with more than half a million peple. Today, Trujillo and Arequipa exceed the million mark.*

steeply to a high Sierra which is studded with massive groups of soaring mountains and gouged with deep canyons. The high land slopes more gradually to the east; the mountains in its eastern zone are deeply forested and ravined. Eastward from these mountains lie the vast jungle lands of the Amazon basin.

In the Sierra, at an average altitude of 3,000 meters, which covers 26% of the country, live about 50% of the people, an excessive density on such poor land. This high level land of gentle slopes is surrounded by towering groups and ranges of high peaks. Ten exceed 6,000 meters. The highest, Huascarán, is 6,768 meters. There are many volcanoes in the south. The South American continental divide is the western rim of mountains looking down on the Pacific. In spite of the handicaps and the lack of written word, Peru has revealed one of the richest pre-Columbian his-

*tories in the Americas, of highly advanced societies that prevailed against awesome odds. There were in fact, many civilized cultures dating back as far as 2000 BC. It is generally accepted that the earliest settlers in Peru were related to people who had crossed the Bering Straits from Asia and drifted through the Americas from about 20,000 BC.*

*The Indians rose in 1780 (against the Spanish conquistadores) under the leadership of an Inca noble who called himself Tupac Amaru II. He and many of his lieutenants were captured and put to death under torture at Cusco. Eventually help came to them from the outside world: José de San Martin's Argentine troops, convoyed from Chile under the protection of Lord Cochrane's squadron, landed in southern Peru on 7 September 1820. San Martin proclaimed Peruvian independence at Lima on 28 July 1821, though most of the country was still in the hands of the Viceroy, José de la Serna. Simon Bolivar, who had recently freed Venezuela and Colombia, sent Antonio José de Sucre to Ecuador, where on 24 May 1822, he gained a victory over La Serna at Pichincha. San Martin, after meeting with Bolivar at Guayaquil, left for Argentina and a self-imposed exile in France, while Bolivar and Sucre completed the conquest of Peru by defeating La Serna at the battle of Junin (6 August 1824) and the decisive battle of Ayacucho (9 December 1824).*

# Lima, City of Kings

We arrived in Lima in May of 1964, the beginning of winter. After a few weeks at the Lima Country Club we moved into a lovely four-bedroom house in San Isidro, one of the fancier suburbs. Peru was at that time enjoying unprecedented economic stability and growth. The Belaunde administration was pro-U.S. and while the 40 families who, for all purposes, ruled the country did not believe in the 'trickle down' theory of economic development, people seemed to be reasonably prosperous. There was considerable optimism in the air and Lima's tag 'City of Kings' still appeared to be justified. The Lima Country Club, in San Isidro across the street from the Lima Golf Club, was the social center of the community and was 'the' place to be.

Braniff was well established and Folger Athearn, Braniff's country manager was socially very well connected and helped us to get established. Braniff had cleverly located a major flight attendant base in Lima and had

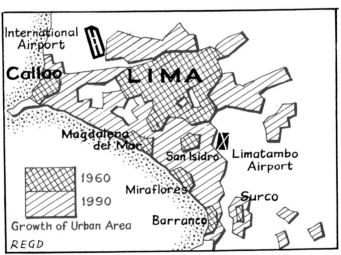

*Founded in 1535, Lima has always been the trading and commercial hub of the Pacific coast of South America. In recent years, it has grown rapidly, engulfing all its neighboring suburbs.*

64

hired socially prominent young men and women, a strategy that gave the airline one of its major selling advantages. We eventually did this in Buenos Aires, Santiago, Bogota, and Rio, and it worked particularly well everywhere. Apart from the cost, which was significantly less than by using U.S.-based flight attendants, these boys and girls knew most of our customers by name (as a matter of record, American Airlines has maintained most of these bases to this day). While Panagra was well established because of its pioneering history since 1928, to some extent Braniff was considered a viable alternative and was well regarded, partly because of the local hiring practice but also because we provided an alternative to what had been, for many years, almost a monopoly situation on the west coast of South America.

> *Lima, capital of Peru, was the chief city of Spanish South America from its founding in 1535 until the independence of the South American republics in the early 19th century. It is built on both sides of the Rio Rimac, lying at the foot of the Cerro San Cristobal. From among the traditional buildings which still survive soar many tall skyscrapers which have changed the old skyline out of recognition. The Universidad de San Marcos was founded in 1551, and a printing press in 1595; among the earliest of the kind in South America. Lima's first theatre opened in 1563. Few cities in the Old World could rival its wealth and luxury. Today it is a sprawling metropolis of eight million inhabitants, unfortunately surrounded by so-called "pueblos jovenes" ("favelas" in Brazil),which are tin-roofed shacks inhabited by squatters from the interior of the country.*

## Settling In

Of our children, Valerie was now nine, Robbie seven, and Guy five and a half. Valerie was enrolled rapidly in San Silvestre and Robbie at Markham. Both were English schools along the lines of the British Schools in Montevideo and dozens of others throughout South America: English teachers from England and the full tradition. My only complaint was that Markham did not play rugby. Guy went to Markham the second year we were there. Lima in the mid-sixties was an island. The wealthy were very wealthy and the poor, were very obviously, very poor. There were few of the former but a large majority of the latter.

Fernando Belaunde Terry had just assumed the presidency after several years of military rule. He was an architect, whose major campaign issue had been the building of the 'Marginal', a highway on the eastern Andes, which was intended to connect the rest of the country with the coastal area. Belaunde was 'old' family. His father had been exiled to Paris in 1924 during one of the periodic political turn-overs. He had been educated in the United States at the Universities of Miami and Texas. He founded 'Acción Popular', a middle-of-the-road political party which brought together all kinds of activists from the left, center, and extreme right. He was elected in 1963 with the help of the military. We subsequently met him and liked him as an honest and dedicated politician.

As a vice president of Braniff we were accepted instantly in the Lima society. This was enjoyable, good for business, and very pleasant. But there was always a nagging concern that something was not quite right. The more exposed we became to the very wealthy, the more we realized that, unlike Uruguay, or even Colombia, the gap between the 'haves' and the 'have nots' was tremendous. This was accentuated by the Indian strain in the largest segment of the population which were called, somewhat affectionately, the 'cholos.' It was not immediately apparent but there was just no middle class as in Uruguay and other parts of South America. Or if there was, it was not very visible.

Braniff's lawyer in Lima was Carlos Neuhaus who was married to Carmen Tudela and we became close friends. They had seven children, ranging from one slightly older than Valerie to one younger than Guy and we spent a lot of time with them at their home in La Rinconada, a suburb to which we later moved. Carlos was very active politically and he eventually became Mayor of San Isidro, Lima's most affluent suburb. But we did find that Peruvians generally displayed an inherent hospitality that was characteristic at all levels of society, from the 'oligarchy'—as long as you represented a foreign corporation and knew which forks to use at dinner—to the most primitive people in the small villages on the coast or in the highlands. Of all South Americans they are probably the friendliest and the warmest-hearted.

## Shelton's Barefoot Airline

One of the first people I met shortly after arriving in Peru was one of the most interesting aviation entrepreneurs of his time, C.N. (Connie) Shelton. We met in the 'Snake Pit' (otherwise: the Grill and Bar) at the Bolivar which was everyone's meeting place. He and I happened to be sitting at the bar, where he was enjoying his favorite 'mortini' (he always pronounced it that way) while I was drinking 'pisco sours.' As obvious foreigners we started a casual conversation. We talked about Braniff and APSA, and how our competition was really Panagra. Unfortunately, to my knowledge, we never met again. I knew and became good friends with Bill Spohrer, who worked for APSA, and who was married to C.N.'s daughter at the time. I was imme-

*The man on the extreme left is Connie Shelton, back in his TACA Ford Tri-Motor 1930s days (and probably after a 'mortini' night).*

diately taken with Shelton. He was quite a bit older than me, having flown for General Chiang Kai-shek during the war. But he liked to drink and we talked about the airline business generally. He told me about his theory which was later coined into the title of a book called *The Barefoot Airline*. He had a theory about the market which was quite simple: if you made it affordable, the market for air travel between the Americas was huge, and Panagra (and later Braniff) was serving only rich gringos and local businessmen. And he was absolutely right. I have always maintained that knowing your competition is as important as knowing your market.

At the time we met he was running three airlines, TAN (Honduras), CEA (Ecuador), and APSA as a single integrated consortium which was giving Braniff and Panagra fits with its reduced fares down the west coast of South America. APSA had recently introduced Convair 990 jets and they were giving us a run for our money. He had invented a form of frequent-flyer program in Peru which had proved to be highly successful. He 'sold' shares (a sort of bond) for $1,000 (U.S.) which gave the bearer 10% discount on all flights as well as a promised profit dividend. They actually sold about 7,000 of these and the bearers were extremely loyal to the airline, for obvious reasons. The dividend never materialized, and the bonds became worthless when the airline folded in the late 1960s. But it had proved to be a successful marketing gimmick and had raised a significant amount of cash for the airline to keep it airborne longer than it would normally have done.

## *Harding Lawrence Takes Over*

Shortly after we moved to Lima, Chuck Beard was replaced by Harding Lawrence. This was the result of a major ownership change in the airline when Troy Post and the GreatAmerica Corporation bought control in 1964. Great America was a three-man holding company which controlled a number of insurance companies worth hundreds of millions. Post was the investor, C. Edward Acker the financial man who analyzed and recommended investments, and Grant Fitts was the chief executive officer.

Acker had come in—a Troy Post appointee—as chief financial officer and after a few months he brought Harding in to be his boss and CEO of Braniff. I had met Ed in the last few weeks in Dallas, but I moved to Peru before Harding came on board. Ed was 6' 4" tall and about my age. He admitted to not knowing anything about the airline business but he was obviously a quick learner. He had met Harding in Los Angeles when Troy Post had sent him out to see if Bob Six would consider a merger with Braniff. Six was not interested, but Ed spent a lot of time with Harding and was duly impressed. At the time, Continental was a major success story and most people credited this to Harding who, as Executive Vice President, ran the day-to-day operation at the airline.

Harding Lawrence was born in Oklahoma in 1920, the son of a school teacher. He graduated from Texas as the war broke out and he became involved with W.F. Long, the Texas aviation pioneer, going to work for his civilian training school which had a contract with the British to train pilots for the R.A.F. Shortly after the war was over, he signed on with a small regional carrier, Pioneer Airlines, as Sales Manager. In 1955 he joined Continental as vice president-sales when Bob Six bought Pioneer. He was Executive Vice President and a director of the airline when Ed Acker hired him away in 1965 to join Braniff.

Some time early in 1965 I was beckoned to Dallas to meet our new leader. As a Staff VP, I was included in the 'Officers Staff' meeting which was an exclusive group of about 20 individuals who were invited to meet informally with Harding. He was charismatic and very direct. I was instantly taken with him. He was in his mid-forties, about six feet tall, and about eight years older than I was. He had a reputation for being very creative and forward thinking. He made a real impression. At a time when airlines were trying every device to lure more passengers (except discounting, which was strictly controlled by the Civil Aeronautics Board), he had put pianos on Continental's aircraft and had helped to build it as one of the most profitable second-tier airlines.

That Staff Meeting was the first of many. He used to go around the table and ask each executive to comment on his or her department (yes, Braniff did have a couple of women executives even then). The meetings were held every Thursday and whenever I could I combined a Dallas visit so that I could attend. I thoroughly enjoyed them, although eventually they became somewhat useless and in the late 1970s Harding dispensed with them.

In that first meeting, when he came around to me, he asked a series of questions about the South American operation, the people and so on. He had clearly done his homework. I realized later that Bennet King's visit earlier in the year had been part of his education. Bennet had shown up in Lima as VP-Public Relations for Continental, about two months before Lawrence moved to Dallas. He was reportedly very close to Harding and had evidently reported in detail about his RSA (round South America) trip. Fortunately Martha and I had liked Bennet and his wife and had entertained them and introduced them around. Harding said he wanted me to organize a visit that fall and asked me to suggest an itinerary. I caught Charlie South out of the corner of my eye, who seemed not like the idea too well but could not do much about it. Shortly after this, Tom King, Bennet's brother, moved in as head of advertising and promotion for Braniff. We hit it off immediately and became close friends.

Harding had just announced that he was placing a major order for Boeing's new three-engined jet, the 727, that domestically we were going to build a real hub in Dallas and needed the smaller airplanes for frequency rather than capacity. The 727 would be the QC (quick change) version and Braniff would be the first airline to fly cargo at night and passengers during the day. This would give us high utilization with the aircraft, probably 13 or 14 hours daily. He talked about his theory that an aircraft had to generate its capital cost in annual revenues. By achieving this kind of utilization, we would generate as much as 1.5 times their capital cost. He loved these rules-of-thumb. Another one, which is still valid, is "a nickel cost (per available seat mile) and a nickel profit (5% on revenues)." He was among the first to recognize the strength of a fortress-hub and built exactly that in Dallas, long before it became widespread in the industry.

About this time Harding had brought John Casey on board, as executive vice president. Casey was the older brother of Al Casey, American Airlines' CEO, and was a former World War bomber pilot. He had had something to do with Hiroshima, but I never knew the whole story. He came to Braniff from Seaboard, having started out in life with American in Tulsa in the maintenance department. He had an Irishman's short temper, but I liked him immediately.

The South American trip in the fall of 1965 was a huge success. Harding brought his (then) wife, Jimmie with him and the couple made a

*Harding Lawrence (left) at a press Conference at which staff VP Booth
seems to have taken over. On the right is Tom King, VP Promotions.*

great impression everywhere we took them. I had organized travel agency and
local airline managers' functions at each stop. Charlie South was with him but
Harding asked me to act as introducer and then translator. This caused much
hilarity because my translations were always longer than his prepared
remarks and he commented on it, accusing me of enlarging on his remarks,
which in some instances might have been the case (when I thought that some
of his announcements needed further explanations). In spite of my sweaty
palms, I enjoyed myself immensely because Harding was 'talking my
language to my people.' He was telling the audience that Braniff was
committed to South America and he advanced some of the ideas regarding
tourism which later became a full fledged program. He also told travel agents
and tourism officials in the audience that Braniff was going to support the
South American Travel Organization because he believed this was the way to
show our 'good citizenship' to the countries we served. Tom King had written
his speech and had already started to lay the ground work for the future. Later
on we would joke that if we wanted to start a new service or approach, all we
had to do was get Tom to write it in to one of Harding's speeches.

The last stop was Buenos Aires where we had the usual round of
calls (the ambassador; the Ministers of Transport and Tourism; and the
head of Aerolineas Argentinas, Brigadier Pellegrini) and travel industry
functions. We had a cocktail reception at the Plaza Hotel for 200–300
people. As the last travel agent left the party Harding asked me to come
by his suite for a nightcap.

## *The Panagra Decision*

It was pretty late, as cocktail parties in Argentina go on until all hours. I knocked on the door of the suite and he was wearing pajamas and silk gown. Jimmie served me a scotch and then withdrew for the night. I was surprised that Charlie was not there. Clearly, he wanted to talk without an audience, and I suspected at the time he was probably trying to size me up. We were catching an early morning flight back to Lima and they were going on through to Dallas. We had a couple of drinks and small talk about the party that evening and some of the people there. After a while Harding said: "Bobby, what do you think about our making a bid for Panagra?"

Jesus, I thought—it was a helluva an idea and told him we should go for it. A Panagra/Braniff merger would make us the strongest airline along the entire Pacific coast and over to Argentina and Brazil and we would be at least as large as Pan American which dominated the Atlantic side of the continent. It would give us a fleet of eight jets and would double our revenue. Braniff had made a pass in 1963 but had not been able to make a deal with Juan Trippe who just did not wish to sell at that time.

I said: "Harding, they have some great people and we are going to have to bend over backward to keep as many of them as possible." Harding agreed. He had the habit of unbuttoning his shirt and scratching his chest while he talked.

"I'm going to talk to Peter Grace when I get back, he's already said he wants to sell their 50%, and once I get him on board I can deal with Juan (Trippe). You know, the airline is going to sell for something like $30 million, and the DC-8-62s are worth that, at least. Its really a steal. I want you involved in meshing the two groups if we succeed. I've been through a couple of mergers and it's the people issues which usually screw them up, okay?"

We talked for quite a while about the combined airline and his philosophy about airline management and where we needed to go with Braniff. He had a real vision for the future and was determined to put the airline on the map. He talked about the need for critical mass and economies of scale, that we must spread our wings east and west but only after we had really consolidated South America. At something like two o'clock in the morning he yawned and showed me out.

I knew enough about Panagra to realize that this would be a major acquisition for Braniff and would consolidate our position. Panagra had a great reputation and following, particularly on the west coast of South America. The airline had been founded in 1929, as something of a shotgun wedding between W.R.Grace and Pan American Airways. Grace had been in Peru and the west coast of South America for more than 100 years. It dominated ocean transport in the region and had blocked Pan American from flying

*Pan American–Grace's (PANAGRA's) Douglas DC-8, which operated its* El Inter Americano *service down the west coast of South America.*

south of Panama down the west coast. Juan Trippe had begun by acquiring local airlines in Peru and Chile and was busy trying to organize a national airline network to circumvent the Grace blockade. Finally W.R. and Juan formed a 50/50 partnership airline, Pan American Grace Airways (Panagra), to be headquartered in Lima, the W.R. Grace base and seat of power.

Subsequently, Panagra built and operated airports throughout the west coast of South America. When Harding made his move, it had a fleet of four DC-8-31s, six DC-7s, and a DC-7 freighter. It also had, more important, seven new DC-8-62s, long range jets and one DC-8-62 freighter. It had bought Douglas equipment exclusively since it bought its first DC-2. It had operated domestic services in a number of countries, partly as an inheritance from wartime operations when it was 'drafted' (along with Pan American) to take over German or German-influenced airlines. Peter Grace subsequently sold off all the Grace interests in South America in the late 1970s and moved the company's headquarters from Lima to the United States.

I knew Carlos Velarde, the Peruvian head of Panagra in Lima, together with several other executives throughout the region; Mike Burbano in Ecuador, Bubi Canelas in La Paz, and Carlos Brunson in Chile, who was something of a legend. They were all politically well connected and the airline had a strong presence in each country that Braniff served, except Brazil. In addition, the W.R. Grace connection gave them incredible strength in each country's political and business leadership. I knew that the acquisition was going to be a major challenge but potentially extremely good for Braniff. We were going to have to work very hard if the acquisition became a fact.

During the mid-Sixties, Braniff had competed head-to-head with both Panagra and the Shelton 'empire' of APSA in Peru, CEA in Ecuador, and TAN in Honduras, which ran as a single entity. APSA's Convair 990 jet operated at discount fares which at the time was hard to prove because it was illegal under internationally-agreed rule-making by the International Air Transport Association (IATA). It was all done 'under the table' through travel agent over-ride commissions and the like.

Fortunately, for Braniff, the APSA management was a disaster. There was considerable in-fighting between the national management and Shelton's U.S.-based managers and the airlines were not as efficient as they might be. Eventually APSA disappeared and was replaced by AeroPeru; CEA was taken over by the government of Ecuador and nationalized; TAN merged with SAHSA, owned by the Lopez family in Honduras.

AeroPeru was sold in 1992 for $54 million (and I personally advised the government on the sale) to Gerardo de Prevoisin's Aeromexico. I had brought in Federico Bloch of TACA as a potential buyer, and TACA became the 'stalking horse' to encourage Aeromexico interest. Federico was legitimately interested and we spent a week in Lima with Julio Flores, his head of strategic planning, but decided against it because they felt the base price fixed by the government was too high.

In retrospect it was regrettable that the TACA Group—as it is now known—decided not to bid for the Peruvian airline. It would have made for a very strong Central and South American combination of airlines. Ecuatoriana was privatized in 1995 (I also participated as an advisor, along with Prudential Securities and SH&E on the sale) and sold to VASP of Brazil; TAN/SAHSA became part of the TACA Group in the early 1990s but was eventually bankrupted and disappeared in 1994, leaving Honduras without a flag carrier. The other government-owned airline with which Braniff competed during the late Sixties and Seventies was Air Panama. It failed in the late 1980s in spite of an attempt to privatize it by a local Panamanian group working with Rollins King, one of the founders of the U.S. Southwest Airlines.

## The End of the Plain Plane

In 1965, Mary Wells, who had left Continental's advertising agency to handle the Braniff account, came up with 'The End of the Plain Plane' campaign which included Emilio Pucci-designed hostess uniforms, different colored airplanes, and Alexander Girard-designed Club Rooms and City Ticket

*(Top) Designer Emilio Pucci, who revolutionized Braniff's hostess uniforms, airplanes, and everything, flanked by some lovely ladies, including my wife Martha (far left). (Bottom) Harding Lawrence (center) with advertising genius Mary Wells, in discussion with manager Roger Piaget, at the opening of the Tambo de Oro restaurant in Lima.*

Offices. Mary was born in 1928 and had started out in life at Macy's in New York as fashion editor. In 1952 she joined McCann-Erickson as a copy writer, and later joined Doyle, Dane & Bernbach, which she liked to say was the best advertising school in the country. In 1964 she was hired away by Jack Tinker & Associates, a 'think tank' where she helped to develop Alka Seltzer's most memorable advertising campaign ('plop, plop, fizz, fizz') before working on Continental Airlines' advertising account under Harding Lawrence.

The 'End of the Plain Plane' campaign completely revolutionized the look of the airline and, in the process, generated millions of dollars of free publicity as the airline made the cover of *Business Week, Aviation Week*, and other magazines, as well as the editorial pages of *The Wall Street Journal* and every other publication, radio and television news programs. A commercial which showed "a little old lady" stuffing her oversize purse with Braniff silverware, blankets, and other items, and ended with her driving an airport tug which was towing a 707, made history and helped to create a rash of pilfering of onboard items. She later joined with Rich and Greene, two former associates, to form Wells, Rich & Greene, which became one of the hottest advertising agencies on Madison Avenue, long after Braniff had disappeared.

During this period, Martha and I spent quite a bit of time with Braniff's vice president of advertising and promotion, Tom King, and his wife, Helen. Mary Wells had fallen for South America and was convinced that we had to do a whole lot more about it as a destination to increase the total market. She knew that the leisure side of the equation is the most elastic of the airline market and Tom and I did nothing to dissuade her. She knew about my involvement with SATO, which continued even though I had changed jobs. I was still on the Executive Committee, and my pal, Eduardo Arrarte, of Lima Tours, had become president.

## Investing in the Tourism Product

We took Mary on an RSA (Round South America) familiarization trip which included a weekend in Punta del Este with Harding but she was enchanted with Peru and decided there and then it was going to be "The Next Place." She convinced Harding that we needed to do some things about the destination and we came up with Tourism Investments, S.A. (TISA) which we incorporated in Panama and Braniff specifically authorized the officers to invest in it along with seed money from Braniff. We developed a whole investment program to develop tourism attractions and facilities which would enhance the destination while Mary produced the advertising campaign which, surprise, surprise, was labeled 'The Next Place.' The advertising included television commercials which featured Machu Picchu, the Amazon, the old part of Lima, the beaches, the Amazon, and other attractions.

To enlist local investors from within the travel community, TISA developed a series of investment opportunities. These included Punta Carnero, a 40-room fishing resort off Salinas in Ecuador; and the *Amazon Queen*, a converted U.S. P.T. boat we bought in San Diego from Kirk Kerkorian and shipped through the Panama Canal, around northern South America, and up the Amazon to Iquitos in Peru. The *Queen* sank one night between Iquitos and Leticia, Colombia, when it hit a log in the middle of the night. Happily, the passengers and crew survived after being in the water for about an hour.

Together with Henry Purcell, who ran a ski resort at Portillo, Chile, we developed a ski lift at Pucon on Lake Villarica, but this was wiped out by the first volcano eruption in a hundred years. And we established the Unicorn Discotheques in Lima, Panama, and Quito. TISA also purchased a Greek Isles cruise ship which was brought to the Galapagos in collaboration with another old friend, Eduardo Proaño of Metropolitan Tours of Quito. At the same time, Braniff had formed Hotel Associates S.A. (HASA) in a joint venture with Western Hotels and Adela Investments, based in Lima. HASA was going to build and manage hotels. The first of these was the Hotel Colon in Quito, also with Metropolitan Tours as a partner. Metropolitan is still the premier tour company in Ecuador with several cruise ships in the Galapagos, a Boatel on an Ecuadorean tributary of the Amazon River, and a host of other tourism resort facilities in Ecuador. Eduardo Proaño was one of the principals in the company—he had started out as a Panagra purser. like Eduardo Arrarte, and understood the airline business. He and his partners built a major tourism company which survives, successfully to this day.

We brought Kemmons Wilson, the founder and CEO of Holiday Inns, to Peru and flew him around the country one day in a chartered Faucett aircraft. All in the same day, we visited Iquitos, Cuzco, and Arequipa as likely spots for a Holiday Inn. He eventually went ahead, I think, with some local partners, and built Holiday Inns in Cuzco and elsewhere. Meeting Kemmons was a highlight. I went to his home in Memphis and met his family. He was a fabulous entrepreneur who had made money before he started Holiday Inns.

A plan to acquire the 16th century monastery, San Antonio de Abad in Cuzco, Peru, never got off the ground. But in 1996, the monastery was finally converted into a 5-star hotel and is now 'the' place to stay in Cuzco. We were also going to build a 5-star hotel on the old prison site in downtown Lima, and this ultimately became the 5-star Sheraton. Two other projects were targeted in Lima, the Tambo de Oro restaurant in a colonial 17th century home, owned by Carlos Neuhaus's brother, Rodolfo, and his wife, Grimucha Wiese; and the

*Basking in the glory of an Alexander Calder print.*

Santa Maria Beach Club, 30 miles south of Lima, a luxurious 25-unit beach resort on the side of a hill overlooking one of the prettiest beaches. The combined opening of both brought in Emilio Pucci, Bill Blass, Cecil Beaton, and other celebrities, the presence of all of whom helped put Lima on the tourism map at the time.

Business was booming and we were all basking in the reflected glory. While tourism had not taken off as much as we had anticipated, Braniff had become the leading airline in the region and traffic was strong. I had introduced Management-by-Objective (MBO), to Latin America and management reacted very positively. Braniff was highly regarded by passengers and shippers as well as by government officials and the business community because of our commitment to the region, and our active involvement in the development of the tourism facilities. We invested a considerable amount of time and effort in selling the value of tourism development to the governments and the public at large. We actually ran an advertising campaign extolling the job creation and multiplier effect of tourism on the local economies.

At the same time, Mary had decided that we needed to centralize all Latin American advertising in Lima and we brought in Horacio Mazza, an Argentine advertising account executive who had worked for the local agency, Eter Publicidad, which handled the Braniff account in Argentina. Horacio quickly organized the agency in Lima, bringing in several hotshot creative and other key people from Argentina. The idea was to take Mary Wells's U.S. advertising themes and adapt them to take account of local nuance and cultural differences for the region. In the past, local agencies in each country had merely translated advertising and commercials which usually failed to provide local flavor, and in some instances, created negative results because of the lack of local creative input. Our approach worked very well and Braniff's advertising took on a major role in setting the stage for the airline's growth.

*The Bogota staff of El Clan Braniff. The Station Manager, Percy Welton, on the far left.*

# El Clan Braniff

hile all this was going on, the Panagra acquisition was completed on 1 February 1967 and I was assigned to merge the two management groups in South America. This was difficult because the two airlines had two of everything and everybody, all the way from Panama to Argentina. By and large we picked the best person for the job in each case, but unfortunately this often involved a close tie for the top job and ended up in our bending over backwards to give the Panagra person the edge. Harding had told me that he wanted to make certain we did not play favorites with our own people. Some of them thus got the short end of the stick, and this created a morale problem with Braniff people thinking that we had 'sold them down the river.' A typical comment was: "Who bought who?" We quickly realized that something had to be done.

About this time I met Dalila Platero, an Argentine psychologist of *Tecnicas Grupales*, a management development company. We organized employee workshops and she introduced me to role-playing and other techniques. Dalila helped to establish a management development program which we introduced across the board from Mexico to Argentina. Some of her methods were controversial but it brought out the best in the people. She would bring a number of employees together, without their bosses, and do a significant amount of role playing. The concept was that people needed to interact with their peers and bring out their frustrations. A sort of Alcoholics Anonymous approach, combined with some MBO (Management By Objective) and Positive Reinforcement (as preached by B.F. Skinner) which worked very well. I think the key to the program was that Braniff was prepared to invest in their development and it produced excellent results.This convinced me that people invariably want to be better and will rise to the occasion.

A direct outcome of some of the findings from Dalila's workshops was the decision to build an advertising campaign around the employees. Sylvia Mazza, Horacio's kid sister and one of the best creative people I have ever worked with, was directed to travel on the airline—as a regular passenger—from one end to the other and come up with an advertising campaign. After 30 days she unveiled her creative approach at a Latin American management

meeting in Lima with Tom King, Mary Wells, and others from Dallas in atten-
dance. The campaign was built around the slogan "El Clan Braniff."

The launch TV commercial showed a bunch of real Braniff employees,
the men taking off their uniform jackets and the girls their Pucci tops and
playing basketball. At the end of the commercial the voice-over said "We love
our jobs, we are 'El Clan Braniff.'" There was mixed response but Mary saw
the potential. Because of some of the controversy, which included a reaction
to the word 'clan', which some of our people thought had a negative conno-
tation (some of the staunch republicans in Dallas thought there was a connection to the 'Kennedy Clan'), Mary proposed that we do focus groups in each
country to see how people reacted. After several weeks around the region we
went to Dallas to present our findings. These were 100% positive, even enthusiastic, for a series of print ads and story boards for television and movie
theater advertising. They showed Braniff people in different work-and-play
environments, all ending in the tag line "We love our Jobs—We're the Braniff
Clan." The implication was that anyone who loved his or her job would
perform more efficiently. Which happens to be true.

More important, Harding loved the campaign. Partly because Mary
Wells loved it. By this time Harding had divorced Jimmie and had married
Mary Wells. I think this was one of the longest-running advertising
campaigns in history, still going when Howard Putnam sold the Latin American routes to Eastern in 1982, just before the airline folded.

## Love Thy Neighbour Sweepstakes

Another major promotion opportunity came along when Braniff inaugurated
Boeing 747 service between Dallas and Honolulu some time in the late 1960s.

*Braniff International Boeing 747, which flew regularly daily nonstop
between Dallas and Honolulu.*

We thought it might be salable in the Latin American Division, even though few Latinos had every traveled to Hawaii. If nothing else, it seemed like an exploitable promotion and would position Braniff as something more than a north-south airline.

Harding had already begun to talk about becoming a 'World Class Carrier' and was even then talking about a route to London which did not happen until the late 1970s. We came up with a major consumer sweepstakes based on "Ama a Tu Projimo—Ponlo en la Lista." (Love Thy Neighbor—Put Him on Your List). Major sweepstakes would run in every country in Latin America. Each would have 10 winners who would get a free, all-expense-paid trip on Braniff's inaugural flight to Hawaii. The mechanics of the promotion involved a 'tie-in' with a major daily newspaper in each market in South America. We would buy advertising space in return for the newspaper running a coupon which had to be filled in with ten names to participate in the sweepstakes. In addition to the ten winners per country, the coupon had to be validated at a travel agent's office so that the winning coupon would also include the travel agent and the newspaper would send a reporter.

The promotion generated something like 50 million coupons. We also obtained an incredible amount of free publicity. Travel agents had entry-blank boxes in their offices to make sure that they participated. The Hawaiian Visitors Bureau produced editorial copy which the newspapers ran without charge.

The sweepstakes drawings were highly publicized in each country and the end result was that 120 people were flown to Dallas and then to Hawaii. In the process, we earned an amazing amount of follow-on publicity. I do not recall if we actually sold much Hawaii business as a result, but the "Love thy neighbor" promo was the talk of the region for months. And it certainly positioned Braniff very favorably. At least one paying passenger had figured out a way to smuggle cocaine to Hawaii in a surfboard, and for a time, at least until he was caught, he was a regular commuter on the flight from Lima to Dallas and Hawaii, always with a couple of surf boards filled with coke. He always flew first class and never quibbled over the price of the ticket, which probably made the U.S. customs people suspicious. He ended up doing time in the United States.

## Faucett Heritage

With the Panagra acquisition we had acquired 19% of Faucett, the Peruvian airline. Faucett had a long history. Started in Peru in 1928 by a group of Peruvian businessmen, including Santiago Acuna, Armando Fabri, and Manuel Gallagher, they were inspired and led by Elmer Faucett. 'Slim' Faucett had

*(Right) Elmer J. ("Slim") Faucett, the U.S. citizen who established Peru's first domestic commercial airline.*

*(Below) by the 1970s, it had joined the jet age, with the British BAC One-Eleven.*

arrived in Peru in 1920 as a representative of Curtiss Aviation and had made a noteworthy flight from Chiclayo to the Amazon River in 1922.

I had met Slim in the early 1950s on a trip to Lima at Folger Athearn's home. He was in the same league of early airline visionaries as Juan Trippe, Lowell Yerex, C.N.Shelton, and others. I was elected to the board of directors representing Braniff's shareholding. Faucett had recently acquired four BAC One-Elevens and was the leading domestic airline in Peru. Polo Pflucker, one of the former Panagra people we had made Country Manager-Peru (except, by this time we were calling them Regional Vice Presidents) was a good friend. Polo's uncle, General Armando Revoredo, was the president and Gustavo Aspillaga, Polo's father-in-law and a super gentleman was vice president of the Board. Gustavo had been educated in England and was a wealthy landowner. Armando was something of a national hero. He had flown in the Peruvian-Ecuadorean war and in the late 1930s had been the first to fly across the Andes to Buenos Aires in a Faucett-modified Stinson Detroiter (of which Faucett eventually built 30 for civilian and military service). One of these is ensconced in the parking lot at Faucett's headquarters at Lima's airport. My Faucett experience was most enjoyable. It was an historic airline and I had a strong feeling for it. Unfortunately, after several ownership changes, the airline failed in 1997 and its future is questionable.

In 1968 a relatively unknown General, Velasco Alvarado, organized a palace coup and ousted our friend, president Fernando Belaunde Terry, who was promptly exiled to Buenos Aires on an APSA flight. Velasco was an active general in the army and came to power as a leftist nationalist with a mission to nationalize the oil companies, International Petroleum among them. The U.S. reaction was to black-list Peru and stop all credits in the foreign exchange market and to cut government aid. Along with other investments, it killed the Lima five-star hotel project. It also hurt tourism across the board, because North Americans cannot tell the difference between a revolution in Peru and a strike in Argentina. The U.S. leisure traveler is consequently more vulnerable to exaggerated or distorted media reports than any other, and the behavior of the Velasco regime had a disastrous impact on the incipient Peruvian tourism industry. While we did not realize it at the time, the impact of the Velasco years had a lasting impact on the economy of Peru. The nationalization of International Petroleum was just one of the factors, a poorly managed agrarian reform probably had more impact as the country became more dependent on imports and the fishing industry—which had been the single largest producer of foreign exchange—practically dried up. Velasco also succeeded, where 500 years of colonialism had not, in putting the Peruvian 'cholo' against the 'white' Peruvian or foreigner.

## What Goes Around, Comes Around

I was scheduled to be in Buenos Aires the day after the coup. On arrival I suggested to Harry Marples, our Country Manager and a close friend, who had lived in Lima when I first moved there and knew Belaunde, that we should call on him. I said: "You know, Harry—the old rule, always be nice to the guy who is down, you never know when he might be up, or 'what goes around, comes around.'"

Harry agreed: "I would like to see him anyway, he was always very nice to Susana and me in Lima. He is staying at the El Presidente."

Belaunde was delighted to hear from us and asked us to come up. Over the past three or four years, I had met him a number of times. He had invited Harding Lawrence to 'Palacio' and had inaugurated the Santa Maria Beach Club. When we arrived at his suite, he opened the door and ushered us in. One of his sons was there and he invited us to sit down and have coffee. He was sincerely glad to see us, although we soon found out why. He was flat broke, that a friend in Argentina had arranged credit at the hotel, and he had a job offer in Boston from Harvard, but did not have the money to buy a ticket to go there. I looked at Harry and he grinned. This was in the days where it was not that easy to grant free transportation to anyone other than a travel agent or other airline employee. Harry knew right away that I was not going to worry about the rules. So we arranged for full-fare first class tickets for him and his son and booked him on the next day's flight. (I had to sign a chit later, charging my account for the cost of the tickets). We told him that we would arrange to have someone pick him up and drive him to Ezeiza Airport, as I was returning to Lima on the same flight, and we agreed to meet at the airport.

The next day as I arrived with Harry at Ezeiza, we were met by Tito Bonaventura, the station manager, with a SITA message from Flight Control in Lima asking that I call in because they had an urgent message but did not want to put it on the teletype. At that time, Braniff had installed a direct line in Flight Control with a 'scrambler' because we had received word that long distance calls were being monitored by the Peruvian Intelligence Service. I telephoned Lima Flight Control and spoke to Gus de la Torre, the supervisor in charge, and he said, nervously: "Bobby, we just got a call from a General Cabrera of the DGAC that if Belaunde is on flight 970 tonight the aircraft will be impounded and Belaunde dragged off to jail. He has been forbidden by General Velasco to tread Peruvian soil. You better pull him off the flight, or we're in trouble."

So I pulled rank and told Harry Marples to do the dastardly deal, but only after we had checked that Pan American had space to New York on its flight which left an hour later than Braniff's, so we booked him and his son in First Class and endorsed his tickets. I said good-bye to Belaunde at the foot of the stairs. In spite of having unloaded him off Braniff, he was very grateful and appreciative. I then boarded our DC-8-62 back to Lima. Six years later, after I had left Braniff, the auditors were still trying to collect the $3,000 value of the two tickets from me. Unsuccessfully I might add.

## Marketing by Motocross

During our time in Peru I interested Robbie and Guy in motocross, off-road motorcycle racing (originated in England as scrambles) which had just arrived in South America. It had started at San Carlos de Bariloche, in southern Argentina, by a former Belgian racer, had spread to Chile, and most recently to Peru. I bought them Honda 50 c.c. bikes and I acquired a 350 c.c. Honda off-road bike for myself. Peru was ideal for off-road motorcycling. The combination of desert and the foot-hills of the Andes mountains provided for the absolutely best terrain, similar to that of Southern California, where it had become popular in North America.

We had moved out of San Isidro to La Rinconada, which was over the hills surrounding Lima and in a dryer desert-like climate. Guy had bad asthma and, as San Isidro's climate was very humid, his doctor suggested it. We first moved into a rented place which was five minutes from the desert where we could ride the bikes freely. We later moved into a Braniff-purchased home with a large swimming pool, big yard, and all kinds of space for entertaining.

Motocross had arrived in a big way and we brought down Gary Bailey and his young teen-age son, David, to teach the sport to young men and kids, the youngest (Guy), aged 11. Valerie had met Gary somehow and we had all read about him. He was the first American to beat the Europeans who had started the sport and had started a very successful motocross school at his home in Tallahassee, Florida. We also managed to persuade the popular Roger de Coster, Belgium's world champion rider to accept an invitation to come and do a demonstration race. Gary introduced us to the 250 cc Bultaco, at the time one of the best motocross bikes on the market, built in Spain. We then created the Clan Braniff motor-cross team and organized the First South American MotoCross championship. Braniff played a major role in providing transport and generated tremendous publicity. We raced every year in Bariloche, and went as far afield as Venezuela, El Salvador, Brazil, and eventually even to California and Houston.

Motocross almost became a national sport. Young children, who would otherwise be in trouble in the somewhat permissive Lima environment, became hooked, along with their parents, and I think we helped to bring many parents and their children together. We actually developed a motocross track at Manchay, in the hills to the east of La Rinconada which, according to professionals like Gary Bailey and Roger de Coster, was as challenging and as much fun as any course in California, Europe, or elsewhere. I was very much involved not only with the racing by Robbie and Guy, but with an 'old timers', loose-knit group that would ride the desert from Lima to Paracas in the south. The desert on the coast was perfect dirt-bike terrain and we spent a lot of time riding the hills and surrounding desert. It was a most enjoyable period, and we made many lasting friends. Braniff was identified throughout South America as the 'Motocross Airline' and I know it was good for busi-

*(Top) Marketing by Motorcross at Manchay, near Lima.*

*I help Robbie (center) and Guy (bottom) to cross the finishing line.*

ness. I still meet people who remember when they were into motocross and when Braniff was 'their favorite airline.'

In spite of this, I received a call from my boss, Charlie South, telling me that the company did not feel I should be riding motorcycles in the desert. I reacted rather violently. I told him that what I did on my own time was my own business and if necessary I was prepared to make a big issue about it. I think he was bluffing but he said it was from John Casey who thought Braniff executives should not engage in that kind of dangerous sport. I told him to shove it. And I never heard about it again. So much for the corporate world.

Indirectly, riding motorcycles off road on the deserted beaches south of Lima was instrumental in my meeting another long-time friend. Nick Asheshov, the editor of the *Lima Times* and the *Andean Report,* wrote an editorial about those "nuts who ride their noisy motorcycles on the beach," and I called him up and invited him to lunch. Nick was another Brit who had 'discovered' and fallen in love with Peru. He was a successful Fleet Street journalist and published *The Andean Report,* one of the most prestigious economic newsletters in South America at the time—long before it became fashionable. Nick and I became close friends in spite of the circumstances and his dislike of noisy motorcycles. Nick helped us much later when we decided to start our own newsletter with excellent advice and counsel. He now owns and manages a fabulous hotel in Urubamba, halfway between Cusco and Machu Picchu in Peru.

## Do You Know the Road to Huarochiri?

One weekend Robbie and Guy came to me with the idea that we should ride to Huarochiri, about 100 miles inland from La Rinconada. Their friend, 'Pelado' Neuhaus, the son of Rodolfo (Carlos's brother) who was also into motorcycles, had a plan to ride over the Andes into a valley to the town of Huarochiri. It sounded good to me and we took off on a Saturday morning. The only problem is that when we met at the main highway there were a dozen other 12-15 year-old kids on bikes. The ride was due east from La Rinconada, up to about 14,000 feet above sea level, where the air was awful thin. The bikes lost a lot of power but we made it over and then straight down hill to the town. We were met by the town mayor and priest in the main plaza and given a hero's welcome. They had never seen a bunch of kids with a grown man all on motorcycles. We overnighted—all 14 of us sleeping on the floor in our sleeping bags in a single room at the only 'hotel', a mud-built thatched-roof affair behind the town bar and only restaurant. We rode back the next day. The trip had been great fun and I had experienced the real Peru, as far removed from the sophistication of Lima as an Appalachian village from New York.

At the same time, Velasco was changing Peru from a warm hospitable place for foreigners to a 'Gringo Go Home' kind of environment. The Peruvian *cholo*, who had traditionally, from the time of Pizarro (in spite of Spanish dominance) embraced all foreigners, were being told that their problems were caused by the 'oligarcas' who had sold out to the gringos. For the first time in Peru I started to feel uncomfortable, and began to wonder about the future.

## Hijack

Early in July 1971 I received a call at 3 o'clock in the morning from Gus de la Torre, Braniff's director of Flight Control in Lima, with the news that a Braniff 727 had been hijacked by a couple en route from San Antonio to Monterrey, Mexico, and was on its way to Lima. I was at the airport before dawn and walked up to the second floor and Flight Control. The aircraft arrived at sun-up, and remained on the ground for 10 or 12 hours. I organized things at the airport where we negotiated with the hijackers by radio. They wanted to go to Argentina and we convinced them to allow the San Antonio-boarded passengers to deplane, and to make a crew change. It turned out they were both Argentine citizens, at least they spoke with a pronounced Argentine accent. We were able to find a volunteer crew (the arriving crew had been on duty for 15 hours or so), Lima-based flight attendants, and a cockpit crew replacement flew in from Dallas. In fact, half the Lima-based flight attendants volunteered, in a demonstration of Braniff esprit-de-corps.

I tried to go on board but the hijackers would not allow anyone on the aircraft. The embassy and the Peruvian Air Force were out in force. Finally the aircraft took off for Rio and then to Buenos Aires where Harry Marples, with a little help from the local gendarmerie, was able to convince the hijackers to get off the airplane. Harry was actually allowed to board and met with them face to face. I envied him because I would have liked to do the same in Lima. After some tense hours the hijackers disembarked and the incident was over with no loss of lives. At the time, and to my knowledge to date, it was the longest running hijack in history.

I forget what happened to them but late in July we organized a big Braniff employee celebration at the Tambo de Oro restaurant for everyone that who been involved. President Nixon sent a letter of commendation to "the men and women of Braniff."

## Sacked—Well, Almost

Some time in 1972 the Braniff Management Club in Dallas asked me to organize a Latin American program. The Club met every month—a major affair which usually involved dinner, entertainment, and/or a featured speaker. I arranged for Peruvian 'anticuchos' to start off the evening, Argentine beef for the main course, Lucho Azarraga from Panama with his organ and sons who played Panamanian music, a Brazilian *samba* band, and an Argentine tango exhibition. The evening was a major occasion and the hotel in Dallas had never seen anything quite like it. I acted as Master of Ceremonies and proceeded to get thoroughly stoned in the process. All accounts are that it was a sensational evening and really gave the U.S. management contingent—from Minneapolis to Kansas City to New York and some 30 other on-line cities— a real 'feel' for Latin America.

At some point I proceeded to make some colorful remarks about my boss, Charlie South, including a comment: "Charlie South is pissed off at me," which he did not appreciate. Next day he called me in to his office and gave me a severe dressing down. He told me that Harding wanted to fire me, but he had prevailed, and that I should take some time off. He characterized it as a leave of absence with pay. It was December and summer in Lima, so I said why not. I could take some time off anyway if I needed to, and had not had a holiday for three years. So I went back to Lima and told Martha that we were going to spend the summer in Punta Hermosa, something we had planned anyway, but I would not have to go into the office. I thought about it is as well-earned vacation. What the hell.

# Dallas—Again

I was down at the beach at the house we had rented in Punta Hermosa, about 25 miles south of Lima. We had been doing this for the past two years, with our friends Costanzo Reiser and Polo Pfluker and their respective wives, Mariolina and Pupi. The north end of Punta Hermosa was not quite high society, but a number of our friends had homes there and it was an easy commute to work. At the south end of the bay were the expensive homes of people like Pancho Wiese, the banker, and other high-society friends. It was a great place to relax, the kids surfed, and we all rode our bikes in the surrounding desert. Costanzo was another transplanted Swiss-Italian whose family had a long-standing business in Peru. He rode a B.S.A. dirt bike that could climb any hill in sight.

One of the kids came down to the beach and told me that Dallas wanted me to call. Mum had the number (as if I needed it).

*Dallas, Texas—Settled in 1841, the city had become the financial and commercial center in the Southwestern United States. With a population of about a million, it is a sprawling city with a bustling downtown—it is also known as the oil and cotton business center of the region. There are a number of universities and colleges, and has more than 70 hospitals and is a major medical center. It was at the time the headquarters of Braniff International and during the period it became the headquarters for the most successful new entrant airline in the early 1970s, Southwest. Love Field Airport served as its major airport until Dallas-Fort Worth Airport was opened in the mid 1970s. Love Field is still used by Southwest Airlines.*

## Saved by the Gong

As it turned out I did need the number because Wally Conrad was the one who wanted me to call. On a Saturday no less. Wally reported to John Casey as Senior Vice President-Sales & Service. He and Charlie South were equals in the corporate hierarchy. I had known him when he was at Eastern Air Lines and I really liked him. He was a Canadian who had joined the Eagle Squadron and fought in the Battle of Britain in 1940. He had joined Braniff a few years previously and was about ten years older than me and a legitimate war-hero, one of those straightforward people with whom you always knew where you stood. Wally came on the telephone and said: "Hey snake doctor, how's it going?"

He always called me that, in a flattering sort of way. I told him I was enjoying my time off, why didn't he come down and we would go fishing or something. He laughed and said: "Look, young fella, I'm going to be in Miami on Monday and want to meet you for lunch at the airport. If you take Sunday night's flight up we can meet and you can be on your way home the same day. How about it?"

I answered: "Sure why not. But would you mind telling me what it is all about, I'm not exactly *persona grata* these days in Dallas and have actually been thinking about making a career change."

Wally answered: "OK, that's what I'm calling you about. I want you to be my Vice President-Sales in Dallas. You'll have all sales, CTOs (city ticket offices), reservations, and a major hand in developing a new sales program. It's a corporate-officer job, pays a whole lot more than you're making but I want to talk to you in person, not on the fucking phone."

I was surprised, to say the least, and I told him that Charlie was on the verge of firing my ass.

"I know, Bobby, but this has Casey's and Harding's blessing. They think you're the only guy for the job, and so do I."

So I met him on the 7th floor of the Miami International Airport Hotel that Monday. After a somewhat liquid lunch (Wally drank gin martinis for lunch, but showed not a sign), we agreed that I would be in Dallas to report for work two weeks from that day. During lunch Wally told me about his ideas for consolidating the eight or nine existing Reservations offices down to two or three, take the savings and build an "inside sales & service rep" program, strengthen the field sales organization, and generally do some of the things I had talked about in the early 1960s when I was in Dallas the first time around. He had found one of my position papers in the files. The idea was exciting, the pay was great, and we agreed that I did not have to move the family but could rent an apartment in Dallas and commute.

As we took the elevator down at about 4 o'clock (we had talked for the better part of three hours) I asked Wally about Charlie South's reaction. "I don't know, Bobby. He and I aren't exactly close, and he doesn't really have a say in the matter. I know all about your pissup" (he often used the English expression, as well as the F word all the time) "remember I was there and had a helluva good laugh. I did talk to Harding about it afterwards and he thought it was all great fun. He happens to think you are one of the really creative guys around, and said 'creative guys have to let off steam.' As far as that was concerned it's an episode in your life, and there will probably be a lot more. John Casey thinks you're a good guy also, so stop worrying about it. As far as I'm concerned I need the kind of energy and leadership I know you can bring to the table."

With that we shook hands, his flight was leaving at 5 p.m. and mine at midnight. So I took a cab and went to Miami Beach to Art Adler's place, the Allison Hotel, to meet him and Mac Seligman for dinner and tell them about my new job. Artie was a great friend and had always stood up for me and all the other chaps in the LAD (Latin American Division). He and Mac were inseparable and very supportive. After a couple of drinks and dinner, I made it back to the airport in time for the flight.

Martha was agreeable because Valerie, who had finished school, could join me, and she herself would come up and spend the odd week there also. I told her I would spend at least every other week in Lima so that I could be with the children and keep on riding the bikes with them. Two weeks later I was in Dallas, ensconced on the 9th floor with Wally and his staff. I was actually replacing Hal Salfen who was moving on to something else. Wally's staff included some old buddies, John Jackson among them. John had worked for me in the early days and was one of the best salesmen around. He was running cargo sales, which was somewhat wasted. Probably the most important member of the team was Art Stellmach, who had joined in the late Sixties to run Reservations. He came from Hertz and was an ex-marine and one of the best in the business. Which was good because I did not really know that much about reservations and I was going to have to lean on him a whole lot. It happened that he and I got along well. For some reason, even though we were total opposites (or perhaps because we were) we found ourselves agreeing on all kind of things, principally that people make the difference. The position was a real challenge, I had the total responsibility for all sales, passenger, mail and cargo—systemwide, which included Latin America.

## The Nixon CREEP Affair

In 1972 John Casey called me up to his office. He said: "Bobby, Harding wants you to arrange for a financial contribution to CREEP", (a very appropriate name I thought), "the campaign to re-elect President Nixon."

I never really knew whether it was Harding's idea or not. Subsequently he denied any knowledge of the source of the funds which Braniff used, and it is quite consistent with his management approach that he could have just told Ed Acker and/or John Casey to "find the money" without bothering about how. I mention this because of the later implications which are described in this chapter.

I laughed out loud. "John, you must be kidding. Are you thinking of the Panama fund? Because if you are, I'm not going to do it. And I don't think Braniff should, regardless."

The Panama fund was something we had set up while I was still running Latin American sales. Because of APSA and other discounting and travel agency over-ride commissions, which were illegal, we had set up the system to generate off-the-books revenues to handle special deals for groups and so on. The system was pretty simple. We had provided Camilo Frabrega, our Country Manager in Panama, with a stock of unregistered tickets which he assigned to the City Ticket Office in Panama to write tickets for direct sales which were deposited in a special bank account and used for under-the-table payments to travel agents or to be used for discounts. The system had been quite successful and was audited by Dallas so that the money was properly accounted for. A Country Manager and either myself, Charlie South, or someone in Dallas's financial services department, had to counter-sign the checks.

Casey became quite annoyed, almost irate. He said he would handle the deal direct. But before I left the office he asked: "Bobby is this a moral issue or are you another flaming liberal?"

Again I laughed and told him it was neither. I just did not think it was the proper use of the fund and if we started doing this kind of thing it would destroy the whole program. In fact I was a flaming liberal and did not like Nixon, but I did not think of it in those terms. Afterwards I found out that Charlie South had gone along with the deal by having Camilo Fabrega bring up the cash and Braniff did contribute something like $60,000 and proceeded to get itself into all kinds of trouble, as did American Airlines for a similar illegal contribution.

All of this did not actually become public until after Watergate; and I had left Braniff by that time. Ed Acker left the airline a year or two later. Most people think he was the 'fall guy' for Harding and that his leaving settled the matter with the Department of Justice and the C.A.B. which had been investigating the 'off-the-books' transactions; first because it was an illegal campaign contribution and the second because it was illegal to pay travel agents over-ride commissions and the like.

I was spending a lot of time on the road, primarily in New York, which was our biggest O&D (Origin & Destination) market, both for the Dallas service as well as for all of South America. This was long before Miami became the predominant gateway to and from Latin America. I loved New York and had many personal contacts in the industry. I always stayed at The Waldorf and spent a lot of time at the Bull & Bear which was an industry 'watering hole.'

## Frank Lorenzo

During this time I met Frank (Francisco) Lorenzo who was born in 1940, the son of Spanish immigrants. He loved airplanes from an early age, growing up in New York City close to La Guardia Airport. After graduating from the Harvard Business School, he joined T.W.A. in the finance department, and later moved to Eastern Air Lines as a financial analyst. In 1966 he and his friend Bob Carney formed Lorenzo, Carney & Co. with $1,000 each and this then became Jet Capital Corporation. They had then taken this company public and raised $1.5 million with which they acquired 58% of Texas International, the beginning of a long and notorious period in the airline industry which included crises at Continental Airlines and the demise of Eastern Air Lines at the end of the 1980s.

The first time I met him was on a Braniff flight to New York when he was still with Texas International, and he offered to give me a ride into Manhattan. A chauffeur-driven limo was waiting for him, an amenity which I thought was a little too much for a small airline president. I liked him but I also recognized how driven he was and the fact that he did not appear to have a lot of time or respect for the 'little people.'

He was interested in the fact that I had lived in South America. When he was with Eastern Air Lines he had sold an aircraft to LANSA, a small airline in Peru and wanted to know all about the airlines in the region. He had actually sold a couple of Lockheed Electras, one of which subsequently crashed in the jungles of the Amazon. I knew the owner of LANSA and Frank wanted to know all about him and the airline.

*Frank Lorenzo, who rebuilt Continental Airlines, and made enemies among the pilots and other unions. The failure (on all sides) to compromise led to the demise of Eastern Air Lines.*

I also tried to do a deal with Texas International which never got off the ground but in the process I met Lorenzo several more times. We were trying to put together a form of code-share arrangement for connecting flights in Houston to points in Texas and across the border into Mexico which Braniff did not serve. Every time we met, a new requirement forced us to revise the proposed arrangement. Finally, Braniff decided he was not serious and we dropped the idea. Frank was known for his habit of re-negotiating every deal until he won by default, or the other side decided to withdraw. Regardless, I always felt he was a fascinating character even though he has been vilified by the unions because of his uncompromising management approach and the confrontation with the unions that led to the ultimate demise of Eastern Air Lines.

## Positive Reinforcement

About this time I re-discovered B.F. Skinner. Dalila Platero, back in Lima, had introduced me by giving me one of his books. Skinner was a psychologist who had written several books and his approach, based entirely on positive reinforcement, whether with raising children or in management, was right up my alley.

I heard about a former Emery Air Freight executive by the name of Ed Feeny who was a Skinner addict and who had started a management development program based on Skinner's approach. I met Feeny, along with Art Stellmach and both of us were convinced. So we hired Feeny's company, which was in its infancy and introduced it in Reservations—with incredible results. The approach was that supervisors would apply 'positive reinforcement' by telling agents they were doing a great job, always looking for something positive they had done to reinforce their action.

We established a self-reporting honor system whereby each telephone sales agent would check off how many sales he or she made on each call, how many times he or she 'upgraded' a normal reservations to first class, and so on. Later on we arranged to use the computer, but in the early stages it was strictly manual. We had meetings with all the supervisors and instilled in them the idea that whatever the agents did, whether they had good or only fair results, they were to look for the positive and then congratulate and pat them on the back; to the extent that even poor performers, as long as they filled in the 'report cards', were congratulated for telling the truth. We had a system for monitoring calls with the agents' knowledge, so the chances that they would fake the reports were relatively slim. The program was an immense success. We started to see more first class revenue, and greater productivity as a direct result. And the agents loved it as we produced report cards by agent. It gave everyone a personal score card.

At the same time we were consolidating the reservations offices from nine down to three. We offered everyone a job so that no one was left out. The savings were mainly in office space and telephone lines, although we did save on some personnel reduction. Some people did not wish to move and we offered them jobs at the airports as they became available so that nobody was left out. This alone was something of a record in the early days of 'downsizing.' We ended up with three reservations offices in Kansas City, Dallas, and Houston. Art was able to negotiate far better long-distance rates based on volume in the consolidated centers and this actually reduced our long distance bill by almost 30%. When you took into account the savings in rent and other fixed costs, we were able to reduce our telephone sales/reservations cost by almost 25% overall, and were achieving better performance across the board.

Wally Conrad was ecstatic about the results. We then introduced Positive Reinforcement in our city ticket offices and the sales representative group, including the newly created 'inside sales & service' organization. Wally and I got along famously. He was probably the best boss I ever had during my entire time with Braniff. He wanted to expand 'Booth's program' to the airport people but we ran into some resistance from above. John Casey, Wally's boss, and the overall head of operations, sales and service, was not convinced. He was very Irish and short-fused. The idea of telling people they were doing a great job all the time was just not his style.

### Goodbye Harding

The job was rewarding in many ways, but although being able to go to Lima when I felt like it was a welcome 'perk', I did not really like the commuting and being away from the family for a couple of weeks at a time. About this time, late 1973 or early 1974, Horacio Mazza was planning to move to Buenos Aires. He wanted to sell *Internandina*, the advertising agency he had acquired from Mary Wells in Lima. Over drinks one evening at the Sonesta in Key Biscayne after a sales meeting, he asked me if I might be interested. He knew I that I enjoyed working with the advertising agencies, especially the creative people, and we had often joked that I would be a good advertising executive. I told him I did not have any money and if I left Braniff I would have to start from scratch. I did not have enough years to qualify for early retirement. Horacio laughed, and said: "Look, the agency is profitable, it has some bank debt which is quite manageable. I'll sell it to you for the debt. You pay that off from operations and the agency is yours. Think about it."

I told him I would. It was an intriguing idea. I had spent 23 years—half of my life—with Braniff, I was 46 and knew I could stay indefinitely but the chances of getting the top job, whether I could make it or not, were remote. Harding, the Chairman, was in his mid-fifties, Ed Acker, who was president and chief operating officer, was my age and would be next in line for the CEO job. And Dallas was losing whatever charm it may have had for me a few years earlier.

At Braniff, Staff meetings were becoming a forum for Harding to chew people out unmercifully. There was one incident, which I did not personally witness, where he supposedly threw a large ashtray at Ned Bosange, head of maintenance, when he lost his temper over some problem or another. Like many such alleged incidents attributed to Harding, I later found out that this one never happened. Another involved my good friend, Roy Brown, who ran Dallas-Fort Worth Airport for Braniff. 'Brownie' was an ex-Flying Tiger and a very strong guy. Harding had returned from a trip, and found something he did not like at the DFW Airport and started out on a rampage, in public, at Roy. The two almost came to blows when Roy stood up and told Harding to jump in a lake. The story ran through the airline. It was probably a sign of Harding's short fuse but reasonableness in the end that Roy continued in his job until the very end. For some unknown reason I was immune from his tirades, but I did not like what I saw.

I also knew that Harding's vision for Braniff was to keep growing into what he called a 'world class airline.' He had this idea that deregulation was going to happen and that unless the airline grew, it could not survive. That there were going to be six or seven so-called 'world class' airlines which would serve all five continents and which would have revenues of $20 or $25 billion. The rest were going to be acquired or would simply fail. And when they did, the government was going to re-regulate the industry. Which has not happened yet and is unlikely ever to happen. But he was right about the consolidation of power with the big airlines getting bigger and stronger as others failed in the decade after deregulation in 1978.

I did not have much desire to be part of that scene. I was tired of commuting and living in an apartment the rest of the time. Braniff was re-organizing its marketing department under Russ Thayer, who had been brought in by John Casey. A close friend of mine, Jack Regan (a former Panagra guy I had met in Punta del Este in the early days) had been made vice president of planning. Fortunately we got along really well but we were usually at odds on strategy.

A few days after the Sonesta Beach meeting with Horacio, I had dinner with my friends, Tom and Helen King, talking about where this whole thing was going. Tom was in advertising, even though he had never worked for an agency. He was very creative and a good writer. He wrote all Harding's speeches and was part of the Harding vision. He had also encouraged my own writing and I had tremendous respect for his judgment. I had gone to his house and Helen had served us a great alfresco dinner. I think it was July or August, which in Dallas is very hot, if dry. Tom and I had several drinks before, during, and after dinner. I told him about Horacio's offer. He looked at me after several after-dinner scotches and said: "Why don't you go for it? I don't think you want to be a corporate animal for the next 20 years."

## *If it Ain't Fun—Quit*

The following day was a Friday, and I was still thinking about the future, John Casey telephoned about something that had happened in Mexico City. I cannot recall the details, but I think our Country Manager, Flavio Manzi, had done something which annoyed Casey. He was in a foul mood and proceeded to lambast me about something I really had nothing to do with. In the middle of my explanation of whatever it was, Casey hung up on me.

I decided then and there it was time to go. I waltzed into Wally Conrad's office and told him I was quitting. He could not believe it but I told him about Casey's tantrum and the fact that I was tired of the whole thing. He asked me to take the weekend off and think about it. On my return he told me that Harding wanted to talk to me about my decision, if I still wanted to quit. I said I did (I had gone back to Lima over the weekend and discussed it with Martha who was in agreement, even though she was worried about job-security and so on). So I went to see Harding who started out saying I was nuts to leave Braniff. I explained that I had enjoyed my time but I felt an urge to be independent and wanted to be my own boss and so on. Harding banged on his desk and said: "Booth, you aren't going to make it on your own, you need the corporate umbrella we provide, give it some more thought, you've got a real future here but not on your own."

I thanked him and told him, not to be rude, that I would think about it some more. But his remark, if I had had any doubts before, just made me know it was the right decision. Harding obviously did not like people quitting on him. It was sort of a personal thing. I knew he could fire people without giving it much thought—actually he never fired anyone himself, but had others do it for him—but few people had actually resigned on him. I was amused but I talked to Wally who said, "OK, if you've made up your mind, you've made it up. But I don't want you to leave mad at Casey so go talk to him and tell him you're not leaving because of the telephone incident."

Which I did, because actually I liked Casey and I did not want to leave with him believing he was the cause of my departure. It was not, it was just the proverbial straw that broke the camel's back. We shook hands on it and he wished me luck. And if I ever wanted to come back, I had an open door, as long as he was there. Which I appreciated. Over the years Casey proved to be a real friend. He was a sailor and many years later, shortly before he died, we sailed to the Abacos together on the *Gilead*, with all, or most, corporate memories long forgotten. I called Horacio in Lima and told him I would take him up on his offer to buy the advertising agency.

Looking back over my 23 years at Braniff, and whether I knew it at the time or not, I left the airline at the height of its entire history. In 1974 the airline broke the $1 billion revenue mark for the first time. It was the eighth largest airline in the U.S. and the 14th in the world. It was also at its most profitable. From a personal standpoint it had been a terrific 23 years. Harding Lawrence had the right idea about the importance of Latin America and in the last ten years had changed the nature of the airline's Latin operations. I had met dozens of people who remained friends and had learned a great deal about the airline business. In particular I learned something about motivating and managing people. In addition to Uruguay and the United States, I had lived in three countries: Panama, Colombia, and Peru; and as a result had a real feeling about a large portion of Latin America, both from the airline standpoint as well as from the cultural and political aspects. I felt that the region had tremendous promise if the people would just get their act together, and rid themselves of populist politics, central planning, excessive nationalism, and government interference. I was convinced that the potential was almost unlimited.

Harding wrote me a nice 'going away' letter, which included: "We all regret your leaving Braniff after our long and most pleasant association, but we certainly understand your desire to take advantage of a good opportunity. We will miss you—you have made a host of friends here—but we look forward to seeing you from time to time. Sincerely, Harding"

And another one from Rex Brack which said: "I have said it so often—and you heard me do so—that you are undoubtedly the best Sales Manager in the industry and I still feel that way."

# AeroPeru

B efore we moved back to Lima, our good friend from Peru, Gonzalo del Solar, and his stunning wife Elena Ivanissevich (her father had been Peron's personal doctor in Argentina), had bought a brand new camper and invited us to join them to drive it from Texas to Panama, before shipping it down to Lima from Panama. It was a two-week trip and I jumped at the idea. It seemed like a great way to unwind and prepare for the future.

Together with Valerie and Robbie, who had just finished a couple of years at Southern Methodist University in Texas, I met the del Solars in Guatemala City and spent ten days with them on the road through Central America and stopping off here and there. It was a good experience and an opportunity to change course, review my personal agenda, and prepare for life on my own. This was long before the Nicaraguan Contras war, and people were friendly and hospitable. We slept on deserted beaches and visited historical ruins. We all thoroughly enjoyed the trip.

Gonzalo was a helicopter pilot. He had the Bell representation in Peru and made a lot of money selling Bell helicopters to the Peruvian Air Force, which was working on oil exploration in the Amazon. He would joke that the Air Force pilots kept breaking the helicopters which meant more spare parts and replacements, which meant more commissions. Eventually he had moved to Argentina where he an Elena had bought a ranch. They were both good companions, and we had been close friends in Lima. Gonzalo later made the mistake of investing in Challenge Air International, which was one of my experiences too that I would like to brush over...

## There is Life after Braniff

Some time late in 1974 I arrived back in Lima as a free man. Braniff had given me a great send-off party, Ed Acker had personally given Martha and me a life-time annual pass, positive space (Pos-A as they were called in the lingo, which meant you could actually book yourself in first class) and everyone had been very friendly. Harding did not come to the party. Tom King had someone put together a book which I still have, filled with clippings and even a complimentary and funny poem (I never did find out who wrote it) which I still have around.

Acker had somehow arranged to transfer to me the ownership in the Braniff house, called Kusi Wasi (Quechua for 'happy home' according to the owners, but later I found out it meant 'house of happy women' or more plainly, a whorehouse) in which we lived in Lima's La Molina district, so I had a mortgage-free home.

Later on I sold Kusi Wasi to Juan Pardo, one of our socialite friends and lived on the proceeds for a couple of years. I did not feel too badly when I found out several years later that he sold it for five times what he paid me. But I could not hold that against him. Juan later helped me to recover from the Challenge Air disaster in the late 1980s when he sent me a check for $5,000, no strings attached. Juan now lives between Mexico City and Lima.

## Earthquake

The day after I returned to Lima I was sitting in the patio overlooking the pool and a hundred yards of front yard when the earthquake of 1974 hit, without warning, as earthquakes are wont to do. The front lawn suddenly had waves in it and the pool emptied in about five minutes. The rumble from the surrounding hills came afterwards. One of the four-foot-wide walls in the den cracked open and everyone came out screaming. It was a 6.5 Richter scale earthquake centered somewhere north of Lima—a heavy one. La Molina was not hit that badly, although our neighbors, the Prados, lost the second floor which collapsed. I had the feeling that perhaps Harding Lawrence was right after all, except I did not think that this was what he had in mind.

I started my take over of *Interandina de Publicidad*, Horacio Mazza's advertising agency, a few days later, meeting the seven or eight full-time employees. Horacio had assigned Eduardo Cermesoni to remain in Lima to be my finance manager and generally help out with the business for a few months. Eduardo had a good feel for advertising and was a great help. When I took over, the agency lived on the Braniff account and a few other smaller ones which included Faucett, the then domestic Peruvian airline, and a cheese producer owned by another Lima friend of mine, Roberto Risso. He was a very good cook, and had developed a cheese manufacturing plant which produced a Peruvian version of camembert and other highly-priced cheese products. Interandina had put the product on the map and it was doing very well, but with a very modest budget. Faucett was fighting the government for international route authority which eventually would present a conflict of interest with Braniff. In the meantime it had about 50 percent of the Peruvian domestic market and was actually complimentary to, rather than competitive with Braniff.

During this period we became involved with a super project: to organize the Lima Gold Museum's tour of Europe and Canada on behalf of its private owner, Miguel Mujica Gallo. The Museum was one of the highlights of every tourist's visit to Lima. Miguel, whom I knew well, had made a lifetime passion of collecting pre-Columbian gold artifacts and had transformed the collection into a museum in his home. He was my good friend Gianmarco Nizzola's father-in-law and we were close friends of both Gianmarco and his then wife, Milagros. We arranged for a very successful tour, starting out in Budapest, then to Helsinki and Vienna, and finally to Toronto. It was not financially very successful, at least not for Interandina, but it paid some of our bills and helped to publicize Peru and the pre-Columbian history of the country. Miguel Mujica did not do too badly either because our deal was that he received a flat fee for every day the collection was on the road. One reason for the lack of financial success was that we had not figured in the problem of converting eastern European currency and took a 10:1 beating on the exchange rate in Hungary, which set us back pretty badly.

Gianmarco had an interest in a printing plant and we tried, unsuccessfully, to promote a book on the Gold Collection. I even got as far as having lunch with Mario Vargas Llosa, Peru's foremost writer, at the Lima Golf Club, about his contributing the introduction and possibly more. He showed interest, or perhaps he was being polite, but nothing came of the idea. Mario was a real gentleman and very friendly. I saw him once after that in London with one of Valerie's Peruvian friends. Many years later he ran for President and lost to President Fujimori. Which was probably a good thing for both Mario and Peru. Although if he reads this, Mario will probably disagree violently.

## Another 'Ché' Alumnus

We needed to diversify our client list. Fortunately Horacio had assembled a professional group of advertising people. The head creative chap was Alberto Nuñez, a former E.R.P. (Ejercito Revolucionario del Pueblo), the Argentine equivalent of the Tupamaros, and an avowed communist. He was a top 'jinglero' (a producer of advertising 'jingles'), and very musically inclined, and creative. Alberto and I worked very well as a team. We also liked each other in spite of our political differences. While I was very much a liberal and had my own thoughts about the need for change in Latin America, I did not believe that armed insurrection was the solution—which Alberto had obviously espoused when he joined the E.R.P.

We spent many an evening drinking good capitalistic whisky and arguing about the best way to bring about a change and to help the poor. We also argued about San Martin and Bolivar. I tried to convince him that Bolivar's plan for South America was the only way for the countries to achieve some kind of political and economic independence; that San Martin was just a gifted military man but had no plan for the region after independence, while Bolivar really did. We never settled the argument but it often kept us up late and the discussion was always stimulating. Alberto was fascinating, intelligent, and very good company. He later went to Spain where he became quite successful and ended up in Mexico as a musician.

El 'Ché'—Ché Guevara—was his hero and he had known him briefly at the university. We also talked about the motorcycle ride through South and Central America which set him on his Marxist-communist campaign as he witnessed extreme poverty and squalor on the one hand and extreme wealth on the other. As well as my meeting with Che in Havana in the early days. I was something of a Guevara fan myself, partly because I admired him for having died for what he believed in, partly because I felt that he was, at least partially, right, even if I did not subscribe to his way (revolution) to solve the basic problem (poverty). But I knew that pure capitalism had not worked either. So I was stuck somewhere in the middle, which is seldom effective, even if compromise is the least of several evils. Alberto had left Buenos Aires in a hurry, one step ahead of the secret police, first to Salvador Allende's Chile and then when Pinochet took over, to Peru.

We set out to make presentations to everyone who would listen. In the first five or six months we picked up several non-airline accounts, including a couple of large clients who helped to balance our billing nicely. I was often amused as we sat in some expensive board room of a major Peruvian bank, brewery, or whatever, while Alberto pitched his creative approach. It these executives knew Alberto's background they would have kicked us out of the board room and called the cops. We also picked up British Caledonian for all South America in a joint effort with Horacio Mazza's Argentine agency. This involved a trip to England which I arranged through some of our contacts.

In 1975 Valerie had signed up with the John Vickers School of Photography in London and Martha and I took advantage of our BCal connection to fly there to see her and watch her progress. Vickers was the official photographer to the Old Vic and a great teacher. His classes were limited to half a dozen students, expensive but worth every penny. Another student was Mario Testino from Lima who has since become famous for his pictures of the Princess of Wales, the lovely Lady Di, of tragic memory. John Vicker's wife was born in Argentina, and we had dinner with them a couple of times. We settled Valerie into a bedroom/studio flat in Knightsbridge, only walking distance from Vickers. After ten days we returned to Lima, knowing she was in good hands and loving it, especially living in London.

In Lima the agency was doing well but I was becoming bored dealing with clients. I enjoyed the advertising challenge and working with Alberto on the creative approach to a marketing problem. But I really did not like working with clients, all of whom wanted me personally to handle the relationship, rather than with our official account executive, young Alejandro Aspillaga.

Alejandro was Polo Pflucker's brother-in-law. Polo was now the Braniff Regional Vice President and our client. Alejandro's father, Gustavo Aspillaga, was another strong supporter. He had been appointed president of Faucett, one of our clients. He had a lovely home in San Isidro where we played tennis on Sunday mornings. But I knew that I had to return to something more satisfying, like airline consulting, which I enjoyed.

After some time I started to look for someone to buy me out. One of our clients was my friend Gianmarco Nizzola, a Swiss who had come to Lima in his early twenties to work for his uncle, a very successful Swiss-turned-Peruvian businessman. After several years with his uncle, Gianmarco had branched out on his own with a printing business and other representations, including setting up the first "Copy-Centro" in Peru, a forerunner of Xerox copy centers. He hired us as his advertising agency more out of friendship than real need. He liked the advertising business and eventually, he and another immigrant from Argentina, Oscar Dufour, a real advertising professional, bought the agency from me for $10,000 which was more than acceptable, considering I had paid nothing for it in the first place.

## El Pub

In 1975 Morales Bermudes organized a coup and deposed Velasco with the intention of bringing the country back to a constitutional Government. About the same time (but no cause-and-effect), with a bunch of my friends, I decided that Lima needed an English pub so we organized "The Pub" on Calle Los Conquistadores in San Isidro. We rented a lovely English style house which was perfect. Polo Pflucker, Yoyo Ferrand, Gianmarco Nizzola, and several others: all became equal equity partners. We hired Andre Aisner to do the interior of the place (I took him to Dallas to look at the closest thing—a 'Steak & Ale' restaurant) and he did a terrific job. We had a typical pub bar, darts, backgammon, shove-ha'penny, the works. It became 'the place' in Lima. We sold it after one year for three times our investment. It still exists.

I still missed the airline business. But I had proved to myself that I could make it without the 'Braniff umbrella', or 'parachute.' It gave me the final level of self confidence that I needed, and convinced me that I was primarily an entrepreneur and not a corporate animal.

## It's the Ownership—Stupid

One day late in 1976 General Javier Oswaldo Cabrera, the former Director of Civil Aviation and recently appointed President of AeroPeru, called me at the office. He told me that General Morales Bermudez, the President of Peru, wanted me to help him to re-organize AeroPeru, the Peruvian national flag carrier. We met at Cabrera's home in a typical middle-class part of San Isidro. He was a retired Air Force General and former pilot. Javier Oswaldo was clean-cut and studious, very straight and honestly dedicated to doing the right thing. The airline had been formed in the late Sixties after the demise of Shelton's APSA. We had several drinks and I stayed late talking about what needed to be done. He was very receptive to some of my ideas and we obviously hit it off, the chemistry seemed right, and the prospect excited me. The challenge and the opportunity to do something significant appeared to be very real.

I had first met Javier Oswaldo when he was Director of Civil Aviation in the late Sixties. We had once traveled to Dallas together when APSA was on the verge of collapse, and the government had asked if we would help to organize the new AeroPeru. We hit it off pretty well even though Braniff's idea of helping AeroPeru—to form a sort of Braniff-dominated step-child airline—had not sold and never took off. In a sense that is what another U.S. airline is now attempting to do in the region, and the jury is still out on the current effort.

Cabrera was convinced that AeroPeru had to acquire wide-bodied equipment and stand on its own feet without government subsidies. He offered me the job of general manager and CEO, reporting directly to him. I asked him about the law which, I knew, required the GM to be a Peruvian citizen. He laughed and said: "Look, Bobby, I have Morales Bermudez on my side. He asked me what I wanted and I told him, you. So maybe you can't sign as General Manager. I will, but you will hold the position. So stop worrying about details. Do you want the job, or don't you?"

Because I liked him and I also thought that Morales Bermudez was a good chap who had really engineered the ousting of Velasco for the good of the country, I decided, there and then, and without giving it a whole lot of thought, why not. The pay was much less than I had made in the agency, but I could live on it. Morales Bermudez was a middle class, intelligent General who had mobilized some of the less radical military leaders, principally the Air Force, and convinced them that the country needed to return to a constitutional government, and he had won a bloodless palace coup, in itself a remarkable and commendable achievement.

I was bored with the advertising agency business and this seemed as if it would be fun. AeroPeru had been a political football for the Air Force and I felt that Morales Bermudez would support whatever Cabrera and I felt needed to be done. The airline had an ideal route map, not only a significant domestic network, but services to the United States and most of South America. It had the potential to operate a real Lima hub, with domestic and international spokes to the major cities in the continent. There was also a feeling that I would be doing something constructive for Peru, which had been very good to us, so it combined a challenging job with an emotionally fulfilling assignment.

## Booth the Bureaucrat

The next week, on a Monday, I checked in to the AeroPeru building and reported for work. Cabrera introduced me to his staff, most of whom I knew. Danny Ratti was the CFO, the son of an old Braniff-ite, Andres Ratti, a long-time sales rep. Danny was in his late twenties, had been to a Jesuit School in northern California on a scholarship and was quite brilliant. He had worked for a government agency for a while before joining AeroPeru. Raul Burneo was head of Planning. I knew Burneo from APSA where he had been commercial manager. He had been CFO and moved over to Planning when Danny came along. The two of them were really bright and became my principal lieutenants. Others who stood out because they were professional and dedicated, included Sandro Francini, treasurer, and Hernando Vasquez, who ran maintenance. Cabrera had also brought in Jorge Salmon, an advertising man whom I knew, to develop a badly needed new image for the airline. Jorge had exiled himself to Ecuador when Velasco took over. He was very creative and produced a great campaign, "Las Rutas del Sol" which not only sold the airline, but above all sold Peru as a leisure destination for non-Peruvians. It also evoked all kinds of emotional ties for the hundreds of thousands of emigré Peruvians, the so called 'ethnic market' outside Peru. The campaign won a number of awards and helped to create a new image for the airline. It was somewhat along the lines of Mary Wells's *End of the Plain Plane* campaign for Braniff in the 1960s.

We also established a Management By Objective program and immediately increased the 7–8 hour daily aircraft utilization to 10–11, which enabled us to add frequency in some major markets such as Argentina and Brazil and to expand the Lima hub. This made the airline more competitive with Braniff by providing daily service to the United States and it significantly improved the airline's market share. Morale was at an all-time high, proving once again that people will step up to the challenge when there is a plan and strong leadership. Cabrera was very good and we had a good team.

Shortly after joining, Cabrera had a meeting with Enrique (Kiko) Dibos who represented Lockheed in Peru and was peddling a couple of L-1011s which had been delivered to P.S.A. in California but which were now being offered at very attractive lease rates. I always suspected that Lockheed was subsidizing the lease because it had failed to place a single L-1011 in South America and really wanted the deal to go through. I knew Kiko socially, his son Enrique was a close friend of Robbie and Guy, and he was into motocross.

This started a horrendous period of on-again, off-again negotiations. A retired Air Force general represented McDonnell Douglas and was pushing the DC-10. The airline needed to move into wide-bodied aircraft. It was competing not just with Braniff but also with other airlines in the region such as LAN-Chile which were all offering wide-bodied service and the lower deck cargo capabilities alone made it the right decision, regardless of the aircraft type. The Lockheed proposal was better financially but the Douglas representative had a lot of friends in the Air Force who still called the shots when the chips were down. There was a faction that liked the L-1011 and no decision was made in a hurry. The L-1011s would be a leased deal and any commission involved would not make anyone rich. The bottom line was the ownership cost and the used L-1011s beat the pants of the new DC-10 proposal, and we did not need the superior range and additional capacity of a DC10-30 for the AeroPeru five-hour mission. The only problem with the ex-PSA aircraft was they had a lower deck galley and lounge and this took up much of the cargo payload space.

*AeroPeru's flagship, the Lockheed L-1011 TriStar.*

Cabrera arranged for a full-blown presentation on the L-1011 decision with Morales Bermudez and the cabinet at the presidential palace with probably 50 people in the room. Cabrera asked me to present the argument and I insisted that we stay away from discussing one aircraft over another, but to present the wide-body principle as the preferred option, as well as discussing the economics of leasing versus buying. Fortunately he agreed so we proceeded, with Raul and Danny to make the case. I think the argument (that the wide-body would also deliver the equivalent of an all-cargo narrow body in the lower deck of the aircraft) is what caught everybody's attention, particularly as Peru was on a major export push. However, no decision was made at the time. But I enjoyed making the presentation at that level, especially answering some of the rather intelligent questions.

Shortly after this Morales Bermudez decided to replace Cabrera with another Air Force general, Frank Tweddle, who had been in Washington for two years in some kind of military mission. I suspected at the time that this had something to do with Tweddle's involvement in ousting Velasco. He had apparently been one of the Air Force generals who supported Morales when he made the push which started in Arequipa.

I happened to know Frank who was socially very prominent at the Lima Golf Club and in Punta Hermosa where he had a house. He had a reputation for being somewhat 'off-the-wall', but was generally liked. He had recently divorced his Peruvian wife and married an American. One evening I received a call from the Minister of Transport, another Air Force General, and he asked me to come to the Ministry the following morning. At the time I did not know that Cabrera was being replaced. The meeting at the Minister's office was to find out if I would stay on with Tweddle. I told the Minister frankly that Cabrera had hired me, but if he was replaced and his replacement wanted me to stay on, I would. I did not see any reason not to—which was my mistake. Later that same day the change was announced and Cabrera took umbrage that I had accepted to stay on. In fact, he took it very personally and would not talk to me when he called the staff together.

The Cabrera incident was very uncomfortable and I knew that I had made an enemy, unconsciously and unnecessarily. Protocol demanded that I should resign as a show of loyalty, but I had inadvertently failed that test and Cabrera never forgave me. After a few weeks I decided that I really did not want to stay on. Frank was a wild, fighter-pilot type, and not in the same league with Cabrera who had been thoughtful and had listened to his staff. Frank went his own way. I talked it over with Martha and we agreed that it was time to move on. Valerie was in London; Robbie had been accepted at S.M.U. in Dallas, with his best friend, Fidardo 'Chueco' Menchelli; and Guy wanted to move to Los Angeles where a friend of his said he could find him a job at Lockheed's Palmdale plant. As he wanted to fly—he had started lessons in Lima—and there was a flying school near Palmdale in the desert, where he could also race moto-cross, I thought it was not a bad idea. Mother had passed away in Porto Alegre where she had gone to live with her sisters, there was nothing keeping us in South America.

## If it Ain't Fun—Quit

I went to see Frank with our decision to move back to the U.S. and he jumped at it, but asked me to take over AeroPeru in North America. He also said that he was going to ask the Minister to approve the L-1011 decision and that we needed to strengthen the U.S. sales and marketing. This seemed like a reasonable idea. It would allow us some breathing space and we could figure out what we wanted to do. Lima was uncomfortable and I did not feel the same about it any longer.

I had already sold the agency to Gianmarco Nizzola and Alfredo Dufour so that was no problem. Tweddle agreed that I could live where I wished to as long as I ran the office in Miami. Because AeroPeru had offices in Los Angeles and New York, and because I would probably travel quite often, it seemed logical that we could live anywhere. I suspect that Frank did not really want me around in Lima, and moving me to the U.S. was a way to remove me from the limelight—which suited me fine.

Some time in 1977 we moved to Los Angeles where we rented a house in Rancho Palos Verdes. Robbie had decided to give up S.M.U., he was not terribly keen on studying, so he moved in with us and found a job with Continental Airlines while Guy went to Palmdale where he also took up flying lessons at a nearby school. I would commute to Miami on Sunday evenings and spend three or four days there. Sometimes I went to New York for a couple of days and managed to spend the weekends in Los Angeles. AeroPeru in the meantime had selected the L-1011 and I was very much involved in re-organizing the United States sales and administration—which I found on arrival was something of a disaster. Valerie had joined us in Los Angeles and shortly afterwards moved to San Francisco which she loved.

AeroPeru's Los Angeles District Manager, George Berrettini, and his wife, became close personal friends. He was an Italian-transplant and his wife was Austrian. He had been with Alitalia and a couple of U.S. carriers before joining AeroPeru. George eventually moved to Miami, where we continued our friendship even though he moved away from the airline industry.

Some time after we moved, the Air Force and some of Cabrera's friends had started an investigation into the L-1011 decision and I was a target of the

General Auditors Office in Lima. They started to make my life miserable with audits and visits and lengthy inquiries (e.g. why did I stay at the Waldorf in New York. Easy—we had a great airline rate and it was cheaper than any other major hotel in the city). The crowning blow was that I was told I was under investigation for kickbacks on the L-1011 deal. I decided there and then that this wasn't worth it. First of all the L-1011 deal was a straight operating lease and Lockheed, which had had more than its share of problems with kickbacks a few years previously, was not about to make that kind of mistake again. Second, the aircraft were being leased by a financial institution which had taken the aircraft back from P.S.A. Third, the decision had been made in Lima, after I left Peru, so I could not claim any credit or otherwise for the decision. AeroPeru was eventually unable to cope with the L-1011 and returned the two aircraft. So the whole affair died a natural death. I was eventually cleared on the investigation in Peru, but I had to hire a friendly lawyer to get the case dropped.

So, in September 1978, I resigned. I had the $10,000 in the bank from the sale of Interandina and we had managed to save a similar amount from the sale of the appliances we had sold in Peru, so I figured we could survive for a few months until I found something. In the meantime Robbie had married Fiorella, his childhood girl friend who had come to live with us in Palos Verdes. Both of them had jobs so we did not have to worry about them. During our sojourn in California I had made friends with a major tour operator who was a friend of George Berretini. He had originally developed an AeroPeru charter program to Peru. When he heard that I had left he suggested that we put together a South American program and actually start an airline. I told him that I had no money and considerable capital was needed. But that we might consider a scheduled public charter company that would sell direct to the public. Something that did not exist in the market along the lines of the European charter airlines. He liked the idea and proposed that we prepare a preliminary business plan; he would finance a trip to South America to set up tentative ground arrangements in Lima, Buenos Aires, and Rio; and then develop a more complete plan that we could use to raise capital, or find an airline that would provide the operating aircraft.

A short time after I had left, Frank Tweddle was picked up at Lima airport with a briefcase full of cocaine. He claimed it was planted, but he spent a number of years in a military hospital more or less under house arrest. The plant story made some sense because he had undoubtedly made a lot of enemies during his career, including at AeroPeru. I never saw him again.

The whole AeroPeru experience convinced me that governments should not be in the airline business. I still believe that while they were terribly important in the early days, providing mail contracts and other forms of subsidy to an embryo industry, this did not apply in today's business environment. Governments should stick to what they do well, which is to provide the legal framework for business, worry about air traffic control and other safety related and anti-trust issues in commercial aviation, and subsidize education, research, and other not-for-profit government-supported healthcare, and so on. Airlines are a business and should be treated as such. While some will argue that airlines are a vital public utility, and will quote the 1997 strike threat by American Airlines pilots which would have ruined the tourism-based economy of half the Caribbean, I maintain that governments are not good owners of airlines. A good example is Latin America today, which has privatized 100% of its airlines (along with a number of other public utilities) and the airlines that have survived are stronger and more efficient than their government-owned predecessors. And profitable, which none of them was under government ownership.

I had met and dealt with some good people in the airline, but government interference and constant changing of the guard in the corner office was the problem. In fact, I coined the phrase which I used constantly over the years: "There's nothing wrong with management, its the ownership." To be fair, this axiom can be applied to just about any business.

Other than my last two Braniff years in Dallas, we had spent a total of 16 years in Peru and made many fine friends. Peruvians are among the most hospitable people anywhere in the world, particularly the 'little' people in the highlands and in the interior. Peru is probably the single most fascinating country in Latin America. Its tourism potential is almost unlimited and I suspect that as the century nears its end, it is finally coming in to its own as a major tourism destination. This may spoil the country entirely, but I do not think so. Peruvians have been conquered, colonized, and culturally dominated for thousands of years but still maintain their own singular character and personality. And the food is great.

# Air Florida

**E**arly in October 1978 I ran into Ed Acker at the Miami airport on my way back from South America. He pulled me over to the coffee shop when I told him I had an hour to kill before my flight to Los Angeles: "So what happened with AeroPeru? The last I heard you were still running their U.S. operation."

I told him I had resigned and was putting together a South American scheduled public charter idea which I had just about completed. He had recently joined Air Florida as C.E.O. and had invested some money in the small intra-state airline. He was intrigued with the charter idea, and said: "Look, Bobby, we've got a real airline going here in Miami. Deregulation will open up all kinds of opportunities for us. Why don't you call me next week and I'll arrange a meeting with the top brass. Maybe we can do something that makes sense to all of us, okay?"

I was still living in Rancho Palos Verdes in California but was thinking about moving to Fort Lauderdale, because Los Angeles was just too remote from Latin America and if the idea bore fruit, I wanted to be based in South Florida. I had traveled to Lima, Rio, and Buenos Aires, which were going to be the three principal destinations and had secured quotations on ground arrangements. The charter flight would leave New York, stop in Rio de Janeiro, and continue to Buenos Aires, with a return via Lima to Los Angeles. The utilization was great, as I planned it, we would run twice weekly with one aircraft. Drop half a 'plane-load in Rio, take the other half on to B.A. and then repeat the process out of Los Angeles. We would sell "air only" (the airline flight) or a seven-day "Air-Land" package in any combination of the three destinations. The economics were simple. Once we were up and running, we would run full loads on each segment. Using a B747-100 with 490 seats, we could reduce the block-hour seat cost to something like $15. We would sell air-only at approximately $30 per seat/block hour which gave us a break-even of 50%. Anything more than 50% was pure profit. At $30 per seat-block hour, the New York-Buenos Aires round trip 'air-only' selling price would be less than $600 and Lima and Rio about $400. This was approximately 50% lower than the going economy fares in the market. I had convinced my tour operator friend that we could contract for the flying with a security deposit which would be much simpler than starting our own airline. And a whole lot less risky.

## The Darling of Deregulation

When I returned to Los Angeles I called Ed Acker and we made a date to meet in Miami the following week. I drove up to the Air Florida headquarters just west of Miami International Airport on the second floor of a two-storey, open-mall kind of building. The offices were low cost but functional. Reservations was on the ground floor behind a restaurant.

Ed took me into the small conference room with Eli Timoner, the founder of the airline, and several other senior executives who included former Braniff executive (and Acker man) John Fasolino, Dick Skully (Vice President—Operations) and Tino Gonzalez, (Chief Financial Officer). Eli had moved to Florida from New York where he had learned the retail business at Bloomingdales in the early 1950s. In Florida he became president of Laura Lee Candies of Florida and later Chairman and C.E.O. of Giffen Industries.

I liked Eli instantly. He was wiry of build, bright of demeanor, and about my age. In 1971 he had started the airline as an intra-state carrier in 1971 with Bill Spohrer, a long-time airline executive, and Jim Woodman, the former PanAm manager I had met during SATO years. Eli had learned the airline business the hard, but probably, the best way—as an owner. He brought much of his retail and financial acumen to the airline. He and his wife Lisa became good friends of ours over the years. For someone with very little airline experience he had an instinctive grasp for the business and what makes it work. He was also one of the few airline C.E.O.s in my experience without an ego, which seems to go with the territory.

Ed had asked me to be prepared to make a presentation to his management team. I showed them the numbers and discussed the marketing approach. I explained that air fares from New York and Los Angeles to Lima, Rio, and Buenos Aires were too expensive to create a real leisure market and that I had several tour operators ready to embrace the plan; that we needed a U.S. airline that would commit the operational resources (the aircraft) to launch the program. I thought I made my case to them, even though Ed Acker did not show much enthusiasm. But knowing Ed from Braniff days, and his financial background, I knew it was a hard sell. Ed asked me to stay over for lunch with Eli.

We went downstairs to the restaurant, Herbets. At lunch Ed told me he liked my idea but that I had the wrong markets. He said, with Eli nodding his head: "Look, Bobby. PanAm has just acquired National Airlines and this is going to open up an opportunity for a second U.S. carrier on the Miami-London route. And we are going to go for it."

Ed waited for this to sink in while I finished chewing on lunch, so I nodded as if in agreement, what the hell, if he did not want to do South

America I would have to look for someone else. He continued: "Bobby, we want you to join us and take your public charter idea forward but instead of South America, I want you to do it between London and Miami. We'll get the aircraft, but we need you to go out and get us a commitment from either a U.K. or Florida tour operator so we can eliminate the risk. After we show the world that we can fly the Atlantic efficiently, we can be a real contender for U.S. designation as the second carrier to London. What do you think?"

I thought it sounded pretty good and we discussed money. They agreed to pay me as a consultant, time and material. Time was $500 a day plus expenses. Material would be the provision of an office, travel expenses and access to one of the 'pool' secretaries. I explained that I had to close down the house in Palos Verdes and move to Florida but I figured I could do that in a couple of weeks. I also had to advise my tour operator friend, who took it very well, and told me that I had to look after Number One, meaning me.

## Harry Goodman, Intasun, and U.K. Charters

We moved into a rented apartment on the beach in Fort Lauderdale which was great except for the 45-minute commute to Miami. Air Florida was then just beginning to look at expansion. Ed Acker had brought in American Financial which had invested several million dollars in the company and then taken it public. By this time it was late in 1978 and the U.S. airline industry had just been deregulated, thus opening up apparently limitless opportunities for aviation entrepreneurship. Founder Eli Timoner had brought Ed in and stepped down from the C.E.O. job to convince him. Eli was a quick learner and the key to keeping a lid on costs. He had previously built a very successful business and had poured his every cent into Air Florida. Until deregulation and Ed Acker, he had struggled to keep the airline alive. Now he had some capital and a chief executive who was willing to 'bet the company' on deregulation. They had just acquired five ex-Singapore Airlines' B737-100s small twin-jets, built especially for Singapore, with low operating costs, and with longer range than the standard model.

My assignment was to go after a U.K.-Miami charter program. By a remarkable coincidence, while I was looking around for an office, I heard from one of my hotelier pals about Harry Goodman an English tour operator who had been in Miami that week, tying up hotel rooms on the beach. His company, Intasun, had announced that it was going to start U.K.-Miami charters the next summer. I took a gamble and called his U.K. office and spoke to a secretary. I told her that I wanted to talk to Harry about a charter program to Miami. I think the fact that I was calling from Miami brought him to the telephone.

"Mr. Goodman, I represent Air Florida, the Miami-based airline, and I want to come to London and make you an offer you can't refuse. I know you are talking to Freddie, but I can beat his price if you'll see me." I was referring to Sir Freddie Laker of Skytrain and Laker Airways fame.

Harry Goodman seemed to appreciate the approach. He admitted that he was talking to Laker but had not completed a deal. We agreed that I would be in his office the following Monday. This was on Thursday. I went immediately to Tino Gonzalez's office. We had already done some work on the direct operating cost of a B747-100. I explained to Tino that we needed the additional capacity of a 747 to beat Laker's DC-10-30. Tino had called a broker friend of his to obtain a quote on a two-year dry lease, including maintenance on a 'power-by-the-hour' basis (the only way to intelligently do a one-aircraft operation; 'power-by-the-hour' meant that we paid all maintenance costs on an hourly basis which eliminated the risk, even though it cost more than the traditional approach).

By the end of the day we had worked out all the numbers and went to see Ed and Eli. They called in Dick Skully, head of operations. We had built in the cost of training pilots and cabin staff and amortized all pre-op startup costs over 12 months. Skully could not argue with our numbers. I had also figured we could probably negotiate a guarantee on lower-deck cargo but we decided that would be our cushion so we did not build in any cargo revenue (I did arrange this later, which added to our profit margin).

We were right at $7,500 per block hour, fully allocated, with a 10% profit contribution. We could sell the rotation at $142,500 and make $14,250 per round trip. The important issue was Intasun's seat price at $291. They could load-factor the flight at 75%, sell the seat at $387 or so, and make a profit on every seat sold beyond 75% of the capacity. I knew enough about the charter business that this was the way the charter operator figured. They would run at 90% average load factor. Which meant they could make an average of approximately $30,000 per rotation, plus profit on the ground arrangements. This would sell.

Acker gave me the go ahead. I asked Tino to buy me a ticket on National's Sunday evening flight (first class, I insisted, if I'm going to sell this thing on Monday I need to be reasonably fresh). They all agreed and we called in the lawyer, Jim Curassi, to write up a contract. I told them to leave the number of rotations and the final price blank so that I could fill that in. Dick Skully wanted to do flight plans to check the fuel burn, but he would not have them until Monday so we shook hands and I made arrangements to pick up the contract on Saturday morning. I also booked a room in London at my favorite hotel, the Hyde Park. Mac Seligman knew the manager and had given

me a good rate. Intasun was out in the sticks some place, Goodman had given
me directions.

I arrived in London early Monday morning, took the train to Victoria
Station, and a London cab to the Hyde Park. I had a real English breakfast,
kippers and eggs, showered, and then took a limo to Intasun's office which
was a good hour's drive. My appointment with Goodman was at noon. Harry
was a big, fleshy man and gave the impression that he had a lot of street-
smarts, from a working class 'school of hard knocks.'

He introduced me around and took me in to the conference room with
three or four of his managers and the chief financial officer. I showed him the
contract and told him we were ready to commit the price, subject to agreeing on
the number of weekly flights and the duration. Startup was May 15 and we
would operate through November 15. They wanted an option to continue
through the winter, but would decide by September 15. We worked until about 4
o'clock. They loved the price, it was well below Laker's offer. They wanted 4
weekly flights and a six-month contract, worth $15 million. We also agreed on a
10% security deposit, or 1 million pounds. About $1,600,000 at the time. More
than we needed for security on the aircraft, training and other startup expenses.

I called Miami and talked to Eli who was delighted and agreed to the
deal. He did not tell me about the flight plans so I figured everything was all
right. The only thing he said was to call him before I went to bed because I
had told him that Harry was going to take me out to dinner in London. We
went to the Savoy, had an excellent dinner, and when I returned to my room I
called Eli and he said: "Bobby, I didn't want to tell you but Dick's godamn
flight plan came in negative, the fucking 747 won't take off from Miami in
July and August with a full load nonstop to London."

Jesus, I thought, here we go. But he then proceeded to tell me they had
worked all day and had a deal on an Icelandic DC10-30. We could match the
seat price. The only problem was that we would have to operate six flights
weekly with the 380-seat DC-10 to provide the same number of seats. I told
him I would call Intasun in the morning and find out if it would still work. I
went downstairs to the lower level bar at the Hyde Park, had a nightcap, and
talked to the bartender for a while to clear my head. I went to bed about
midnight, totally bushed.

The next day I called Harry and told him the 'good news.' We could do
it better with a DC10-30, keep the same price per seat. He loved it, he
preferred six flights weekly anyway. We agreed that Miami would courier a
revised contract. He agreed to deposit the one million pounds in escrow that
day in our Miami bank. I took the rest of the day off, went to a pub, and got

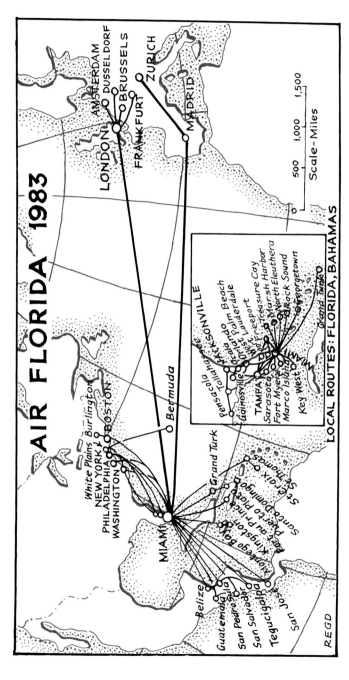

**AIR FLORIDA 1983**

AMSTERDAM
DUSSELDORF
BRUSSELS
ZURICH
MADRID
LONDON
FRANKFURT

Scale – Miles
500   1,000   1,500

White Plains
Burlington
NEW YORK
PHILADELPHIA
BOSTON
WASHINGTON

Bermuda

Grand Turk

St. Thomas
St. Croix
Santo Domingo
Port au Prince
Kingston
Montego Bay
MIAMI

Belize
Guatemala
San Pedro Sula
San Salvador
Tegucigalpa
San José

REGD

**LOCAL ROUTES: FLORIDA, BAHAMAS**

Pensacola
Tallahassee
JACKSONVILLE
Gainesville
Ocala
Orlando
West Palm Beach
Fort Lauderdale
Freeport
Treasure Cay
Marsh Harbor
North Eleuthera
Rock Sound
Georgetown
Grand Turk
TAMPA
Sarasota
Fort Myers
Marco Island
Key West
MIAMI

*Sadly, memories of Air Florida are overshadowed by the spectacular srash into the frozen Potomac in 1982 ( see page 137). Few remember that , before the management crisis precipitated by Ed Acker's departure ( page 132), Air Florida's network ranged from Europe to Central America, from New England to the Caribbean, and had created a major hub at Miami.*

sloshed at lunch. That night I went to the theater, and flew back to Miami, next day, feeling like a hero of sorts.

I came to know Harry Goodman subsequently. As I mentioned before, he was an interesting character and later started Air Europe with partners in Spain and Italy. His approach was right on, but the execution stank and the whole thing eventually collapsed.

Eli and Ed had negotiated with Icelandic for the DC10-30 and were talking about adding a couple more sister ships. They were all worked up about opening up additional charter flights to and from the continent. The down payment from Intasun more than covered the up-front costs of leasing the first DC-10, training crews, and everything else. We had ninety days to be ready to start. At the time I appointed Roger Felber as our General Sales Agent in the U.K. I had met him during the AeroPeru days, he was English, married to a Peruvian, and had done a good job as the off-line General Sales Agent for the Peruvian airline, generating several million dollars of business in the U.K. and Europe; I was convinced he could do the same, only better, for Air Florida. In fact, he did such a good job that Ed Acker later bought out his contract and made him a senior vice president. Roger was paid in Air Florida stock and became a millionaire in the process.

## Back to the Corporate Jungle

The next three or four months, while we were gearing up, I travelled throughout Central America to negotiate traffic rights and look for General Agents. Eli, Ed, and Don Garvett went with me to Honduras where we had decided to start service. I impressed all three of them by forgetting my passport and giving the immigration officer my business card with a "free trip on Air Florida—anywhere" in lieu of a passport. And it worked. I happened to like Honduras a lot. Not just "T-Goose" (Tegucigalpa), but also San Pedro Sula and nearby La Ceiba which I visited because it was a United Fruit Company bastion with many U.S. citizen employees who travelled frequently and lived there.

I also went to Europe and approached potential tour operators in Brussels, Amsterdam, Paris, and Zurich, seeking additional charter contracts for the winter months, the prime travel season to Florida. I returned from one trip in early May or June and had a message that Acker wanted to see me right away. I checked in with his secretary and she ushered me straight in.

"Booth, I've been looking at your invoices. Do you realize you are making more money than Eli or me on an annualized basis?"

I played dumb and told him I had no idea how much money he and Eli made. "Well, let me tell you, Eli and I make about 100K, and if you continue to get your $500 per day and I don't count weekends, which you invoice for more often than not, you will make $125K this year. So I've got an offer for you. I know you don't want to be an executive because you told me that back at Braniff. So here's the deal. We make you Senior VP-Marketing at $75K salary and we give you a straight grant of 100,000 shares of Air Florida stock. That makes you a partner, or you can pack your things and go be a consultant someplace else, how about it?"

I laughed and told him that was different, so I would take it. I did not really have any other option. We shook hands and then he called Eli in and told him we had made a deal, and Eli congratulated me and welcomed me on board. The stock was selling at something like $3 at the time so I figured I was ahead of the game. Later on the stock actually hit $17 which made me a millionaire on paper. I replaced someone who had come to Air Florida from Continental Airlines, but had not adapted to the small, hands-on kind of organization, where everyone did their own typing and telephoning, with no personal secretaries.

## No Amount of Planning Replaces Dumb Luck

By this time we had bought a house in Miami and acquired *Gilead*, a Westsail 32, (otherwise known as a "wetsnail" because it was slow and low in the water) from Robert Dupont, the former manager of Air France in Miami. The house was fine but the sailboat was even finer: it was terrific. I had not actually owned a sailboat—although I had sailed a lot on O.P.B.—Other People's Boats—as opposed to O.P.M.—Other People's Money—since *Spoonbait* in Paysandu. *Gilead* was about ten years old but in great shape. It had a new set of sails, including a chute (spinnaker) and everything you could have asked for, if you loved sailing. I had my good friend, Art Adler to thank because he was a sailor and had introduced me to Bob Dupont who was selling his boat.

*Gilead* was great to sail even though slow. The first winter we sailed across to Hopetown in the Abacos and actually left the boat there for the season. We would fly back and forth (on Air Florida which had a very convenient 737 flight to Marsh Harbor, a 30-minute water-taxi ride from Hopetown) every Friday and Sunday evening. Guy, who had finished his California experience at Lockheed in Palmdale, and most recently with Mexicana at Los Angeles Airport, had come to Miami and spent the entire winter looking after *Gilead* and getting to know everyone in Hopetown. He subsidized his bar bills at the Hopetown Lodge by conch fishing with some Bahamians he became friends with.

Robbie and Fiorella had moved to Miami where Robbie found a job (on his own, with no help from me) in the Revenue Accounting Department at Air

Florida; while Guy then went to work for Arrow Air at the airport as a ticket agent. This was before Arrow terminated its passenger business as a result of the accident in Canada several years later.

## Building a Team

Getting back to business in early 1979, and in my role as senior vice president and one of the three senior people, I decided that I would have to build an organization that had hitherto been sadly deficient. The airline had grown topsy-turvy with a significant amount of 'cronyism'—something endemic to the airline industry. I brought in some ex-Braniff men who exceptional experience in their field: Art Stellmach to head up reservations and John Jackson, one of the best salesman in the business, to organize and supervise sales. Shortly afterwards we brought in Dan Brock (in fact, I had hired him as a sales representative straight out of school, a really bright young chap) and made him Agency & Interline Manager. Some good local talent was already in place. Don Garvett had worked at Air Florida as an intern. He was a part-time rocket scientist working on the space shuttle after graduating from MIT, and was probably in his mid-twenties, one of the best strategic planners in the industry. I made him VP-Planning. Another was Emilio Dirube, a Cuban-American and another great salesman. He had come from Air Sunshine, a small feeder airline that Ed and Eli had acquired, and was running the sales department practically by himself along with Vickie Thoen, a Dutch girl who had been married to a Peruvian. Both Emilio and Vickie became long-time friends. Vickie went to Uruguay for me and fell in love with a Uruguayan musician by the name of Faux and they make the best 'mejillones a la provencal' (mussels) in the United States.

About this time, Eastern and Delta announced that they would not be undersold. I told everyone that we were now in the unusual position of setting the pricing policies for three airlines. We would set the fares on the north-south corridor and any place else where we competed with them. We knew we could fill aircraft at $99 on the New York-Florida corridor, and when the competition matched us we jointly stimulated more traffic than we needed to fill our 737s without having to steal passengers from the other airlines. And because the established airlines did not match us completely because of all kinds of restrictions, our 'All seats, All flights' pricing paid off and people flocked to our product. Interestingly, Air Florida was among the first to apply the Southwest pricing technique, which has now become standard procedure for startups from ValuJet to Reno Air and all the others.

Ed and Eli did the financial planning and left the rest up to me and my team, although Ed considered himself the best scheduler in the airline industry and kept changing schedules. They kept adding B-737s and this type became the mainstay of the fleet. We opened up most of Central America, contracting out (before it was popularly known as outsourcing and standard operating procedure) everything we could, and then starting service to Jamaica, Haiti, the Dominican Republic, and the Virgin Islands. The B737 was ideal for these relatively short runs and we were able to break even almost from the first flight. Air Florida had terrific appeal in these markets, which had been dominated by a complacent Pan Am and our staff's enthusiasm was refreshing. The customers loved it. Also, our General Sales Agents were usually successful local businessmen and this did not hurt either.

As a result of my travels in Europe, I came to know Dick Marx at Transavia in Holland, a smallish charter airline which also operated B737-200s. Together we engineered what became a major aircraft exchange program which was particularly successful. We leased-in as many as five Transavia B-737s during the winter months when European charter activity fell off; but when the Florida winter season was at its peak; and we sent them back to Transavia, together with five Air Florida B-737s for the European peak summer. It worked like a charm because both carriers added significant capacity when they needed it most, Air Florida in the winter, Transavia in the summer. I also met many tour operators in European capitals with whom we established a relationship.

## The First Frequent Flyer Program

Other programs involved what I believe was the first frequent flyer program ever instituted when we introduced Green Stamps for flying Air Florida in the summer of 1980. It was tremendously successful—at least it attracted a great deal of media coverage. Our station manager in Florida's State capital, Tallahassee, told me that the Florida legislature, which flew frequently on Air Florida, were not allowed to accept green stamps, so he had to deliver them every week to the state administration. I am not sure what they did with them, but the number of stamps delivered would indicate that we were generating substantial traffic.

I also read somewhere, many years later, that Tom Plaskett, American's marketing head who was credited with creating AAdvantage, the first real frequent flyer program, had based his decision on Green Stamps. Perhaps we can take credit for having stimulated Plaskett, and what has undoubtedly become the single greatest marketing tool of the 1980s and 1990s.

We were also the first startup to participate in every major C.R.S. (Computer Reservations System). We made a deal with American's SABRE computer program, almost by accident. We called Tom Plaskett at American and suggested that we wanted to participate in SABRE. When we met at Dallas Fort Worth Airport in November of 1980, with Don Garvett and Art Stellmach, Plaskett had a flip chart showing a menu of products available.

I saw the word "Cohost" at the head of the list and said: "That's what we want." To everyone's surprise, Plaskett agreed, albeit over the objections of some his staff. This put us on a par with American in terms of travel agency display and was probably worth millions of dollars in revenues. To this day Garvett gives me credit for this inspired insight, yet at the time I did not know what the term meant, except that it was the top of the list. On the way back, Art and Don congratulated me and celebrated. They felt it was a major achievement. I reminded them of the sign in my office: "No amount of planning replaces dumb luck."

We worked on a potential Air Florida/AeroPeru interchange service which would have provided a through DC-10 flight from New York to Lima and beyond via Miami. It was a great idea but it never saw the light of day. I do not remember the reason, but probably some corporate bureaucracy at AeroPeru may have killed it, although Don Garvett remembers that he was against the idea for some reason.

About this time, PanAm was pulling out of a number of markets. In early December 1979 we found out that they were pulling out of San Jose, Costa Rica, and we applied for and were awarded the route within a week, something of a world's record. On 1 January, 1981, with very little advance planning or marketing, I flew down on the inaugural Air Florida flight from Miami. We organized this in 48 hours and were warmly received by the local government, the travel industry, and the community in general, all of whom were dependent on U.S. carrier service.

During the inaugural ceremonies in San Jose, I met one of the gentlemen of the airline industry, LACSA's long-time president, Otto Escalante. Later on we tried unsuccessfully to organize a joint venture which would have involved an interchange flight between New York, Miami, and San Jose. This could have been highly successful, but the LACSA pilots opposed it because Air Florida flight crews were to be used initially. Much later, Otto became Director of Civil Aviation in Costa Rica and signed one of the first Open-Skies bilateral with the United States.

Later in 1980 PanAm pulled out of one of its traditional routes between Miami, Port au Prince, Haiti, and Santo Domingo, in the Dominican Republic. Again we reacted quickly and were operating the route within a few days. We were greatly assisted by Jerry Theophile who was the Air France General Sales Agent in Haiti. We convinced him to guarantee our flight profitability by buying a certain number of seats on each flight in return for appointing him as our General Sales Agent in Port au Prince. We never used the guarantee because the flight was profitable from the start, but it helped to sell Ed Acker on doing it in the first place. This one turned out to be our most profitable flight and made money until Air Florida's demise in 1984.

I had brought Daniel Ratti in from Peru to head up budgeting and soon afterwards hired another AeroPeru alumni, Sandro Francini to handle foreign exchange hedging and repatriation. Sandro saved us hundreds of thousands of dollars, perhaps millions, in potential exchange losses in some of the Central American and Caribbean markets we served. At the time, there were no BSPs (Bank Settlement Plans) in most countries so we were not bypassing IATA which would have been a problem. After Air Florida's demise, Sandro joined with a partner and they developed a real expertise in handling otherwise "blocked" currencies which they sell to U.S. corporations, including, at one point, American Airlines. Sandro is now living in Kenya where he handles currency and investments throughout Africa.

Together with Don Garvett, we experimented, probably the first airline to do so, with discounted pricing and a very preliminary form of yield management, which had not yet been invented. I think Air Florida was the first airline to introduce non-refundable fares, which were the deepest discount of them all. Just like buying a ticket to a theater or sporting event, if you did not show up, you lost it. It eliminated the 'no show' factor, something every airline is still battling with, and is today called 'ticketless' travel.

## We Win 'The Battle for Britain'

By this time late in 1980, we had been awarded the Miami-London route, replacing National which had been acquired by PanAm, thus eliminating one of the two U.S. airlines designated to match the British ones. The Department of Transportation (DOT) wanted a second U.S. carrier on the route because British Airways and Laker were both flying to Miami from London. With the help of Tony Linney, our resident 'Brit', we had organized an amazing 'Battle for Britain' campaign throughout the State, generating hundreds of thousands (I think we came close to one million) of petitions to support Air Florida for designation. We actually beat out Eastern Air Lines, among others in the 'establishment', for the prized route designation. The party at the 94th Squadron restaurant was a major company-wide blast. We even had a Winston Churchill look-alike to act as master of ceremonies. "We shall fight on the beaches..." was the theme of the party where everyone got plastered, had a lot of fun, and helped to consolidate a real team spirit which lasts to this day among former Air Floridians.

*At the London inaugural: (left to right) Cesar Alvarez (Exec. VP); Cathy Alvarez; Lisa and Eli Timoner.*

For the London inaugural Mac Seligman (I had hired him to handle public relations, or 'corporate communications' as—in line with his contemporaries—he preferred his activity to be known) had rented every chauffeur-driven Rolls Royce in the state of Florida and we arranged a reception at the Sheraton River House, a few blocks from Miami International Airport. We then drove all our guests (200 plus) in a single column of Rolls Royces. A picture of something like 75 Rolls driving up to the airport made the front pages of a number of papers and we also made the 6 o'clock network news. We had advertised that our premium service, 'Upper Class', would have chauffeured limousines for free transfers between Gatwick and any London hotel, and vice versa. Virgin Atlantic later copied both 'Upper Class' and the limo idea, but we were long gone so could hardly complain.

For a number of months we had been operating scheduled charters on the route with considerable success. After the successful London-Miami Intasun charters we had opened up Brussels and Amsterdam which at first were a disaster. The tour operator we had selected had over-committed and within a couple of weeks the program was falling apart. Ed Acker sent me to Europe where I spent three or four weeks finding a replacement. Finally we

*Air Florida operated four Douglas DC-10-30s from Miami to London (taking over from National Airlines) until its demise in 1984. It offered "Upper Class" service, a term that was later adopted elsewhere.*

found the kind of operators we needed and the program took off. But it was a scary time. If we failed to fill the airplanes we would have been in deep trouble because we did not have the scheduled authority to fully utilize three wide-bodied aircraft.

We had appointed a Norwegian friend of Ed's, Johan Stenersen, to be our cargo agent in Europe and the U.S. He had a company called Air Contact and we effectively sold them the belly of the DC-10s on the Atlantic. The deal was pretty good for both sides. They guaranteed $5,000 each way across the Atlantic and we split the face value of the revenue (airway bills) 40/60 (their $5,000 came out of our 60% of the revenue, unless they did not generate that much on a cumulative basis). The formula was particularly good because unlike most of these deals, we had the upside on yield and Air Contact had an incentive to go for the highest yield cargo. My son, Robbie, later copied the formula when he created Cargo Services, Inc., which did the same with Carnival Airlines

We were also operating DC-10 charters (we had acquired three from Trans America) from Zurich and Stockholm to Miami. The additional programs fully utilized all three aircraft. 1980 revenues exceeded $300 million and with a fleet of some 35 aircraft, we were profitable. The fleet comprised four DC-10s and a whole bunch of 737-200s in addition to the original five B737-100s which Air Florida had obtained from Singapore Airlines earlier on. The stock was selling for $16 or $17 and the media had decided that we were the 'darling of deregulation.' Admittedly, charters probably contributed more to profitability than scheduled service. And because I had developed the charter side almost single-handed, I was feeling very good.

The following is an excerpt from a typical media story, of literally dozens, which ran in the May 1981 issue of the prestigious *Air Transport World* magazine:

"Air Florida is on the prowl..and no market is safe from its competition"

At Air Florida Booth is the Merlin of the charter operations. "Charters are a hell of a way to get identity in a marketplace," he says. While many observers, and even some inside Air Florida, considered the airline's DC10 charter foray into Europe as merely a stepping stone towards C.A.B. scheduled approval, Booth sees it differently. "Its first purpose was an opportunity to make money and expose the U.K. and Europe to Air Florida and the Florida vacation product. The proof to CAB was just a dividend." During that year of U.K. charters, the airline flew 100,000 passengers, and was booked through Intasun's network of 2,500 agents. "So now 2,500 agents and 100,000 passengers know Air Florida before we start the scheduled route. Charters are a hell of a way to open a scheduled route, but they also are complementary." Although the Swiss won't approve Air Florida's scheduled fares, a successful Zurich charter program now has Air Florida known from northern Italy to southern Germany, Booth said. He has high hopes for his end of the business, and those immediate hopes are for $100 million in charter revenue this year, one-third more than the optimistic forecasts of the airline. But Booth's responsibilities do not end at the charter market, for Air Florida's bulk fares are part of his plans...Booth goes into each new market with a bulk fare deal the local agents cannot refuse, thereby guaranteeing break-even loads during the initial service introduction period that is usually the most painful for airlines with an eye for the bottom line.

By early 1980 we were operating scheduled services all through Central America and much of the Caribbean. PanAm was pulling back all over the place and it gave us a an opportunity to replace their larger aircraft with fuel-efficient 737s. We established a major presence in Jamaica and worked closely with the government tourism agency to help develop a charter subsidiary for the government in conjunction with Air Jamaica. We always worked closely with our local competition because we believed that cooperation was the key to our future development. I became close to a number of people in Jamaica, including Tony Hart, then chairman of Air Jamaica, Butch Stewart of Sandals, the all-inclusive Jamaican resorts fame (and much later the individual that privatized Air Jamaica). I also worked the Dominican Republic and a number of other countries. In the Dominican Republic I met and made friends with Rafael Trujillo, the son of the dictator, who later started his own airline, APA International.

## Air Berlin

Late in 1980, Mort Beyer of Avmark, a Washington-based consultant who knew Ed Acker from Braniff, came to see us with the idea that Air Florida should acquire a West Berlin-based U.S. Part 121 airline called Air Berlin. The airline operated charters and had recently been awarded scheduled rights in the I.G.S. (Internal German Service). It operated four B-737s, and had also recently started a 707 charter operation into Orlando from Berlin and Brussels. The airline was owned by the Lundgren family which lived in Oregon.

*Air Berlin Crew.*

We spent quite a bit of time on this, traveling to Berlin, where I met John MacDonald, the president, and one of the founders of the airline. John had generated international publicity on the 707 charter program when he hired a bunch of topless waitresses and put them in Air Berlin flight attendant uniforms (without the tops) and had photographs taken which received wire service distribution around the world. The girls were from a local night spot and he paid them $100 each for the photo-op.

John had worked for Mort Beyer at George Batchelor's Capitol Airlines and was an interesting character, born in the Dominican Republic of a Scots father. He had started his career at Pan Am, like so many of us, and had lived in Venezuela and Miami. He and I hit it off from the start. He had a great, low key, sense of humor. Air Berlin was a neat operation. Its only competition was PanAm's I.G.S. which was not promoted energetically. But for some reason we never managed to conclude the purchase. The Lundgrens' son had been a Pan Am pilot based in Berlin, and I suspect he did not want to sell the airline. He is still running it today, although it is now controlled by a German group. I enjoyed Berlin which was at that time still a city divided by a common language and the Berlin Wall.

## Scandinavian Diversion

About that time we also met Jan Carlson who had just taken over as C.E.O. of the Scandinavian Airlines System (S.A.S.), the airline consortium of

Norway, Sweden, and Denmark. He was a fascinating character and we tried to work some kind of joint venture. Eli Timoner and I spent some time in Stockholm where Johan Stenersen, our cargo G.S.A., introduced us to Carlson. We did do something on the Stockholm-London route with them but this did not really develop into anything much. Carlson and S.A.S. later acquired a significant shareholding of Continental Airlines as well as of LAN Chile when it was privatized in the late 1980s, beating out PASUR, the employees of LAN who had retained my services to assist them.

## The Big Apple

In the spring of 1981, Pan Am's president, Bill Waltrip, on a visit to Miami, made a major announcement. He told the employees and the media that the airline was going to "go back to its roots" and concentrate on international service, with only those domestic flights that actually fed the international gateway flights. We were in a staff meeting that morning and heard the report first on a radio news flash. Ed Acker and Eli were ecstatic because it meant that Pan Am, which had spent $400 million to acquire National, the airline that had competed head-to-head with Eastern on the New York-Florida route (known in the industry as 'the gravy run'), was going to pull back to a couple of flights a day, exclusively serving to connect to its international services across the Atlantic and into Latin America.

Everyone went into a frenzy of planning. Our 737, which is slower than the 727s and L-1011 that Eastern had, was not the right aircraft to build the route. Ed, who always knew which aircraft were available where, picked up the telephone and called someone at Boeing. He knew that Braniff had canceled an order for five B727-200Adv aircraft which were sitting in Seattle waiting for a customer. They had -17 power (Braniff had ordered them for use in Latin America and needed the additional power of the -17 for high altitude airports at La Paz, Quito, and Bogota) which was 'overkill' for Air Florida but no one seemed to mind. We needed -17 power like a hole in the head but the 'planes were painted and delivered within 30 days and we began to build up the Florida-Northeast schedules. The aircraft were acquired through a financial lease with interest rates at their highest point in 20 years. The monthly ownership cost for each aircraft was around $200,000, which was awfully high. I recalled Harding Lawrence's rule of thumb. I did not see how they could generate their capital cost in annual revenues.

## Sir Freddie Bites the Dust

I was in London some time in 1980 when we heard that Sir Freddie Laker had been put out of business because of alleged financial difficulties. In fact, the demise of Laker was caused by an unwarranted bank foreclosure, made under pressure by a group of airlines whose Trans-Atlantic traffic was being eroded by the Laker no-reservation Skytrain service, possibly the most innovative airline service in air transport history. In spite of some reports at the time, Sir Freddie was never bankrupt and always paid his bills. As one writer has described the affair, the demise of Laker Airways was "A Case of Corporate Murder."

I had met Freddie Laker, before he was Sir Freddie, in 1978 when I was with AeroPeru. We met at the Statler Hilton in Los Angeles to discuss a possible joint venture with AeroPeru to Latin America. The meeting had been arranged by a mutual friend and we talked for several hours. Nothing ever came of the meeting, partly because I left AeroPeru shortly afterwards, and partly because the timing was not right. But I was taken by his personality and charm. I had met him again more recently when we started Air Florida charters into the U.K. and he was very friendly.

As soon as I heard that he was grounded, I called Miami and got hold of David Tait, a Scot who handled Laker in the United States, and I offered him a job with Air Florida. I had met David with Sir Freddie and he was another real asset. David accepted the job offer and went to work for Air Florida even before I returned to Miami. In the meantime I called Sir Freddie and he invited me to dinner at his home, south of Gatwick airport, in Sussex. I had brought him an annual pass on Air Florida which was timely now that he no longer had an airline. He and I had a few drinks and he told me some war stories (mainly about the Berlin Air Lift which helped him to start in the first place). Before leaving I gave him the annual pass, quite casually. He was very touched and thanked me. The annual pass was good for positive space and first class travel. He had a girl friend in Miami and an apartment on Key Biscayne, and I know that he made good use of it in the months ahead. I met him again later when I was at Northeastern where I introduced him to Steve Quinto and he became a board member for a short time. By this time he had won a multi-million dollar out-of-court settlement against British Airways and McDonnell Douglas which, according to Sir Freddie, had been major players in the attempt to put him out of business. So he was not hurting, financially.

# "Iaccoca Goes to Chrysler"

Late in 1981 I went in to see Ed and Eli one morning with, I thought, a terrific idea. Braniff was going through all kinds of trouble. Harding had been sacked by the Board which had appointed John Casey to replace him. Shortly after this the Board had brought in Howard Putnam, a former Southwest and United Airlines marketing man, to replace Casey. I had met Putnam at a travel agency affair in West Palm Beach, where we were both on a panel and I was not terribly impressed. Some of my old Braniff pals had told me that Putnam announced at an early staff meeting that he did not have a U.S. passport and was going to rebuild Braniff into a low cost, domestic airline. He was not remotely interested in the Latin American operation. My idea was that we offer to buy the division, lock, stock, and barrel: planes, pilots, installations and several decades of goodwill, some of which I had been a part of.

At the time, Braniff was generating $300 million a year in Latin America and was profitable. Even though the system of expense allocation used by Braniff (supposedly to avoid paying taxes in the region) showed a loss from the operation on the books, I knew this was sheer nonsense. The yields were high and Braniff had a 50% or better share in every market it served. The DC8-62s which it had acquired along with Panagra were the perfect long-range aircraft at the time. I figured that the operation was worth $100 million to us, based on my figures: that it was making at least 10% on sales, or something like $30 million per year. I argued that by tying our existing Northeast service along with our Central American and Caribbean presence we could add significantly to the profitability. Ed and Eli were intrigued, and they asked Don Garvett and me to put together a position paper, which we did. The plan was to keep the Braniff system intact, and even talked about keeping the name, if possible. I think we came up with $100 million price tag which I know would have been accepted instantly by Putnam, who later sold the division for $30 million to Eastern. Ed's cousin, Bobby Stewart, was president of First in Dallas, Braniff's lead bank, and he was on the Board of the airline. Ed promised to follow up, but nothing happened.

However, Eli decided that he wanted to meet with some government official in Peru to sound out their position, in the event that we were either successful with the Braniff ploy, or to position Air Florida to go after the route independently. I told him that I could arrange a meeting with President Belaunde (who had recently been re-elected president of Peru after the military stepped down). Eli was duly impressed (I did not tell him about my 'who goes around, comes around' and the Argentine interlude) and I went ahead and made arrangements for a visit to Lima.

## It Comes Around

We arrived in the morning and met with president Belaunde, Carlos Velarde (the former Panagra man), who was head of AeroPeru at the time, and Manuel Ulloa, who was prime minister in Belaunde's cabinet. Both the head of AeroPeru and Manuel Ulloa were close friends of mine—our time in Lima—and could not have been nicer. The meeting was very successful and they assured Eli that Air Florida would have a very warm reception in Peru. After the meeting I took Eli to lunch at the Tambo de Oro where we ran into Polo Pflucker and Yoyo Ferrand. We had a somewhat liquid lunch and then collapsed in the hotel for the afternoon. We came back the same night and Eli thought I could walk on water in Peru. Not that it helped our case, as it turned out. But it was nice to prove my theory about helping people when they are out of office.

By the late summer of 1981 Air Florida had something like 16 or 17 daily flights in the Northeast-Florida market,

*The key players in Air Florida when it was in top gear: (left to right) (rear): Eli Timoner, Ed Acker, (front) with inseperable pipe and drink, Bob Booth.*

serving JFK as well as La Guardia and White Plains in New York and Washington National. We also served Toledo, Ohio, and Orlando and West Palm Beach in Florida. By the Fall we were offering almost as much capacity as Eastern Air Lines, which had practically 'owned' the route after National was acquired by Pan Am.

## The Bermuda Triangle

Our Norwegian G.S.A., Johan Stenersen then introduced us to the Prime Minister of Bermuda, who was married to a Norwegian. Bermuda wanted to establish its own flag carrier and the idea was that Air Florida would provide the aircraft (DC-10-30) to operate on behalf of Bermuda on a U.K.-Bermuda-Florida route. Nothing came of this one, except that we did operate a White Plains-Bermuda-Florida route for a while. Ed Acker had bought a home in Bermuda and this probably influenced the decision. The route was quite successful, particularly on the northeast-Bermuda segment. Florida was not bad because the only alternate route was via Atlanta, but it was very seasonal. As a result I managed to spend quite some time in Bermuda and got to know a number of people in the tourism sector.

Another, similar deal, involved someone who had an oil refinery in Antigua in the Caribbean. Through one of Ed Acker's contacts we were invited to meet the Prime Minister of Antigua, Lester Bird. Don Garvett and I went to a couple of meetings, one in Zurich, Switzerland, of all places and another in Antigua. I remember the Antigua meeting because it was on a 75-foot power yacht. Everyone drank a lot and we did put a proposal together, but this one also never saw the light of day. I think the oil magnate lost interest when we told him how much it would take, in money.

## The Captain of the Titanic

Some time in the fall of 1981 I was in London with Eli and Tino Gonzalez for a European G.S.A. meeting. Roger Felber, who ran the U.K. for Air Florida, after having started out as our G.S.A., had brought in the managers from Zurich, Amsterdam, and Brussels. I think we were also talking to a major tour operator in Paris about this time regarding a Paris-originating charter program and he was going to be in London to meet with us. We were sitting in Roger's conference room, just the four of us, Eli, Tino, Roger, and I, when Roger's secretary came in to announce that Ed Acker wanted to talk to Eli, from Miami.

We watched Eli as he listened to Ed. We saw him go pale. He did not say much except to wish Ed luck. After he hung up he told us Ed was leaving to take the job of CEO at Pan Am, replacing Bill Waltrip. We were astounded.

Ed was a major stockholder in Air Florida and his leaving would certainly hurt, particularly by going to Pan Am. Eli said: "You guys know what he's going to do there, he's going to turn Waltrip's strategy around and re-enter the Northeast-Florida market, probably with 747s, we had all better get back as soon as possible. He's only going to be around for the next week."

To state that we were shocked would be an understatement. Ed had really been the driving force at Air Florida and his departure would create a major void. On the flight back Eli and I talked about the future. He told me he was going to look for a Chief Operating Officer, or even a CEO, someone with plenty of airline experience, as well as credibility in the financial community, to fill the void. As I have stated before, Eli was one of the few senior airline executives without an ego. His only concern was the survivability of Air Florida. He was very honest: "Bobby, I don't think I can promote any one of the four of you (he meant Dick Scully, John Fasolino, Tino or myself) because I can't see any three of you working for any one of you. What do you think?"

I had to agree. I felt I was qualified for the job, but I knew that John Fasolino and Dick Skully particularly would balk at reporting to me. At the same time, Tino was a good financial man but he really did not have the operating experience. I could not see the other two in the slot of chief operating officer. I also told Eli that I was certain Ed was going to make a play for Braniff's Latin American routes. It made sense that he would try to acquire Pan Am's major competitor in the region. I suggested that he should call John Casey who was either out of a job at Braniff or was probably very unhappy about being replaced by Putnam. Eli agreed. Nothing came of this, although I know they talked. Later I heard that Ed had called John and offered him the COO job at PanAm.

Back in Miami the Board of Directors proposed hiring a head hunter to find Ed Acker's replacement. Eli actually suggested this because he was smart enough to know that our stock price was important and the perception of Acker's departure had already had a negative impact. Bringing in a strong operating executive from a large airline, whether as C.E.O. or C.O.O. would be a positive move.

That winter, (1981-82) was one of the worst periods in my business career (there was worse to come). My brother, Ronald had died in Brazil at 60. His wife, Patsie had died several years before so we brought his children, Michael and Jenny to stay with us for a while. They were about the same age as ours, and it was nice having them but both wanted to return to Brazil after a few months.

Some time shortly before the season, Pan Am did what we had predicted. Ed Acker filed a schedule with a bunch of New York-Florida B-747 flights and came out with a $69 unrestricted "all seats-all flights" promotion which obviously killed our advance bookings for the normally high season. We had to match this bargain-basement fare to stay alive. Pan Am could not make any money, in fact we figured they would lose more than we would on a seat-mile basis. But they filled up their airplanes and we saw a softening in our load factors even though the resulting fare war stimulated the market and created a new stratum of traffic (Eastern had to match as well, albeit with capacity-controlled fares). But Ed's strategy at Pan Am had a dramatic impact. Shortly after joining Pan Am he had sold his significant Air Florida holdings which did not help our cause. I know now that Pan Am's legal counsel advised him that he must sell the stock. But the perception was that he had abandoned a 'sinking ship.' His remark, which was quoted in The Wall Street Journal at the time: "I always wanted to be the Captain of the Titanic" was typical of Ed's sense of humor, but it also was not appreciated by many. While many at Air Florida blame Ed for our demise, and there is no question that his Pan Am strategy did not help us, he did it because he felt it was the only thing to do. In retrospect, Bill Waltrip's decision to pull out of the northeast-Florida corridor had more to do with our demise in reality. If he had not done that Air Florida would not have acquired the expensive B727-200 Advanced aircraft which were a major reason for our problems.

## Wolf in Sheep's Clothing

Shortly afterwards I started to receive reports from the field that PanAm's sales people were telling travel agents to 'plate away' from Air Florida and to use a PanAm plate even if they were booking on us. U.S. travel agents have a standard ticket form but use the airline's plate (somewhat like running a credit card) which determines which airline receives the proceeds from the sale. The rules are that agents must use the airline plate which is providing the transportation. But in fact, they can use any airline plate and the ticket will be honored, the difference is which airline receives the revenue directly from the travel agent, through the Airline Reporting Corporation (A.R.C.). The argument they gave the agents was that Air Florida was doomed to fail and that this way the agents and their customers would be protected because PanAm 'paper' was good and they could always obtain a refund or use the ticket on PanAm. The process was doubly bad. Instead of being paid on a weekly basis through the A.R.C., we would be paid through the Airline Clearing House (the A.C.H.) once a month, plus an additional 15 days. The impact on cash flow could be devastating.

I decided not to call Ed Acker about it but went to my then counterpart, Steve Wolf, who was Senior VP-Marketing, at PanAm. I sent a pretty strong message which stated: "I don't believe this is corporate policy but it sure as hell smells of 'dirty tricks' of the worst kind. I would appreciate your investigating and putting an end to the practice." I also gave him names of specific travel agents who had reported the practice to us. I had a response within 24 hours, stating that this was not PanAm corporate policy and that instructions had been sent out to the field to 'cease and desist' if they were doing it. I always appreciated Steve's quick response, whether he was cognizant of the practice or not. For the record, I believe it was merely over-zealous sales people using any argument they could think of to sell Pan Am at our expense. He later went on to become C.E.O. of United, then went to Air France and most recently, USAir, where he has changed the airline's livery and name to USAirways.

## Bob Crandall Nice

Late in 1981 we called a meeting with Federico Bloch, executive vice president of TACA and a couple of other Central American airlines, TAN of Honduras, and LACSA of Costa Rica, to discuss travel agency override commissions which were way out of line. I had met Federico on one of my early trips to El Salvador and had immediately liked him. He was probably 30-something at the time, the son of a middle class Salvadorian doctor. He had gone to Stanford University in California where he obtained an engineering degree, and then an MBA from Harvard. He had previously been at school in El Salvador with Roberto Kriete, the son of the principal Salvadorian shareholder of TACA. The two of them had privatized the airline in the late 1970s, from its former status as a U.S.-based publicly-owned company. The two of them had bought 90% or better of all the outstanding shares and brought the ownership back to El Salvador, with the Kriete family owning control. Federico represented everything I liked about young Latin Americans. He was bright, well educated, and totally committed to his job. Many years later when someone asked me to describe Bloch. I said: "Bob Crandall Nice."

Which was not totally fair, but he did have the 'killer' instinct which is required in this highly competitive business. The use of the Bob Crandall analogy was intended as a compliment in that Crandall is universally acclaimed as one of the sharpest airline executives in the business. Federico could easily be the C.E.O. of a major U.S. airline or corporation. He has the ability and is also (which no one has accused Bob Crandall of being), a people-person who understands the importance of the human side of the equation. But he also understands what it takes to make a profit, which he demonstrated many years later when he engineered the acquisition and control of four airlines in Central America, to repeat history be re-creating a Central American consortium of airlines that derived strength by national association rather than self-destructive competition.

## No airline quite like TACA

Founded in 1932 by Lowell Yerex, a New Zealander who had flown in the Great War of 1914–18, TACA had an amazing history. Yerex started airlines throughout Central America and even in South America, with TACA de Venezuela and TACA de Colombia as well as Aerovias do Brasil, in which Yerex had a minority stake. He also founded British West Indian Airways in Trinidad & Tobago.

Lowell Yerex was born in New Zealand, educated in the United States, at a university in Indiana, and received his flying instruction when he joined the RFC (Canada) in 1917. In May 1918 he was shot down behind the German lines and became a prisoner of war. After the war he returned to the United States, where he worked in a San Francisco shipyard to save enough money to buy a surplus military aircraft. Late in 1932 Yerex was requested by the Honduran government to make some reconnaissance flights over mountains where guerrilla strongholds still supported the former president. Flying low to drop pamphlets, he was shot in the eye by a stray bullet, but he flew back to base where doctors found that, in addition to losing an eye, he had also fractured his skull. In the eyes of officialdom in Honduras, Lowell Yerex was a hero and could do no wrong, and he made most of his privileged position by obtaining an exclusive mail contract, and founding TACA.

Thus founded by the purest chance,TACA was launched on its way by a remarkable example of entrepreneurial opportunism, expanded to become an international consortium throughout Latin America, attracted the covetous attentions of large corporations in the United States, and came very close to becoming a giant airline in its own right. It eventually collapsed to a mere shadow of its former stature. It finally revived, phoenix-like, in the early 1980s, to take its place in the airline world of Central America. From one aircraft and one route in Honduras, Lowell Yerex had developed TACA to a fleet of more than fifty, and a route network which served 235 points on a scheduled basis alone, and many more on contract work and charters to sixteen countries, reaching from Miami to Rio de Janeiro.

My brother, Ronald, had flown for Aerovias do Brazil, the TACA affiliate, for a short time after the war. I met Yerex during my stint as a travel agent in Punta del Este where he had a home after selling TACA in the mid-to late-1940s. He was a big man, very friendly, bluff, and somewhat boisterous as I recall. We had talked briefly about the airline business, and he had known Tom Braniff and many of the early pioneers

## Grand Jury Anti-Trust Investigation

Getting back to the travel agent override commission meeting: it was probably a border-line anti-trust situation but Bob Silverberg, Air Florida's legal counsel, thought it was all right because it really did not have to do with pricing, which was definitely illegal. TAN's General Manager, Arturo Aceituno, brought along his assistant manager whom he subsequently fired; who, as a result, decided to go to the Justice Department in Washington and reported that the three of us, Aceituno, Federico Bloch and I, had met to set fares.

All three of us were targets of a Grand Jury investigation into illegal airline pricing practices, a situation which placed us in pretty good company, because a year or so later Bob Crandall was caught in a taped telephone conversation with Braniff's Howard Putnam proposing a fare increase. The experience was not amusing and fortunately we had O&D (Officers and

Directors). It cost Air Florida about $25,000 to prove that we had not indulged in price fixing. In the process I found out, once again, who were my real friends. Even though I had left Air Florida by the time of the Grand Jury investigation, Eli and several board members stood by me and insisted that the company provide legal counsel. Emilio Dirube was given immunity to testify (he had been at the meeting, but was not a target), and swore (truthfully, I might add) that the whole thing was a personal vendetta by the man from TAN.

## Tragedy on The Potomac

Then, on 13 January 1982, Air Florida Flight 90, a 737 plowed into the Potomac River after taking off from Washington National in a snow storm. The accident was on prime time news for weeks. Apart from the tragedy and the loss of life, it had a terrible impact on our forward bookings. Many have blamed the accident as the main cause of the airline's demise. I do not agree, but there is no question that it had an impact. By this time Pan Am had gone back to higher fares and our yields were back to normal. After a few weeks we seemed to have regained our market share and things were beginning to look better. While the accident had a profound and far-reaching impact—they always do with new entrant, or upstart airlines—the effect on Air Florida's finances did not last beyond a few weeks in spite of the massive prime-time and front-page media coverage.

A word about the impact of airplane accidents on the demise of airlines is perhaps in order. Many have made the analogy of the Pan Am Lockerbie accident on Pan Am's demise and the more recent TWA's Flight 800 disaster which could spell the end of another great airline. Not to mention ValuJet which has since changed its name in an effort to live down the terrible publicity surrounding its highly publicized (equal to or greater than the Air Florida accident in Washington 15 years earlier) crash into the Florida Everglades. I discuss Air Florida's demise later in this chapter. While Pan Am was an 'endangered species' at the time of Lockerbie, my own theory is that Pan Am's demise can be traced back to the unnecessary and poorly executed acquisition of National for $400 million, the sell-off of assets, such as the Pacific route, the Intercontinental Hotel Chain and eventually the European routes to Delta. An interesting aside: while Delta bought Europe, it allowed Pan Am's Latin American routes to collapse and be picked up by United for a song. Only now is Delta moving into Latin America after ignoring the region for decades. TWA looks healthier today and while not 'out of the woods,' is making significant progress as I write this.

## *Putnam and Braniff's LAD*

In the spring of 1982, Acker and Putnam reached an agreement on Braniff's Latin American routes. They announced the deal as a route-lease but in essence it meant that Pan Am was going to acquire its primary competitor in Latin America. I was particularly annoyed, having (with Don Garvett) written the original paper for Ed about the whole idea while he was still at Air Florida. We raised all kinds of hell, and Bob Silverberg, our Washington attorney, filed immediate objections pointing out the anti-competitive aspects of the proposed deal and stating that if the routes were going to be sold there should be a route case because Air Florida wanted to go after the same authority, and we were prepared to match Pan Am's $30 million offer to Braniff. Eight years later American paid Eastern close to $400 million for the same deal.

Eastern Air Lines then jumped on the bandwagon and filed objections of its own. Eastern's Frank Borman later took credit for the opposition, but in truth we were there first. The DOT disapproved the transaction and advised Braniff that it should find another party that would maintain competition. We were on the telephone to Braniff instantly and Putnam agreed to have his people meet with us. Eli gave me the assignment to go to Dallas with Don Garvett and Bob Silverberg.

We arrived in Dallas to discover that Pan Am was in town. We met in one room while Bill Waltrip and others from Pan Am were closeted next door. Braniff did not think we had the cash to do a deal but they had to listen. Putnam did not attend but Sam Coates, the lawyer, and some others, attended the meeting. They gave us their list of assets in the region, and the aircraft that we might take with the routes. Our idea was that we should take everything, including pilots and ground personnel, and particularly the flight attendants. Our proposal was much more attractive to middle management because we would be hiring most of the Braniff staff in Miami whom PanAm had already said they did not need. PanAm had a major station there and could add the Braniff operation without having to hire any of its personnel. Nothing definitive was decided. But Braniff left the door open for further meetings to be held in Washington later in the week.

At the Dallas airport I ran into Waltrip who was also coming to Miami on the same flight. We had met briefly before and so I suggested we sit together and talk about 'the deal.' I outlined to Bill that we did not have to have the whole package and would be quite happy with a piece of Latin America. Waltrip was interested and we played around on a yellow legal pad as to how we might split up the Braniff assets. We both agreed that this would solve the anti-competitive issue for the D.O.T. I told him we wanted Panama, Colombia, Ecuador, and Peru. He could have the rest, Brazil, Argentina, Bolivia, Paraguay, Chile, and

Mexico-Dallas. This made a lot of sense because Pan Am already had the east coast of South America. It added something to what Pan Am already had, eliminated excess capacity, and strengthened their presence in those markets. I liked the northern tier because I felt it made more sense to us and the 727-200s were perfect for that operation. We could use the DC-10s to some extent, but the Boeing trijets would give us frequency rather than capacity. We agreed that we would put our lawyer, Silverberg, and Pan Am's Dick Mathias together in Washington to work on the specifics.

Eli called Ed Acker and they worked out a tentative agreement, at least that was how we understood the conversation. We would have the northern tier countries and would sell three B-737s which we owned to Pan Am, and which Ed wanted to use in the Internal German Service. At the same time, Ed had gone to the White House and had obtained a letter supporting the original PanAm/Braniff deal, although we were not aware of this at the time. We were supposed to finalize the Air Florida/Pan Am agreement later the same week. We were in Washington on Friday and Bob Silverberg had hammered out the Air Florida/PanAm/Braniff agreement which they took to the D.O.T. Over the weekend Braniff's Howard Putnam met with Frank Borman of Eastern in New York and negotiated for Eastern to take over the routes for $30 million. On Monday the D.O.T. approved the Eastern/Braniff take-over. Acker was furious when he heard that they had been working over the weekend. We were not exactly delighted at the outcome either. The Braniff pilots tried to intervene because they were left out in the cold—Eastern's flight crews would take over the flying in Latin America, so that the Braniff pilots were out of a job. My friend Captain Phil Bradley, who was the head of Braniff's pilot group in Miami, took Braniff to court but it was too late and nothing could be done. The D.O.T. decision prevailed and a few weeks later, the negative cash flow from South America put Braniff out of business.

Putnam had given up Latin America, the only profitable part of Braniff for $30 million (which, incidentally, he never received in full because the airline failed before he collected) and Eastern sold the network to American eight years later for $400 million. The interesting point that says something about the quality of Braniff's local management (I do not pretend to take credit for this, but it makes me feel good) is that both Eastern, and later American, kept all or most of the Braniff management team in place, in fact, promoting some of them. Perhaps the saddest aspect of all this is that Braniff, Eastern and the original Pan Am, are all gone. I often wonder if the Air Florida/Braniff acquisition, as originally envisioned in late 1981, had occurred, a lean Air Florida might have succeeded where the others failed. Wishful thinking, perhaps.

## The Beginning of the End

Early in 1982 Donald Lloyd Jones, a former senior executive at American Airlines, who had been passed over for the C.E.O. job when it went to Bob Crandall, joined Air Florida as Chief Operating Officer (C.O.O.). Don was a strong operating and financial executive with 20 or more years at American. He had strong credentials and we welcomed him onboard.

That summer we were doing one of my Saturday morning sessions with the Reservations gang, and anyone else who might be interested in joining us. It had been a tradition which Art Stellmach and I had started. Every Saturday we took over Herbets, the local eatery on the ground floor at the Air Florida headquarters and held open house between 10 and noon. We had coffee and sat around and listened to what the agents or others had on their mind. It was a sort of 'hair down' gripe session. The sessions were great for morale and people were invited to tell us what was wrong and in many cases came up with some good ideas for improving systems and procedures. We also used the sessions to brief people on how things were going with the airline and to recognize outstanding performance by handing out commendations.

On this occasion, unusually, Eli had shown up. He talked for a while and answered questions. After coffee he left and went to his Miami Beach masseur—something he did every Saturday. Later that day we heard that he was in intensive care, after a major stroke. Donald Lloyd Jones took over as C.E.O. Eli recovered gradually but he never came back to take an active part in the airline, although he was still on the board and was a significant shareholder.

## If it Ain't Fun—Quit, Part 4

Eli's stroke was a set-back to morale and some of the old-timers in the airline were concerned that both the original leaders, Eli and Ed, were gone and people did not yet know Donald Lloyd Jones. Earnings that summer were terrible. The 727-200 ownership cost was killing us, and we really had no logical market to deploy them because they were too big for Central America and the Caribbean, so we kept them in the northeastern corridor, which was the reason we acquired them in the first place. Since there was no market for the aircraft it was preferable to use them than to sit them on the ground, one alternative that I think we analyzed at the time. But PanAm's re-entry into this market, while having a stimulative impact on the total market as a result of the deep discount fares, was definitely hurting us in what had become a major segment of the total operation.

Lloyd-Jones began a 'downsizing' program (at least we did not use the term 'rightsizing' the other popular euphemism), reducing the headcount, and canceling routes, which also meant lower utilization for the 727s which we owned. We pulled out of some domestic and international markets. This did not work. Airlines have always had a hard time trying to reduce themselves into a profit. You cut schedules and the revenue dries up instantly, but costs have a way of lingering on, even after you have stopped flying. The morale was terrible. Some of the smart young people, like Don Garvett and Dan Brock, among others, left for other airline jobs. Don to PanAm and Dan to Piedmont. Everyone was waiting for the other shoe to drop. The financial community had lost their confidence and the stock was down to $2 from its 1981 high of $16–17 per share.

In December 1982 I went to Don and suggested that the downsizing was not working because it was all 'bottom-up.' We should cut some of the higher-salaried senior jobs. I wanted to leave anyway and if he would complete my stock deal (Ed had never issued me the 100,000 shares which was part of my verbal employment contract) I would leave on 31 December. Cesar Alvarez, who had been involved with Air Florida, first as outside counsel with Greenberg & Traurig, and for a while as Executive Vice President, confirmed my stock agreement and Don Lloyd Jones jumped at the idea. My job could be consolidated with John Fasolino's, who ran airport services. Lloyd Jones even gave me a going-away party where he made nice noises about my contributions to the airline. Air Florida actually survived for another 18 months, until 4 July, 1984. Airlines take a long time to die.

My time at Air Florida had taught me many lessons. It had given me a real education in the airline business in a deregulated environment, something that none of us had any experience with before 1978. I had personally taken to deregulation like a fish to water. I suppose it was my entrepreneurial bent because I had always felt that the airline business was too restricted in terms of freedom to do those things which made sense, especially using pricing as a real marketing tool, along with brand loyalty (frequent flyer) and other programs. The whole approach to the business had changed dramatically. The airline 'industry' had truly (at least in the United States) become the airline 'business.' And I, for one, loved it. Including the freedom to fail. Which until 1978 was unavailable.

When it went under in 1984, Air Florida had gone from three DC-9s in 1977 to a fleet of 45 aircraft, including four DC-10-30s and $350 million in revenues, with routes in the Caribbean, Central America, and to Europe. I had brought in some young fellows who worked very well together, in spite of different backgrounds, education, and cultures. Most of them have gone on to better things since, and that gives me a good feeling. These included David Tait (now Senior Vice President-The Americas for Virgin Atlantic), Dan Brock (USAir), Don

Garvett (Simat, Helliesen & Eichner), Emilio Dirube (running his own charter airline), Daniel Ratti (who went on to be C.E.O. of Carnival Airlines), Tom Redding, C.E.O. at Reno Airlines, among others. One of these recently paid me the greatest compliment when he told me that I had truly given everyone a chance to make mistakes. I suspect that is because I have made so many myself.

## *Lee Iaccoca Went to Chrysler*

Some time later, after Air Florida failed, I was asked by a reporter who was writing a piece on deregulation what happened at Air Florida. I gave him my short answer: "Lee Iaccoca went to Chrysler." Ed Acker had gone to PanAm about the same time that Iaccoca went to Chrysler. Had Acker gone to Chrysler and Iaccoca to PanAm (not that either was ever mentioned as a candidate for the other), Air Florida might still be around. PanAm's strategy to return to the Northeast-Florida market sealed Air Florida's fate; while the controllers' strike, the crash of Flight 90 in Washington, D.C., Eli Timoner's stroke, and several other factors played their part, not to mention a series of decisions (internal) and factors (external) over which we had little control. Certainly the B727-200 acquisition decision was a contributing factor. American having invented Yield Management another; which allowed the big guys to offer discount fares on a portion of their capacity which took away the discount carriers' pricing edge while maintaining yields at levels required to remain profitable, filling up other-wise empty seats. And frequent flyer programs. Books have been written about Braniff's, Eastern's and PanAm's downfall. And one should probably be written about Air Florida's. But not this one...

# Northeastern

When I left Air Florida we re-organized Airline Management & Marketing (A.M.& M.) with David Tait and my younger son, Guy. I had originally organized A.M.& M. in Peru when I took the AeroPeru job, and then again when I went to Air Florida. The company had been dormant since I joined Air Florida as an executive. We took offices in the Air Florida building, in the shopping mall, printed up some stationary and business cards. We had few prospects, but I figured that anything was better than waiting around for Air Florida to go out of business. And I had 100,000 shares of Air Florida stock which I sold as quickly as possible. The proceeds served as working capital.

## Randolph Fields

Shortly after that, Randolph Fields, an American lawyer who lived in the U.K. called me. I had met him during one of my Air Florida trips to London. "Bobby, I need someone to help me develop the business plan for a British airline, can you meet me in Miami next week?"

We agreed to meet at The Mutiny in Coconut Grove. Randolph had gone to a public school in England and then to Oxford, where he had graduated as a barrister. He had a very profitable legal practice, had specialized in liability litigation, and had made a bundle in the process. We met in the bar and he told me about his plan. He wanted to start an airline, British Atlantic Airways, which would fly from England to the Falkland Islands. Because I knew something about that part of the world (even though I had never been to the Falklands), he thought I was the right one to work on the plan. Apparently some former British Caledonian people were working on it for him but he wanted an outside opinion. He also told me that the Falklands might not work so he wanted to look at other options, possibly an all-first-class London-New York service.

We did not have any clients at the time so we jumped at it. Randolph was taking some vacation in the U.S. and would not be back in England for three weeks so I would travel across in 30 days' time. He left me a copy of the preliminary business plan which he and the former British Caledonian managers had put together. I was to review, analyze, and make some recommendations. He agreed to a modest retainer and expenses. I did not tell him that I had nothing else on our plate anyway.

By the time we met in London, the Falkland Islands had been ruled out. The government did not want a civilian operation because the RAF had recently instituted L-1011 service by way of Ascension Island and was operating Combi aircraft which carried the much-needed cargo for the 'kelpers' who did not grow anything except sheep and vegetables. Randolph then wanted the business plan based on an all-first class London-New York schedule. Since Laker had failed there was an opening for a second U.K. carrier on the route. I tried to convince Randolph that no one had yet succeeded with an all first-class approach, and that there were several examples of failures in the U.S. On the other hand, if we could produce an available seat-mile at the right cost, and we offered first-class at the full economy fares, it might work. So he gave me the assignment to work on the plan. Something on the order of 150–200 seats was a small enough percentage of the total seats in the market, that the business person, who could not afford first class, and the restrictions attached to the deep discount fares, might jump on the aircraft. In other words, the 10–15% of the market which paid full economy, might be sufficient to provide profitable load factors across the Atlantic.

After a couple of weeks we came up with a plan using a DC10-30 with 150 seats, two+two+two, which was extremely comfortable with a 40-inch pitch or thereabouts. The plan worked on paper at least. I left him with the plan and returned to Miami. He was going to go forward with his BCal people, Roy Gardner, a technical chap, and a couple of others. I had to come back later on to act as an 'expert' in the British C.A.A. certification process. The C.A.A. kept delaying him, questioning our traffic forecast. I had Don Garvett do some moon-lighting for me on Q.S.I. (Quality Service Index) which the British did not understand. I was not too clear on it myself even though it is a standard methodology in the United States, assigning traffic by market (city-pair) based on existing and projected capacity. I had to call Garvett several times during breaks in the hearing to make sure I could explain it. I spent a couple of weeks in the hearings which seemed to satisfy the C.A.A.—at least on the traffic.

## Richard Branson

Finally it became an issue of insufficient capital and Randolph either did not have it or could not raise it. This is when he arranged for a meeting with Richard Branson, of Virgin Records, who liked the plan and agreed to fund it as long as the name could be changed to Virgin Airways. Randolph had gone to school with Richard but they were not close friends. I met him on the inaugural flight, with David Tait in New York. He is unique, totally unlike any other major airline player I had ever met, except possibly Herb Kelleher of Southwest. He is informal and casual and very English in many ways: somewhat unassuming and yet very much a celebrity even then. We met briefly in New York but did not spend much time together; I immediately liked him and felt he was going to be very good for the industry. He had a very fresh and non-traditional approach. Like his own airline hero, Sir Freddie Laker, he was a master of publicity and managed to generate worldwide media coverage with his balloon trips and other escapades. Later on he took Freddie's advice to heart when British Airways started a campaign of 'dirty tricks.' "Sue the bastards" said Sir Freddie, who had himself been the victim of a dirty tricks campaign. He did so—successfully.

By this point I was not being paid and I helped David Tait to be hired by Richard Branson to run New York. Richard and Randolph did not get along and Richard finally bought him out for something like a million pounds. I think I was 'tarred' as one of Randolph's people or I might have had some ongoing consulting. Richard Branson has since built Virgin Atlantic to become one of the most successful airlines in the world.

## Another Child of Deregulation

I met Steve Quinto during the Air Florida years, probably 1980 or 1981, in some kind of airline panel. I was filling in for Ed Acker and there were two or three startup airline C.E.O.s there, plus a couple of travel agents. It had been organized by a TV station in Miami, and we were being interviewed on the pros and cons of deregulation. Steve had recently started Northeastern International, a Fort Lauderdale-based startup which was operating two or three B-727s between Fort Lauderdale and MacArthur Field at Islip, New York. He was an extremely attractive, rather Mephistophelean-looking character who chain-smoked Cuban cigars. I suspect that we both made an impression on each other. A short time after leaving Air Florida, and while I was playing around with British/Virgin Atlantic, he invited me to Fort Lauderdale for lunch.

He had been very successful with the Islip business because he had really discovered a niche, the Islip-Fort Lauderdale market—one of the potential sources of traffic that the majors had overlooked. I went up to Broward for lunch with him and his South African-born Anglo wife who was his deputy in just about everything. Both of them were charming. He had once been an actor and was a consummate host. Steve was an odd-ball character, had been a pilot and had flown cargo aircraft in the Caribbean. He wanted me

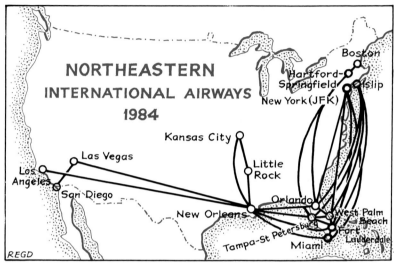

*Northeastern was one of the many post-deregulation airline start-ups that seemed to hold great promise, but could not stand the pace.*

to join them as Executive Vice President and Chief Operating Officer. I was flattered, he told me that I would report directly to him and all the operating heads, including finance, operations and marketing, would report to me.

Northeastern was operating four Boeing 727s and was looking for expansion. Steve thought I could help. The money was less than I had made at Air Florida but he held out all kinds of promises, stock option deals and so on. I took the job and made arrangements to sell the house in Miami and move to Fort Lauderdale. We actually bought a house even though we had not yet sold the one in Miami, but we never moved in. The house was on a canal and had a dock for *Gilead,* which was convenient. We eventually rented the house to Ed McNair, Northeastern's vice president of operations. During the whole time I was at Northeastern I commuted from Miami to the headquarters in Fort Lauderdale.

The job was interesting, we went from 4 to 15 aircraft in ten months. We added JFK (New York) and then transcontinental service via New Orleans to San Diego in California. Airbus made us an offer we could not refuse for four A300-B4s. I met some good people and enjoyed working with them. One of the best was Warren Ullman who was the chief financial officer and we have remained friends ever since. Another was Lawrence (Larry) Smith, a former C.A.B. attorney and one of the nicest people in the business. He later joined us at Aviation Management Services. Guy Tirano, an Italian-American

*Northeastern International Boeing 727, 1984.*

former travel agent, who had identified the Islip-Fort Lauderdale opportunity, ran marketing and sales. Bob Vermilion was head of maintenance, with Ed McNair, head of operations; former Braniff captain, Stan Midnight, chief pilot and some others. All of them real good chaps and I enjoyed working with them. As Chief Operating Officer (C.O.O.) I ran the 8 a.m. morning briefing which meant I left the house in Miami before 7 a.m. and most evenings did not get back until midnight. I patterned the morning briefing on John Casey's practice at Braniff: 20 minutes maximum and everyone from operations and maintenance, finance, sales, and other departments reported on what happened yesterday and today's highlights. The airline was growing at a tremendous rate. In ten months, we went from about $20 million in annual revenues to more than $100 million.

Early on, I introduced Steve to Freddie Laker, who was living in the Bahamas and spent much of time in South Florida. They hit it off to the extent that Steve nominated him to his board of directors. This generated some favorable publicity, and helped to give the airline some credibility. Some time after I left they parted company, not on the best of terms as I understand it. Another character at Northeastern was Michael Gillis, another Brit whom Steve had known from Jamaica. I never really understood his role but he was some kind of financial advisor to Steve. Michael had gone to Highgate School in England and was impressed when he found my father's name in the school roster of Old Boys. He was a mysterious character but was enjoyable company and knew a lot of people in the Caribbean.

Michael also brought in another personality with whom I hit it off rather well. His name was Dr. Hervey, a Hungarian who had been educated at Oxford in England and moved to Jamaica. He had been appointed chairman of Trans Jamaican by Prime Minister Seaga who was a personal friend. The airline was Government-owned and operated a fleet of small Islander and Trislander aircraft based in Kingston with routes to neighboring islands, the Turks and Caicos, Caymans, Haiti and the Dominican Republic. We tried to organize a joint venture with Trans Jamaican, but Northeastern would have had to serve Jamaica, which at the time it did not make any real business sense. After I left Northeastern, Hervey invited me to come to Jamaica to try to privatize the airline. Unfortunately, we were ahead of our time and there was no interest, but I enjoyed doing business plans and projections of what it might be as a Kingston-based regional commuter serving the islands. Many years later, 'Butch' Stewart, the successful Jamaican hotelier, bought control of the flag carrier, Air Jamaica, and then folded Trans Jamaican into it.

## Island-in-The-Sun Project

During my time at Northeastern late in 1984 and early in 1985, we spent as much time as possible on *Gilead*, sailing to the Bahamas and the Florida Keys. We discovered an island, Devil's Key, in the Berrys, in the eastern Bahamas, which was for sale. It was about 100 acres, facing the open Atlantic on the one hand and the Bahamas Bank on the other. My old Lima pal Andre Aisner developed a plan with me to buy the island for $150,000.

*Bobby, Robbie, and Guy on the good ship* Diderot.

Gilead, *family, a pipe, a bottle of beer: what else is there?*

I had met Andre on a sand hill east of Lima on a motorcycle. I had just taken a fall and cracked a couple of ribs. He helped me back on the bike and then drove me to the American Clinic in his pick-up truck with the bikes on the back. He had moved to Miami in the late 1970s where he became involved in a fish-import business. He was an architect, having studied under Belaunde at the University in Lima. He and his wife, Lacky, were good friends.

We did not have the money but this did not stop us from planning. We spent several long weekends on the island which was totally uninhabited, with good anchorage on the leeward, or western side. A hill overlooked a natural bay on the Atlantic side and we figured we would build bungalows and a lighthouse on the hill and dredge a marina on the lee side. Valerie was enthused with the idea of raising goats. I wanted to build a mini-brewery, before these came into fashion. Beer in the Bahamas was 100% imported and expensive. The marina would be strictly for sail boats. The project never got off the ground because we just could not come up with the money. But it was fun dreaming.

## If it ain't Fun—Quit, part 5

I had some good times at Northeastern and some not so good times. Steve was Machiavellian. He would have employee meetings at his home and he was always fascinating. He would put people against each other and had no idea of decent management practices. One Monday I learned that Warren Ullman had resigned and left, without warning. I called Warren at home and he told me that Steve had fired him over the weekend. As Warren reported to me, I realized this was time to move on.

So I quit and kept my record of never being fired from a job and quitting ahead of that possibility. The airline finally failed a year or so later. It was a shame, because it had great potential but a bunch of good people were out of a job as a result. I met Steve later when he was trying again to start another airline unsuccessfully. He did not seem to resent my having left him. In retrospect, the Northeastern experience was worth while. We had to sell the house in Fort Lauderdale at a loss so the financial part of it was a disaster. But I met some great people. Many of them are still scattered around the industry, and I see some of them every now and then.

# *Challenge Air International*

E li Timoner and Danny Ratti had teamed up around this time and I re-joined them to reactivate Airline Management & Marketing. We took office space and put up our shingle as consultants. Eli and I were good friends and have remained so to this day. He had recovered from his stroke although he still needed a cane to move about, but his mind worked as well as it always had.

## *If you can't get a Real Job—Consult*

We did a couple of interesting jobs. One was for a couple of Airbus chaps whom I had met when Northeastern acquired the A300B4s. The project was one we had talked about, but had never implemented. It involved an A300B4-QC (Quick Change) program which we tried to sell to Airborne Express. The aircraft would operate as freighters at night, Sunday through Friday, and we would create a passenger division to operate the aircraft during the day and on the weekends. Utilization would be as much as 15 hours which was pretty high. We took the idea to Airborne's chief executive officer, Graham Dorland in Seattle. He liked the idea, particularly because it gave him a wide-bodied aircraft at a fraction of the ownership cost because of the day time and weekend passenger operation. The passenger division would operate as a low cost, point-to-point airline, terminating at spoke-ends of Airborne's Columbus central sorting hub. We planned to sell seats on simplified non-refundable tickets (our old theater-type distribution method). Weekends would be devoted primarily to charters. Based on the high utilization and low cost approach we could deliver an available seat mile for less than 5 cents. This was even lower than Southwest's 7 cents, because of the longer average stage length—we would be using city-pairs that were approximately 1,500 miles apart. Graham Dorland arranged for us to meet with his staff in Columbus where we presented the full-blown business plan, utilizing six aircraft. Fortunately, Airbus Industries paid for the entire exercise, but unfortunately, the whole thing died a natural death. Someone at Airborne killed it, to prove, once again: ideas are one thing; execution is another.

Shortly after that Danny, and I were retained by the Colombian Flower Growers Association to establish a wholly-owned all-cargo operation to sustain the exporters from Colombia. We were paid for the study but it did not go anywhere, although it proved that the flower growers in Colombia could have profitably operated their own airline. It was later used by another former AVIANCA executive and friend, Hernan Galindo, as the basis for setting up a wholly-owned indirect-air carrier in Miami called Aerofloral, which has become the largest Colombian flower importer in Miami, chartering B-747s and DC-10s in the same market.

## The Res Center

Art Stellmach had joined us to create a Reservations Center for foreign and/ or small carriers under contract (later known as 'outsourcing') and Art would run this operation. The idea was that most foreign carriers have small reservations and telephone sales offices where they do not enjoy the economies of scale of their large U.S. competitors, and have relatively high union-labor costs. We would offer the service at a revenue passenger-boarded flat fee which made it a variable rather than a fixed cost to the airlines. No waste, no union problems; with benefits including 24-hour, 7-day-a-week coverage, better long distance rates because of purchasing clout, and lower real estate costs. We were probably 15 years ahead of our time.

## Leisure Air

Almost at the same time Ed McNair joined us with the idea of starting Leisure Air, a no-reservations, non-refundable ticket (theater ticketing-type) airline between Florida and the north-east. This was before 'ticketless' was invented, but it meant the same thing. The customer calls a 1-800 number, gives his credit card number, and books a seat on a specific flight. The boarding pass is sent by mail or the passenger picks up his boarding pass at the airport. It reduces distribution cost substantially because it not only eliminates paperwork; eliminates 'no-shows' and the travel agent. Again, our plan was for a fully allocated available seat mile cost at less than 5 cents. The eastern corridor of the United States, because of its extremely high leisure and V.F.R. (Visiting Friends & Relatives) content, is the single, most price sensitive air travel market anywhere. Eli was enthusiastic and said he would bring in some of his friends as investors. All of us were excited about the prospects for both projects. The Res Center would also handle Leisure Air, so it all made a lot of sense as the center would have an

*Challenge Air International was one of several post-deregulation airlines that tried to combine the northeastern USA–Florida market with the Miami gateway to Central America. Like the others, it was unsuccessful with its passenger operation but survives healthily today as a specialist air cargo airline.*

immediate airline client. Years later, in September 1995, the new PanAm and the Eastern Air Lines estate did exactly this. Eastern's OASIS Reservations Center was set up for Pan Am, using facilities that were no longer being used since the airline's demise. 'Ticketless' has now become the norm for discount airlines such as Reno Air, ValuJet and others.

Then we were side-tracked. In the fall of 1984 we were visited by the former Air Florida General Sales Agents in Honduras, Ricardo Suarez and Ricardo Martinez. They wanted to start a U.S. Part 121 operation to replace the Air Florida service in Central America, which had filed for Chapter 11 in July. The void in the market was now dominated by TACA and Pan American, which only flew to a couple of markets, Guatemala and Panama. Eastern had not yet entered the market, although they did later.

The idea was good, but the basic objective was wrong, to start an airline to justify the General Sales and Handling Agency ('GS&HA') network in Central America. Martinez and Suarez had set up the G.S.& H.A.s for Air Florida from Guatemala to Costa Rica. At Air Florida we had agreed early on, to contract out as much as possible, before it became fashionable as 'outsourcing.' And the two of them had invested in ground equipment, offices, and the rest. When Air Florida failed they were stuck with a basic business framework, but no business. They had some capital but not enough to start an airline, so they approached us. Eli liked the idea and committed to invest, if we could find some others to share the risk.

I called Dick Marx at Transavia in Amsterdam to see if they might be interested in participating. He loved the idea and committed a couple of B737-200 Advanced aircraft with -15 engines, which we needed because of the altitude at certain airports in Central America, which would be the basis of the operation. In the meantime we did the business plan which called for expanding the airline from two to five aircraft in the first year. Transavia liked the idea—it had previously worked very well with Air Florida on a contra-seasonal aircraft exchange arrangement. It would own 24.9% of the airline, the legal voting limit for foreign ownership. Dick Marx came to Miami and we worked out the details.

## Bill Spohrer

We then started to look around for an existing certificate, as we did not wish to go through the lengthy process of certification. Someone mentioned Bill Spohrer and Challenge Air Transport. They had their offices on the fourth floor of the same building we were in, near the airport at Miami. Challenge was a small cargo operation which Bill and Michael DeBakey, the son of the famous doctor, had bought and were trying to grow. Bill had been with APSA, the Peruvian carrier founded by his then father-in-law, C.N. (Connie) Shelton in the early Sixties. Shelton had started TAN in Honduras, CEA in Ecuador and APSA in Peru and operated all three of them as a single entity. Before acquiring Challenge, Bill had done a stint as President and

*Bill Spohrer, Chairman of Challenge Air Cargo, and one of the great gentleman of the business.*

CEO of 'Tacho' Somoza's LANICA airline in Nicaragua and previously had owned TAN for a brief time before selling it to the Lopez family in Honduras. Both Bill and Michael were friends of mine and had been involved with Eli Timoner in the early days of Air Florida.

I called Bill and asked: "how would you like to have a passenger subsidiary?"

He was immediately intrigued and suggested that we come upstairs and talk about it. The idea was that as Challenge was already a Part 121 airline, it would be much easier, and faster, to start a passenger operation as a division or subsidiary. We would pay Challenge a 'royalty' for the use of the certificate but we would handle 100% of the costs, and assume all the risks. Bill liked the idea. He knew both Ricardos from his days in Central America. Martinez had been Director of Tourism in Honduras and was a partner in Suarez's travel agency business. We agreed to pay Challenge $10,000 per month per aircraft operated for the first year. With five aircraft, this meant $600,000 in the first year, which was less than it would cost in terms of delays to obtain our Part 401—the DOT economic authority. The FAA Part 121 would probably take even longer, but we would accelerate the process this way and could be up in the air in 90 days. At the end of the first year we would have the option of spinning off the passenger division and buying it from Challenge at a price to be negotiated. It all seemed to make a lot of sense.

We proceeded to complete the business plan. Ricardo Martinez, who really wanted to run the airline in the worst way, would act as General Manager. Because he was not a U.S. citizen, he could not be C.E.O. But as it would start out as a division, these rules on foreign citizenship and ownership really did not apply. We put in Daniel Ratti as C.F.O., Art Stellmach as head of Sales & Service, and Emilio Dirube, who had been involved with the Ricardos, as head of operations. Working capital was put up by Eli and Transavia contributing the first two aircraft. Eli, Ed, and I were on the board of directors, but were going to continue to pursue the idea of starting up Leisure Air, which was what we really wanted to do anyway. The Central American passenger division of Challenge Air Transport would start out with San Pedro Sula and Tegucigalpa in Honduras and then rapidly expand into El Salvador and Guatemala.

Extracted from Cadogan Guides—"Honduras"

After Nicaragua, Honduras is the largest Central American republic—a little smaller than England and about the same size as Ohio. Ninety percent of the population is mestizo, with only a small indigenous population, mostly living in the Mosquito region. There is a sizable black population, who live all along the north coast of Honduras and on the Bay Islands, where you also find a unique people, who are descendants of pirates, slaves, Indians, and Spanish colonists, They are known as the Islanders, and they speak the lilting English of the Caribbean. On the island of Utila, in particular, there are still many whites, keeping their blue eyed, blond features to this day, even if their English is now a bit rough. Everyone on the islands, also speak Spanish and the schools here are all bilingual. Honduras has a special character of its own, and while its treasures are not so easily found, there is the attraction of traveling in a country where tourism has made little impact on the local way of life, and where there is the additional bonus of relative safety, as guerrillas are not active.

Honduras won its independence from Spain in 1821, after which it became a member of the United Provinces of Central America in 1823 along with Nicaragua, Costa Rica, El Salvador and Guatemala. Most Central Americans, however, have never fought for independence, and a significant number did not even want it. As a result the union was split right from the start. Fighting soon broke out, and the Honduran pro-union forces were defeated in 1839, a year before the Central American experiment dissolved into the countries we know today. The defeated Honduran general, Franicsco Morazan, died a few years later, but he is still regarded as a hero, and the most opulent boulevard in Tegucigalpa, the capital, is named after him.

*Author's note: The airport at Tegucigalpa is notorious among veteran pilots in the area as one of the most daunting in the Americas, and is still so even after substantial improvement by removing an offending hill which effectively used to block one end of the runway.*

## C.A.I., Not C.I.A. Please

C.A.I., for Challenge Air International, was how we decided to identify the passenger division of Challenge, the cargo airline. Someone had figured out that Challenge International Airlines, the logical name, spelled C.I.A. which at the time was not exactly a propitious name for an airline serving Central America. Remember that this was the time of the Contras in Central America, where an undeclared civil war was raging.

The airline got off the ground early in 1985 with two B-737s leased from Transavia, starting with San Pedro Sula, Tegucigalpa, and San Salvador

*The first Transavia B737-200, in Challenge livery.*

service. It also applied for and obtained rights to serve Jamaica. The airline had some interesting features. Flight attendant uniforms were tuxedos for the men and fancy evening gowns for the women. Onboard service was a real cut above the competition. Bar cart with free drinks, hot meals, and a "touch of class" was customary. We quickly added Newark behind Miami, Jamaica, and Guatemala City. The airline did quite well in terms of load factors and acceptance was good. But very quickly we started to have problems with the management, and with the GSA structure which was far too costly because the Ricardos did not have any real experience running an airline and were operating it to a large extent to benefit their structure on the ground. Handling was too expensive and we were having problems with Transavia because they were highly critical of the management, and were talking about pulling out. In addition we were still only operating two aircraft, and while the management in Miami was lean, we still did not come close to the required critical mass.

After six months into the operation we decided to make some changes. Eli and our group decided to shelve the Leisure Air project and concentrate on Challenge. We negotiated with Bill Spohrer and Michael DeBakey to spin off the passenger airline and pay them—I think—something like one million dollars for the certificate. The board asked me to take over the position of C.E.O. which I agreed to do. This was a huge mistake, but those three little letters have tremendous appeal to the ego (after all, I am not immune). Transavia decided it needed the 737s in Europe so we had to scramble for replacement aircraft, and ended up wet-leasing BAC One-Elevens—not the right aircraft for the mission, calling as it did for more seats and lower deck space for baggage than the One-Elevens had. An airline cannot make money by operating wet-leased aircraft. The operator of the wet-lease aircraft builds its profit margin into the A.C.M.I. (Aircraft, Crew, Maintenance, and Insurance) cost which it charges, and this means there is not enough left for the contracting airline (in this case, C.A.I.) to make a profit.

I approached Ed Acker at PanAm to try to convince him that C.A.I. would make a good PanAm 'feeder' at Miami. I wasted several weeks trying to get a decision, but after several meetings with some of his planning people, nothing came of it. And then we were hit over the head.

## Eastern Air Lines Goes West & We Go South

In the spring of 1987 Eastern Air Lines announced that it was expanding into Central America. I tried to convince George Lyall, Eastern's Vice President-Latin America, that, rather than compete with us with their far higher costs, we should sell the airline to Eastern as its low cost 'feeder' airline. We played around with that idea for about a week but Eastern did not buy the idea, and instead launched their service with daily flights to all our markets.

Eastern reduced fares to gain market share, but its most significant marketing tool was its frequent flyer program which we could not come close to matching. The spring was a disaster. We tried our own form of frequent-flyer program with a "Seven-Eleven Coupon Book" which we promoted on the basis of "Buy seven-get-eleven" which was a pretty good deal. We picked up a significant amount of advance cash sales but the yields were horrible and it did not help the P&L. The cash did keep us going for several months but you can not live on cash flow alone.

We never had enough aircraft or capital. During my 18 months or so, we (mostly Eli, with $2 million or more) had to raise money. Eli brought in several investors, including Bart Lewis, the heir to the Sealy Mattress company, and a very successful businessman. He agreed in principle to invest and we seemed to be on our way. We needed to add a couple more aircraft, and with them, to survive for a few months. We figured, and our customers told us, that if we could stay alive for five or six months, Eastern's lousy service would eventually turn customers back to us. It was a finite market and there were only just so many passengers for the two airlines.

Ed McNair and I went to New York on one occasion to meet with Bart Lewis. Ed became Bart Lewis's guy and by July 1987 he took over my job with Bart's support. I do not really blame him, he was probably right in the sense that he had Bart's confidence and I was identified with the lack of profitability. It was probably the only way to persuade Bart to agree to invest. On the other hand, I made the stupid mistake of staying on in a sort of non-executive-capacity, ostensibly to provide marketing support.

This was the one time when I did not quit in time. I guess the motivation was—partly at least—a mistaken idea of loyalty to the other investors, primarily Eli and to the employees. Bart Lewis wanted to see some significant improvement at the 'bottom line' as we headed into the high season in July and August. It never happened. July and August were disastrous. Early in September Bart Lewis decided that he was not going to invest any more money and that was that.

To cut a long story short, the airline lasted 36 months. By mid-1987 Challenge Air International was broke. We made some bad decisions, among these to use our credit with suppliers and vendors to keep the airline going while we were waiting for Bart Lewis to invest more capital. Rather smartly he decided not to pour good money after bad. At least, he made the right decision. We filed for Chapter 11, and I was D.I.P. (Debtor In Possession). This means that I was appointed by the court to work with the creditors and the court to liquidate the assets of the airline in order to try and pay off the liabilities. Unfortunately, Challenge had no assets to liquidate. There were really only two options: re-capitalize the airline to get it back in the air so that over time it might be able to pay off the creditors; find a buyer who would purchase the certificate and the operating rights and negotiate to pay off the creditors who were, in fact, the owners at this point. The shareholders were completely wiped out.

## Carnival

As D.I.P. I spent several months trying to find a way to put Challenge International back into the air. The problem with being D.I.P. with an airline like Challenge, which had no assets or strength, other than some routes in relatively liberal bilateral-countries, is that you have very little to offer, not to mention liabilities. But as often happened in bad times, good things also happen. In this case it was getting to know Richard Baron, a former Greenberg & Traurig attorney, who was specializing in bankruptcy. Richard was very helpful to us and was a pillar of strength.

We talked to a dozen aspiring investors who kicked the tires. and of these, Ted Arison of Carnival Cruise Lines, was seriously interested. He and Eli were friends and he agreed to take a look and we set up a meeting with Reuven Wertheim, a school-chum of Ted's who was running a tour company responsible for the Arison Bahamas hotel project. I arranged to meet Reuven on a Saturday in late October of 1987 and took Danny Ratti with me. Carnival wanted an airline to fill the Nassau hotel property it owned, and while we assumed that they also wanted to fill cruise ships this was not the main thrust. Wertheim was a shrewd business man with airline experience, I think he had been head of catering at El Al in Israel before joining Ted Arison in Miami.

He was definitely interested and we talked about price and what it would take to re-launch Challenge as a Carnival subsidiary. It would not take much, probably $2 to $3 million at most. This, would at least solve the IRS problem—we had unwisely used withholding taxes to keep the airline alive during the last few weeks. This would take management off the hook, and of course wipe out Eli and all of us as shareholders. We agreed that the lawyers would start on the paperwork on the following Monday. That weekend we thought we had it made. We were not going to recover any of the investors' money, but at least the creditors would receive some of their money and the airline would be back in the air which meant that the employees, pilots, flight attendants, and others (except senior management) would keep their jobs.

On Monday, Carnival's lawyer called me. He told me that over the weekend Ted Arison had purchased P.I.A., an airline in Las Vegas from an old Israeli friend of his. The airline was a one-B727-100 charter operation. Less risky and perhaps less expensive than acquiring C.A.I. out of bankruptcy. It was a blow to everyone, except Danny who was hired by Reuven to be the C.E.O. of the new Carnival Airlines because Reuven was not a U.S. citizen and needed a surrogate. Danny was also eminently qualified. He had a good feel for numbers and understood the business.

> Carnival grew rapidly to a 27-aircraft operation, generating some $270 million in 1996. It operated a fleet of A300s, B737-400s and a couple of B727-200s. It was opportunistic, jumping into markets, and jumping out equally as fast. It was a major discount carrier with a presence in the Northeast-Florida, Puerto Rico and South Florida-Los Angeles market. Danny Ratti was very good at doing deals with lessors during a time when aircraft were sitting in the desert and most were on a 'power-by-the-hour' basis which means they only paid for the ownership when the aircraft were in revenue flying. This is good for a charter carrier but not so good for a scheduled airline which needs high utilization. After the ValuJet disaster Carnival lost $75 million in the Fiscal Year ending 30 June 1997 and later that year the "new" Pan Am acquired 100% of the airline from Ted Arison's son, Mickey, which had taken over Carnival from his dad. The airline was never owned by Carnival Cruise Lines.

I was at the Dinner Key Marina in Coconut Grove, checking on *Gilead* some time in October, when Claudia, my then future daughter-in-law who was holding down the fort at the airline, called. She said: "Bobby, Art Stellmach's wife just called to say that he has had a heart attack."

I was shaken. Art was actually younger than me by a couple of years, and much fitter. I realized that the airline failure had hit him very hard. He was tough on the outside but soft on the inside. By the time I got back to the office he had died. We had worked together at Braniff and Air Florida. He wore his hair crew-cut like the marine he had been in the Korean war. He was a strong people-person and I have missed him ever since.

## Out on the Streets (or the Water)

With the only real investor, Ted Arison, blown away, I called the Board and told them it was all over. Except for the liquidation of the few remaining assets, some computers and furniture at best, which first Danny, and then Richard Baron handled. This was the low point in our lives. I was 59, had no job, and no prospects. I decided to go sailing and sort things out in my mind. I called John Casey and invited him to come down and spend a week in the Bahamas. My buddy, Andre Aisner agreed to join us.

# Hanging In There

ohn Casey, Andre Aisner, and I were sailing up the east coast of the Abacos, in the Bahamas, on *Gilead*. It was blowing about 15 knots from the northeast and the sea was choppy and quite rough. *Gilead* actually pointed quite well for a double ender. This means that it would sail well in to the wind. The sun was setting and we were approaching landfall. The entrance on the southeast side of the Abacos, just north of Hole In the Wall, was always tricky and we made it inland right after dark. We dropped the anchor and broke out the scotch. We had been sailing for 36 hours and were bushed but feeling great. The next morning we sailed up the inside of the Abacos to Hopetown and picked up a mooring in front of the Hopetown Lodge, which belonged to our friends, the Malones.

## John Casey

We spent the weekend at the anchorage at the Lodge, and sailed during the day and drank a lot in the evenings. A terrific hideaway in one of my favorite

*Andre Aisner and John Casey prepare dinner on* Gilead.

places, one of those incredible, undiscovered jewels. We had been there in the late 1970s and early 1980s and it had not changed. During the weekend John said: "Bobby, how about doing some marketing work for PanAm World Services? We need Latin American business and have the best maintenance and repair service available."

As a result I picked up my first consulting client. The deal was a small retainer and a success fee on business generated. John flew out on Monday morning from Marsh Harbor, a 30 minute sail from Hopetown. Andre and I sailed back to Miami with an overnight stop in Bimini, another favorite of mine. We went ashore to the Complete Angler, one of Hemingway's watering holes, where he wrote part of *Islands in the Stream*. The next morning we sailed back to Dinner Key where I kept *Gilead*. Andre is a great sailor, but best of all, he is good company on a boat and cooks like a Frenchman. A few days after John Casey had arrived back in New York, where he was Chairman of World Services (having held the position of Chief Operating Officer for PanAm under Ed Acker previously), he sent me a personal note with a check for $5,000. The note said: "I know this will help. You repay me from your first million dollars."

John Casey was a gentleman. I eventually repaid him even though I have still not made my first million. He died several too short years later and I miss him. During this period I relied heavily on his judgement and friendship.

## On Our Own, or Once more into the Breach

By this time, the latter part of 1987, I had decided that I would concentrate my activities in Latin America. It kept me out of the way of dozens of other former airline executives-cum-consultants, all of whom were concentrating on the Pacific, Europe, and Asia. No one was interested in Latin American aviation. I had picked a region which I knew well, but which could be, to coin a well-worn phrase "the sleeping giant." For a while I thought I had made a horrible mistake. No one called me and no one seemed to be the least interested in aviation in the region. We incorporated the company as Avman, Inc., d/b/a Aviation Management Services. My children, Robbie, Guy and Valerie, owned the corporation. I was merely a paid hand working for them.

Robbie and Fiorella had started Hi Tech Air Shipping during the Challenge period and had organized the lower deck cargo on a 60/40 contract (something we had invented at Air Florida, the agent keeps 40% of the revenue but handles 100% of the job, marketing, loading, unloading, collecting). After the airline folded they had entered the courier business, representing courier companies who needed contacts in Central and South

America. While they were just beginning they were doing quite well and had two or three employees. They had taken a small office and a tiny warehouse behind the airport and offered me a desk and a place to hang my hat.

I printed up some stationery and business cards and was all set. I organized a couple of Pan Am World Services financed trips to Central America, looking for business. The World Services assignment petered out because Casey left and we never did any business, although we did arrange a number of appointments, including one with my old friend Otto Escalante at LACSA. But it helped me back on to my feet and to keep myself occupied.

By this time Eli Timoner had decided he was going to stay home and maybe dabble in real estate, He had had it with the airline business, having dropped at least couple of million on the C.A.I. project. Ed McNair had joined his buddy Pete Seidlitz at Bristol Associates, an aircraft brokering business in Washington D.C., and Danny Ratti was off and running with Reuven Wertheim at Carnival as president and C.E.O.

In the meantime, Guy had met a couple of Frenchmen who had converted a 110-foot French river barge, or 'peniche', the *Diderot*, and brought it across to New York. They hired Guy as captain—even though he did not have ticket, and he moved on board and cruised it from New York to Miami's Dinner Key Marina. The Frenchmen had planned to sell replicas of the *Diderot* as 'live-aboards'—the concept was to use the Diderot as the model, offering to buy peniches in Europe and build them to order—but they never sold one and had run out of money. They left the boat in his care to pay the dock and insurance—with the understanding that he would keep whatever income he managed to generate from local charters in Biscayne Bay. He and his new wife, Claudia moved on board and did charters and parties on the bay, very successfully.

Meanwhile, Avman's second customer was Evergreen International which wanted to develop charter and subservice business in Latin America. Evergreen had a reputation as a former C.I.A. 'company' (or front) but I never did find out whether this was true or not. Someone introduced me as the 'guru' of Latin American aviation and I was invited to McMinville, Oregon, their headquarters. I also invited Juan Ucros and a couple of other close friends from South America and we had an all-day meeting with Evergreen's C.E.O., Del Smith and his senior staff, answering questions about the region. Bearing in mind that this was 1988, my optimism about the region was as much intuitive, laced with some wishful-thinking. They had us all out for dinner and I was hired.

We did a couple of tours with Del Smith and his key people on the company G-4. The mission was not outstandingly successful, mainly because Del did not really want to do business. Every time we quoted a rate to someone for a wet-lease or all-inclusive aircraft charter, it was way out of line. He also surrounded himself with former military men (who might have had a C.I.A. connection), but they only helped to confuse the situation when they tried to go around us to the local military. This might have worked a few years previously, but no longer.

In 1989 Patricio Sepulveda, then president of LAN Chile, approached me about putting together an employee buy-out to privatize the Chilean airline. I had met Patricio when he was the planning person at LAN during Carlos Lathrop's time and we had tried to do something with them at Air Florida. Patricio had been named C.E.O. after Carlos left the airline to run his own aircraft brokerage business. Patricio could not pay for our services so we did it on a 'success fee' basis, i.e. we would be paid if we were able to arrange the financing. At the time I was happy to have any kind of an assignment. We put together a plan and I took it to Del Smith at Evergreen who was interested but never came up with the necessary cash. So Guillermo Carey, a former president of Ladeco, the privately owned Chilean airline, convinced SAS's Jan Carlson (the Scandinavian consortium had recently invested in Continental Airlines and were interested in building a closer association in Latin America—which, incidentally never really materialized) and they stole the airline for something like $25 million. Later on the airline was sold to the Cueto family and friends, who have made it into one of the most profitable airlines in Latin America and a model of privatization

In Brazil we tried very hard to do something with Omar Fontana and TransBrasil, but nothing came of it. Omar had previously acquired a couple of B727s from Evergreen, but we were unable to do anything significant. We did manage to do a helicopter deal in Chile but my local representative went around my back and cut a deal with Del Smith, screwing me out of a commission. No problem, except that it hurt—but, as I like to say, what goes around comes around.

## Writing for a Living

Starting in 1989, I managed to get some writing assignments on the subject of Latin American aviation. I submitted articles, some on request, which were published in Airline Business, AirFinance Journal, LatinFinance, LatinTrade, America Economia and The Journal of Commerce among other, lesser, publications. Some of these actually paid me for them, and I appreciated being paid for writing about my favorite subject. During the early years it appeared that there was no one else around who either cared, or knew anything about the subject.

A couple of these articles are worth mentioning because they served to establish our role, which some have called, facetiously, "the defenders of the poor." The first, published in Airline Business in December 1989, "It Takes 28 To Tango" outlined a concept which we called "Latin Leasing, Inc." whereby Latin American and Caribbean domiciled airlines should form a consortium to negotiate with the manufacturers of heavy transport aircraft, to acquire new jets at competitive prices with their U.S. competitors, and then lease the aircraft to the airlines. The concept being that the airlines would themselves own Latin Leasing, Inc., and thus build their balance sheets through ownership of the aircraft as opposed to having them owned, in a large majority, by leasing companies such as General Electric Capital Aviation Services (GECAS), I.L.F.C. and others which owned 80% of the fleets used in Latin America. While nothing came of the idea at the time, in 1997 three airline groups, among the most successful in Latin America, actually placed a record order for approximately 90 narrow-bodied jets with Airbus Industrie. The single largest order ever placed by Latin American airlines. The three airline groups are TACA of Central America, the TAM Group in Brazil and LAN-Chile. The three groups have 13 airlines in their fold and a current fleet of approximately 120 narrow-bodied jets. The 90 Airbus jets will replace their entire fleet and will provide for substantial growth over the next ten to fifteen years. I also predicted, correctly, that South America was to become the fastest growing airline traffic market in the decade ahead.

The second article, "Unfriendly Skies", was published in LatinFinance as the April 1991 cover story in this prestigious financial publication. The in-depth article reviewed the current situation in Latin America and the threat from outside the region as American Airlines takes over Eastern Air Lines routes and other U.S. carriers begin to look south. We suggested that the only solution for the 30 some Latin American and Caribbean airlines which oper-ated to the United States would be to form cooperative associations among themselves to provide sufficient strength to survive in what was going to become a highly competitive, and globalized, aviation market. Again, we cannot take credit for everything that has happened since, but it did set the stage for our involvement in a number of such activities, i.e. the TACA consolidation in Central America, LatinPass, the frequent flyer program owned by a dozen airlines and others. Others, incidentally, in which we had no involvement, include the Aeromexico/Mexicana and AeroPeru consolida-tion, the LAN/Ladeco/Fast Air in Chile, and the VASP/Ecuatoriana/Lloyd Aereo Boliviano joint ventures.

All of these consolidations have allowed the airlines involved to nego-tiate from far greater strength with American, United, Continental and more recently, Delta Air Lines as they establish marketing agreements with their U.S. competitors.

## PanAm's L.A.D.—For Sale By Owner

In 1988, PanAm's Tom Plaskett, who had replaced Ed Acker as C.E.O., came to Miami and publicly threatened the union that if they did not give what he wanted he was going to sell the Miami maintenance base and the Latin American Division. I was on the telephone the next morning to John Casey (who had left PanAm) and we agreed that it was a great opportunity—for someone. John called Plaskett who confirmed that he was serious and had the board of directors' approval to do the deal if necessary. We arranged for a meeting with Julius Maldutis of Salomon Brothers and I called a Peruvian investment banker friend, and we met in New York after I had put together a summary of the opportunity. The idea was exciting. PanAm's maintenance base in Miami did third party work and the Latin American Division had generated revenues of $600 million and $43 million in operating profit in 1987, while the airline as a whole lost $124 million.

The Peruvian connection was the Romero family which owned the Atlantic Security Bank in Miami and Banco de Credito in Lima. They were extremely wealthy and had previously shown interest in acquiring an airline. My contact there was one of the Monteros of Peru, who was an investment banker, and was married to the daughter of our friend Chabuca Sala. Montero lived in New York and represented the Romeros in the United States. He was well known to Salomon Brothers and this lent credibility to the project.

The whole project was killed when Plaskett decided, in spite of the unions, not to sell. Later on, in 1991, he sold Europe to Delta and kept Latin America, which then failed because Delta decided not to support the division. United then stepped in and bought the Latin American routes for $100 million, as it had done previously when it picked up the entire Pacific Ocean for $700 million from Ed Acker.

For the next two or three years it was slim picking. I borrowed money from a number of old friends who came through like gangbusters—proving my theory that what goes around comes around. The loans subsidized my otherwise meager income. I mention their names because, in some cases, this kind of support, John Casey and John Phillippe (a former Braniff associate), was unsolicited; and in others I did not have to beg. Others included Juan Pardo, who bought our house in Lima, and came through with a loan when he had no reason to do so; Herbert Buencristiano, my first boss at PanAm in Montevideo, who did not question what I needed it for; Gianmarco Nizzola who bought Interandina; Ricardo Healy, who had worked with me at Air Florida and was doing very well in the airport handling business, and Horacio Mazza in Argentina, who had sold me Interandina. Years later, I managed to pay most of them off without interest.

## Charlie Bryan

In October 1989, John Casey called me. He was in Miami at the Hilton Blue Lagoon, by the airport: "Bobby, get your ass over here. I'm meeting with Charlie Bryan, and we have something we need to talk to you about."

Charlie Bryan was a local leader of the International Association of Machinists (I.A.M.) and Eastern Air Lines' nemesis. I was surprised. I knew who Charlie Bryan was and John was not exactly a union man. I had heard that John was doing something about Eastern, but I had no idea what this was all about. It had to do with Lorenzo and I spent most of the ten-minute drive over there speculating. I knew quite a bit about Charlie, although I had never met him. He was one of the most aggressive union leaders in the industry, starting out as an A&P mechanic at Eastern, and rising to the position of general chairman of the I.A.M. in 1970.

The two of them were having a drink with a character called Larry Spivey. I later read about Spivey in "Grounded—Frank Lorenzo and the Destruction of Eastern Air Lines" by Aaron Bernstein. He had written about Spivey as follows: "The tale of Loehr H. (Larry) Spivey is one of the strangest chapters in the saga of Eastern Airlines. Union leaders knew little about him at the time and it was many months before they found out much more. A small, thinly built man with a sincere air and a proclivity for saying embarrassingly personal things about himself, the 45-year old Spivey was an unlikely candidate to become a middleman in the war between labor and Lorenzo. ..In his early Twenties he had been arrested on moonshining charges in Columbia S.C. Two years later, he got five years' probation on a worthless-check charge. Altogether he had been arrested five times, including once on felony charges for aggravated assault on Charlene Spivey, who was divorcing him at the time....in 1975 he contacted the Georgia Bureau of Investigation (GBI), a state counterpart of the FBI, saying he had been approached by two acquaintances who wanted his help in a drug-smuggling scheme. Spivey claimed he spent time in Guatemala, Mexico and Jamaica in pursuit of drug-smuggling leads....Spivey told a dramatic tale that included names of his alleged contacts, such as Henry Kissinger, fugitive Robert Vesco, and Omar Torrijos, the former president of Panama..."

After the introductions they asked me to help myself from the open bar. John then told me that he had been brought in by Larry Spivey, who was from

Atlanta, and who was trying to put together an employee buyout of the airline from Frank Lorenzo. He was a colorful, rather mysterious lawyer who had approached Charlie and the union leadership, and had taken them out on a fishing boat in Isla Morada in the Florida Keys over the Labor Day weekend. He told the union leaders he could raise the money to buy the airline. Spivey was about 45, wiry, and dropping names freely. He claimed that he had Bill Marriott, Ross Perot, and Louis Kelso, the father of the Employee Stock Option Programs (ESOP) backing him. He had formed a corporation, Grandview, to manage the buyout.

After the fishing trip Charlie had been in Houston and had dinner with Frank Lorenzo who agreed to sell the airline if Charlie could put together a viable plan. They had enlisted the former senior vice president of marketing, Mort Ehrlich, who would be the C.E.O. of the airline. I knew him from my days at Air Florida but was not all that impressed. In my opinion, while he was a professional airline marketing type, he did not have the 'charisma' or the kind of public perception that it would take to make this happen.

Charlie Bryan was a tough, 5' 10", stocky, and very plain-spoken individual. By tough I mean someone who is both bloody-minded and resilient. He and John Casey were exact opposites, but at the same time they were both tough—in different ways—they had a common background in maintenance, seemed to hit it off, and respected each other.

"So what do you want me to do, Charlie?" I asked.

Charlie looked at Larry and John, who answered for them: "We thought you might have some potential investors in South America who might like to come in and take a minority position because of Eastern's Latin American routes."

John was obviously thinking back to our failed attempt at PanAm's Latin American routes. I thought about it and came up with an idea: "Maybe, but first of all I think what you need is a real figurehead, I've nothing against Mort Ehrlich, but he is not exactly a name that will conjure up people's imagination."

## Peter Ueberroth

"You need someone like Peter Ueberroth, the Baseball Commissioner," I said.

They loved the idea. The next morning I called his office in New York and then sent a fax: "Peter, we have an airline situation that you ought to know about that's an exciting opportunity."

Within 30 minutes Peter called me. He remembered me from my Braniff and more recently, AeroPeru days in Los Angeles, even though we had not talked in years. I explained the deal that Spivey and Charlie Bryan were working on. He was very interested and knew about the employee buyout idea because he had met a few days before with Frank Lorenzo, but had not thought about playing a role. He was very close to Carl Pohlad, one of Eastern's directors, who thought this was the only way to save the airline. He agreed to meet in New York later that week.

I attended the meeting in New York where Spivey and Bryan had assembled some Easterm pilots and other union leaders, as well as some financial types, including Louis Kelso and Aaron Gellman, an airline consultant I had met previously. Gellman had put together a plan which involved a $200 million 'give-back' by the employees which would become their investment. They had taken a suite at the Marriott and the place was like a war room, with fax machines, PCs, even a paper shredder. I had brought in Horacio Mazza from Buenos Aires who thought he might enlist some heavy-hitter investors from Argentina. I had also talked to some of my Peruvian friends. The meeting was something of a farce. No one knew who was doing what, but Peter did agree to take the lead and organize a buyout team. Louis Kelso was particularly interesting and spent some time talking about employee ownership—I happened to agree with his views even though they are still being argued about in the industry. He and his wife had agreed to invest $100,000 of their own money, committed as they were to the idea of employee ownership.

## Death of Eastern

The rest is history. Eventually Frank and Peter did not agree to the terms. The major issue was the unions and Peter wanted a trustee named to represent them while the transaction was being completed and Frank would not accept. Spivey had tried to claim a 5% ($23 million or so, depending on the final price) 'finder's fee' for bringing in Ueberroth, which further complicated the whole issue. The other problem was bickering between Frank and Peter over who would get how much if the deal fell through. I wonder now whether I was just too naive. I had never asked anyone how much was in it for myself in trying to help save the airline. Eventually the lack of a deal between the two high-ego players doomed the airline. I never even received a thank-you note. So it goes.

## The 900-lb. Gorilla

And then in 1990, American Airlines acquired Eastern Air Lines' Latin American Division, the former Braniff L.A.D., for something like $400 million. This changed the face of Latin American aviation and at the same time gave Aviation Management Services a mission: to work with Latin American carriers to help them to survive the onslaught of competition, the likes of which they had never experienced since Pan American dominated Latin American aviation in the 1930s.

American's approach to Latin America was totally different from Eastern's, or, for that matter, Braniff's, albeit in the latter case the time and the rules were different. Bob Crandall's strategy was 'to take no prisoners.' He immediately built a fortress hub in Miami with double-daily flights between Miami and every major city in the region. Instead of sitting aircraft on the ground at the end of the line, he turned them around quickly and added daylight flights northbound which gave him far greater aircraft utilization and with the emphasis on frequency rather than capacity. He introduced B-757s and A-300s rather than larger DC-10s, L-1011s and B-747s.

The competition was ferocious, American was a real 900-lb. gorilla of an airline in a zoo inhabited by small, inefficient, mostly government-owned lesser mammals. Bob Crandall had given Peter J. Dolara the top Latin American posting and he did a remarkable job. Peter is a native Uruguayan who had migrated to the United States in the 1970s. He had started out as a reservations agent with a Caribbean airline which was later acquired by American. Peter rose through the ranks strictly on merit. He is an interesting character, tough as nails, and determined to make it to the top.

He ran Latin America with a nice blend of Crandall's 'take no prisoners' approach and a certain Latin *geito* or 'touch.' We are not close friends but had mutual acquaintances—he had worked at one time for Herb Keilsen, who had later worked for me at Air Florida. Herb told me about Peter as a real comer at American Airlines, even then. Peter and I would occasionally meet for breakfast at the Hyatt Hotel in Coral Gables to exchange views and—probably—misinformation. I have a lot of respect for this fellow-Uruguayan (by adoption, in my case) who has really carved out an important position for himself with American—no mean feat. He told me an amusing story one day which is worth repeating. I had written something in the newsletter about American Airlines which really annoyed his boss, Bob Crandall, who called Peter and asked him: "Aren't you a friend of this guy, Booth? Where the hell was he born?" Peter told Crandall he had no idea. After all, why should he admit we were compatriots, of sorts. It would somehow show a lack of control if he could not control a compatriot.

## What Goes Around

Some time in the early 1990s, Pedro Heilbron, C.E.O. of COPA, the Panamanian airline owned by the Alberto Motta group, called me and we did some work for them on their Miami-Panama startup, which was a lot of fun. Pedro's father, and Motta were partners and apparently I had been nice to them during my Braniff years and they wanted to help. I had to spend some of the time in Panama, which was like "going home." I did strategic marketing for them until they hired a full-time General Manager-North America, who decided they did not need me any more, but that is the nature of the business. Pedro and I continue to have a relationship which I enjoy almost as much as if under contract—perhaps more so.

At about the same time, Dick Haberly of Arrow Air and indirectly George Batchelor of International Air Leases—who owns Arrow Air—hired us. George, who is probably one of the most interesting and controversial people in the business, had told Dick to hire me. He had started out as an A&P mechanic and had built up a billion-dollar business. I had met him during the AeroPeru years. General Cabrera, my boss at AeroPeru at the time, had agreed to lease a couple of aircraft and had sent me to negotiate the deal. After we had signed the L.O.I. (Letter Of Intent), Cabrera had decided against the deal and I had to tell George about it. He could have taken the airline to court but did not. I suspect that he had Dick hire me out of the goodness of his heart, a Batchelor characteristic that no one has accused him of in the past, but true, none-the-less.

The Arrow assignment was to assist the airline in securing wet-lease, (Aircraft, Crew, Maintenance and Insurance) and/or all-inclusive charter contracts for the airline's DC8-62 freighters in the region. We made a couple of trips to Brazil and Argentina. Dick was a knowledgeable air cargo executive and had his own contacts, coming from Flying Tigers, at that time (before it was acquired by Federal Express), the premier all-cargo airline in the world. Among his contacts was Pablo Faracci of Argentina, with whom Arrow and I.A.L. (George Batchelor) had a joint venture, which involved using Arrow aircraft on Argentine and Paraguayan airline certificates which the joint venture controlled in one way or another. The problem with our assignment was that it really was not clear as to whether George wanted to build an airline or to lease aircraft. We did put one deal together with our friends at COPA in Panama. But the relationship, while positive, did not go very far. It was not our primary focus, but it paid some bills for a year or so.

## Last flight to Carrasco

In 1991 Tom Plaskett engineered the sale of Pan American Airways' European routes to Delta for more than $1 billion, with a commitment from the Atlanta-based airline to support the remaining route structure of PanAm in Miami and Latin America. In November of that year the loads on the remaining PanAm flights were a disaster and Delta's stock took a plunge as the analysts predicted that Delta had taken on more than it could digest. On 4 December 1991, I was on an Arrow mission to South America and had managed a pass on PanAm to Montevideo where I was going to overnight before spending a couple of days working for Arrow in B.A. I had also managed to be upgraded to First Class, courtesy of my friend, Fred Kells at PanAm in Miami. PanAm still had one of the best First Class B747 sections in the business. As we left São Paulo at about 9 a.m. the Captain, whom I knew, came back and sat next to me. He said: "Plaskett has just announced that Delta has pulled out of the deal and we're filing Chapter 11 this morning. This flight will be ferried back to the United States."

He had tears in his eyes. I felt pretty misty myself. Here I was, about to land at Carrasco Airport where it had all started some 43 years ago, on PanAm's last flight. I spent a night at the Victoria Plaza, another old haunt, where I proceeded to get thoroughly pissed. The next morning, with a major hangover, I went to B.A. for a couple of days and talked myself into a cockpit ride back on an Arrow DC8-62F.

An interesting afterthought is that late in 1997, Delta Air Lines' new C.E.O., Leo Mullin, announced that the Atlanta-based airline was going to expand into Latin America in 1998 and compete with the three other incumbent U.S. airlines, American, Continental and United, to carve out a significant share of the market. If Delta had acquired Pan Am's Latin American Division, instead of Europe, in 1991, it would undoubtedly be a force in the region at least equal to American today. United would not be a player because Pan Am's routes would not have been available.

# "The Darkest Hour is Just Before the Dawn"

D uring the early 1990s, more in self defense than because we were committed to being charter brokers, we had organized several northbound charter programs quite successfully. In Brazil we convinced a group of tour operators to join together to develop a charter program. We then arranged for a Rich L-1011 to operate a 16 week program into Miami and Orlando. We made our money from a flat $50/hour commission from Rich. We also put something together in Argentina where we managed to have Horacio Mazza and his partner, Eduardo Cermesoni, involved—so much so that they are still operating charters into the Caribbean. The trouble with this kind of business is that once you put the parties together in the first place there comes a time when they do not need you. I was not smart enough, or perhaps it was not possible, to protect the future and after a good couple of years we were no longer involved in the business.

In 1990 a friend at Pratt & Whitney had hired us to provide market intelligence on the region. As part of this assignment we started a bi-weekly Faxnews on the region. Through our contacts in Latin America we were able to assemble a specialized source of intelligence. We subscribed to a number of local publications and periodically gleaned from some of our friends in the airlines the kind of information which was not otherwise available. Over a period of a year, the Faxnews became a valuable mine of information. It included facts and editorial opinion about events and trends. My contacts at P&W thought the material was invaluable and told me so repeatedly.

In spite of all this, after a couple of years, Pratt & Whitney canceled the intelligence-gathering assignment because of budget cuts. Claudia, who had joined me as my personal assistant-bookkeeper-office manager, suggested that we convert the fax into a hard-copy newsletter. We came up with a name—highly unimaginative but precisely descriptive: AVIATION-Latin America & Caribbean. My old public relations guru and friend, Mac Seligman suggested that Lora Erickson, a former Eastern manager and graphic designer, who did that airline's collateral material, i.e. brochures,

174

promotional literature, should design the newsletter. Lora died a couple of years ago but we still use her smart design. we still produce the monthly newsletter and enjoy doing it immensely; primarily because it allows me to pontificate, opinionate, and generally write about my favorite subject in my favorite part of the world.

## *The Airline Club*

Late in 1990 Eduardo Gallardo, then General Manager in North America for LADECO, the Chilean airline, came to see me about an idea to create a frequent-flyer program. He had tried to sell it—unsuccessfully—to his counterparts at other Latin American airlines and thought I might have better luck as an outsider. American had launched its highly successful AAdvantage frequent-flyer program in Latin America and Eduardo knew that it was going to become a major competitive factor.

I enlisted David Hedley-Noble, a Brit who had done a terrific job for us as the advertising agency for Challenge and Mac Seligman of Creative Resources and they both agreed to speculate. David came up with the creative approach: The Airline Club, and we approached all the carriers in the region. We finally made a presentation with advertising copy and the works on Guy's

*Diderot* during a three-hour cruise on Biscayne Bay. The presentation included a plan to develop a Private Airline Club at Miami International Airport for the use of the airlines which would serve as a model for other Clubs at other major airports. The whole idea was well thought out and presented. There was interest but no one would make a commitment. American's entry had not yet shown its teeth and demonstrated the amazing strength of its frequent-flyer program, so that the Latin American airlines' apprehension had not yet reached a crisis level. We were plainly ahead of our time.

## Another Great Idea

Early in 1992 we put together a marketing plan to common-brand the five-airline consortium that TACA's Federico Bloch had put together in Central America. From its El Salvador base and starting with Aviateca in Guatemala, Federico had made equity investments in four other carriers, Aeronica (Nica), TAN/SAHSA (in Honduras) and LACSA in Costa Rica. He had convinced the owners in each case to give up management control and was actually running all four airlines, as well as TACA. He also brought in COPA from Panama, as a non-equity partner, so in essence he had buttoned up all the carriers in Central America from Guatemala to Panama.

He had consolidated purchasing, ground handling, and a bunch of other services, all aimed to achieve lower unit costs and was well on his way to achieving an effective consortium. In essence he was doing what Lowell Yerex, his predecessor and founder of TACA, had done during the 1930s and 1940s when TACA (plus BWIA in the West Indies) came under a single management from Central America to Venezuela and Brazil.

We enlisted Mac Seligman for public relations and David Hedley-Noble on the advertising side and put together a presentation to common-brand the five airlines. We came up with a logo and brand name, "America Central", and went to San Salvador to make the presentation. Federico brought in some of his senior managers and Roberto Kriete, board member and majority stockholder. They loved it and thought it made a lot of sense. Unfortunately, for us, they liked the idea so much that they hired Bain & Co. of Boston to execute the plan, partially, because they did not common-brand the five airlines until much later.

Later on, Federico did hire David Hedley-Noble's company, Public Image Limited, to design the whole new look for the combined airlines, now known as the TACA Group, or Grupo TACA, and the first aircraft with the new and spectacular livery started operating late in 1997. Mac had retired in the meantime, but his friend and fellow-public relations expert, Bill Kofoed, took over the public relations function. While Aviation Management Services was not involved in this, we continue to have a cordial relationship and do not feel left out of things because of *LatinPass*—which is dealt with later in this story.

In August 1992 Hurricane Andrew hit Miami and sank *Gilead* and drove *Diderot* onshore. Guy joined us at Aviation Management after he sold the hull. The insurance company paid me for *Gilead* and we used the proceeds to subsidize the business for a couple of years. While the hurricane was a major disaster, it indirectly kept us alive for a while. And my last grandson—who was in the process of being born—was named, appropriately, Guy Andrew. Better known as Gandi. It really was the beginning of building the business.

## After the Storm

Following Andrew, things seemed to become much busier. We started to receive calls and business picked up in general. We had moved, together with Robbie and Fiorella, to more 'presentable' offices, still in the warehouse/airport district. I now had a separate entrance to a suite of offices including, that status symbol, a conference room. John MacDonald, my old pal from Air Berlin, had moved to Orlando and had started up Trans International, a subsidiary of Trans America. The airline had been shut down by the parent after a couple of years and he moved in with us as a senior associate. He brought some business with him which involved consulting work for Rich International, a Miami-based charter airline. We provided John with an office, telephone, staff, and equipment and he became an important member of our team. John is still with us and contributes famously with his skills and expertise, as well as with good advice on just about everything.

Larry Smith, whom I had enjoyed working with at Northeastern, also joined us. He was great to have around with a wealth of knowledge, particularly on regulatory matters. Unfortunately, about two years later, he decided to retire. I still use his legal briefcase which he had had since he was at Airlift—which dates me back to the Sixties every time I board an aircraft. I miss Larry.

Jorge Bedoya, a Paraguayan businessman who had been appointed CEO of Lineas Aereas Paraguayas (L.A.P.), hired us to look at the airline and make recommendations on restructuring. I enlisted my Caribbean associate, Ian Bertrand, to work on this project, which was a lot of fun. We spent a week in Asuncion, which was a new experience for Ian. We did some research into the kind of hub-and-spoke operation that made sense for L.A.P. The plan was to continue the long-haul U.S. route with small aircraft serving eight or nine points in the region. British Aerospace was involved with them at the time and proposed the BAE146, which worked very well. Our recommendations were never implemented because of political problems, although Jorge Bedoya and his Board of Directors were all for it. Unfortunately the Air Force wanted DC-10s to fly to Europe. The airline was finally sold to SAETA of Ecuador and most recently to Rolim Amaro's TAM of Brazil, and he is doing exactly what we had proposed, using Fokker 100s.

## The Privatization Years

During this period we worked for SH&E (Simat, Helliesen & Eichner), the New York-based aviation consultancy, as a subcontractor. They first hired us to work in Peru on the AeroPeru privatization, because it was during the Sendero Luminoso (Shining Path) years when car bombs were exploding in Miraflores and other smart, Lima residential districts. No one in the New York office wanted to go there. The assignment was to place a value on the airline in preparation for its privatization. I managed to convince SH&E's Don Garvett that it was safe to go and we spent a week or so at the airline's San Isidro headquarters, where I met a number of people I had worked with in the late 1970s. I learned a lot about valuing an airline. I think we said the airline was worth something like $30 million. Interestingly, when it was finally privatized, Gerardo de Prevoisin of Aeromexico paid $54 million for it. We also had some help from Federico Bloch of TACA who was interested, but felt that the asking price was much too high. But he helped to create the demand which might otherwise not have existed.

　　　We also worked with SH&E on the successful privatization of Ecuatoriana. We did this job together with Prudential Securities, and managed to sell the airline to the Brazilian airline VASP, and the jury is still out on how well the 'born-again' Ecuatoriana will turn out. VASP has re-introduced DC10-30 service to the United States, and also acquired control of Lloyd Aereo Boliviano, within months of the Ecuatoriana deal. We were not involved in the privatization of the Bolivian carrier even though we had earlier worked with SH&E in connection with its fleet planning and possible restructuring as a preliminary to its privatization. VASP reported a profit of $1.2 million at L.A.B. in 1996, the first time in history that the carrier has been in the black. The VASP strategy to build a South American consortium was now taking shape. It also acquired control of a small regional airline in Argentina, Transportes Aereos Neuquen.

　　　Earlier during this period, the U.S. Agency for International Development, (A.I.D.) called and I did some work in Nicaragua on the privatization of Aeronica which was sold to TACA. Andy Duarte of Linea Aeropostal Venezolana (LAV) hired me to help with the (eventually failed) attempt to privatize the airline. Andy was a successful businessman who had been appointed C.E.O. of LAV in order to privatize it. The airline was grounded in 1994 when the government decided to stop subsidizing it, and it was eventually sold for $20 million in 1996 to a private group. We were then hired by the Venezuelan owners to develop the business plan and find them a strategic partner.

Another interesting assignment, with Don Garvett, was for TAESA, the upstart Mexican airline which had taken advantage of Mexican liberalization of domestic aviation. Under the leadership of Captain Alberto Abed, a former pilot who was politically connected, it had grown from a small air taxi operation to become the third largest carrier in Mexico. We made a number of recommendations but I do not think the execution was very well done. As an aside, I have always felt that consultants are only as good as the final implementation of their recommendations and I still believe that consultants need to be involved in the final execution. TAESA almost failed after the two Mexican carriers, Aeromexico and Mexicana, were acquired by the banks and joined forces in early 1996. While in Mexico, we met an old friend, Rafael Montero, a Spaniard who had been the first manager of the Punta Carnero Hotel, the Braniff-sponsored Tourism Investments S.A. (TISA) investment company resort in Ecuador, and was now executive vice president for the airline in New York.

We also did some work for the Rodriguez Banda group from Arequipa, a Peruvian trucking conglomerate, which wanted to buy AeroPeru, after the valuation assignment was concluded. Unfortunately they were not serious and did not follow through and failed to pay our fees and some expenses.

## A Labour of Love

The 1993 Study of Functional Cooperation for nine Caribbean-based airlines was almost a labor of love. We did it in conjunction with Ian Bertrand, a really bright former C.E.O. of B.W.I.A. It identified some 35 cooperative actions that the airlines could take which would add some $60 million annually to the income statements of the nine carriers involved. The study was commissioned by the Caribbean Tourist Organization, but like many such projects, nothing has happened so far, except lip-service. At the time all the airlines involved were government-owned and the C.E.O.s had their own agendas, which did not include cooperation with each other.

## The First C.E.O. Conference

In 1993 Phil Bradley called me. Phil is a former Braniff captain who started Advanced Petroleum, an airline fueling company which he later sold to World

Fuel Services. He had an idea that we should organize an airline conference in Miami which would bring together the Latin American and Caribbean airline chief executives. Because of American Airlines' inroads in Miami and at the airport where they were taking over much of his aircraft fueling business, he felt that a conference with Latin American airline chief executives would make the point that American was not the only game in town.

Thus, more by accident than design, we started the International Airline C.E.O. Conferences. Phil wanted to hire us to organize it but his chairman balked at our quoted fee. By the time that Phil advised me of his Chairman's decision not to pay us to do it, I had approached a number of Latin American airline C.E.O.s who thought it was a great idea, so we went ahead and did it as a profit- generating affair. I called all my friends in the industry and enlisted enough sponsors to pay for breakfast, lunch, and dinners, and sundry other sponsored events so that we were not at risk.

John Casey was the Conference Chairman and he did a great job. We were able to corral a couple of dozen C.E.O.s and more than 200 paying delegates, so we made a small profit—again proving that 'no amount of planning replaces dumb luck.'

In 1998 we celebrated our sixth C.E.O. Conference and everyone who has attended any of them tell us it is the single most effective Latin American airline conference because of the level of executives that attend. Bob Crandall of American, Gerry Greenwald of United, and Gordon Bethune of Continental Airlines, have been keynote speakers. At the Bob Crandall speech we gave him a bullet-proof vest, a tongue-in-cheek admonition that some in the audience were not his staunchest friends. He took it very well and actually wore it for the media pictures which made the front page of the *Miami Herald* and several other papers. Crandall actually outlined his "Divide-and-Conquer" strategy (not his name) which involved alliances with selected carriers which would jointly dominate the markets. No one believed him at the time. They do now. Today, American Airlines has more than 70% of the U.S. flag market share between the U.S. and all of Latin America and more than 50% of the total. In fact, American Airlines is larger than Eastern Air Lines and Pan American were combined, serving more cities and more countries with more nonstop flights.

After John Casey died we turned to Bob Papkin, a partner of *Squire, Sanders & Dempsey,* the prestigious Washington aviation legal firm, who has become the C.E.O. Conference "Lifetime Chairman", while Ed Pinto, publisher of *Aviation Daily,* the most prestigious aviation newsletter in the business, is the breakfast 'opening speaker.' Jeffrey Shane, a former Deputy Secretary of Transportation, has been the final banquet speaker and wrapper-

*The CEO Panel at the 5th CEO Conference, April 1997. Left to right: Juan Maggio (Southern Winds, Argentina); Gilleas Fillatreault (BWIA); Juan Emilio Posada (ACES, Colombia); Fazel Khan (Guyana Airways); Frans Kramer (Santa Barbara Airlines, Venezuela); Federico Bloch (TACA).*

*(Top) Continental's Gordon Bethune tries his hand with the 'boleadoras' at a C.E.O. conference. (Right) Bob Crandall tries on his bullet-proof vest.*

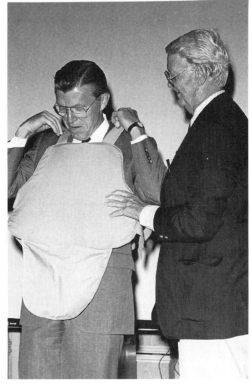

upper. All three of them do a terrific job and help to make the conferences truly memorable. We have now organized C.E.O. Conferences in Miami, Orlando and Santiago, Chile.

As a direct result of the first C.E.O. Conference, the then President of Avianca, Alvaro Jaramillo, called a meeting of a dozen Latin American C.E.O.s in Cartagena, Colombia, and decided that they needed to do something about AAdvantage, American's successful frequent flyer marketing tool. Alvaro represented a new breed of airline C.E.O., bright and willing to try a different approach. Unfortunately, he was replaced shortly afterwards. Someone in the group remembered the The Airline Club project and they assigned Federico Bloch to call us and we met in Miami at the airport. He said: "Look, Bobby, this is serious and we are determined to do something about it. I remember your pitch back in 1990. At the time none of use believed that we needed to do something, now we are all convinced."

Federico was one of the first to believe in the need for a cooperative approach and he provided considerable leadership and drive to make it happen.

## LatinPass

So we were hired to do the study, and we brought in SH&E and Bob Mann who had managed AAdvantage at American Airlines, Randy Petersen, the 'consumer-guru' of frequent flyers, and publisher of Inside Flyer, the prestigious monthly newsletter. In May 1994 we presented the study to the C.E.O.s of the 15 Latin American airlines which agreed to the formation of a multicarrier frequent flyer program and this became LatinPass. The group retained

David Hedley-Noble and his new advertising agency, Public Image Limited to create the distinctive logo and the launch advertising. The name LatinPass was proposed by

*Federico Bloch, the head of TACA, who assembled (or re-assembled) a group of Central American airlines into a cohesive consortium, and who came up with LatinPass as the name for a unique frequent flyer program.*

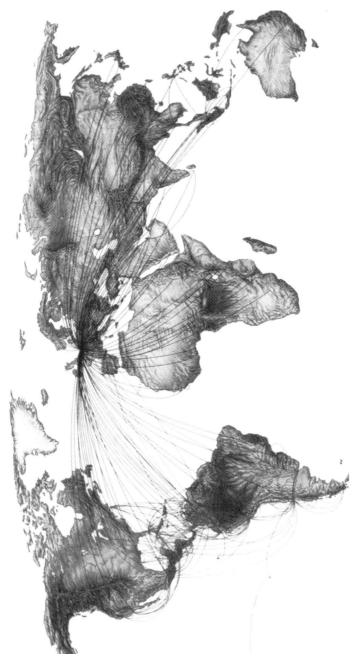

*Through membership of LatinPass, airline passengers can fly almost anywhere in the world, with considerable flexibility for constructing unusual itineraries to combinations of romantic places. And, at the same time, earn miles which they can redeem around the world*

*Sir Freddie Laker selects a LatinPass T-shirt.*

Federico Bloch. We did not particularly like the name and suggested that a survey should be conducted by Randy Peterson's Inside Flyer magazine, sug-gesting a variety of options, including LatinPass. Surprisingly to us, the majority voted for LatinPass, so we went ahead with it.

And then, to top it off, they hired us to manage the program. Aeromexico, one of the original supporters, offered to manage but the majority did not want another airline handling the database, preferring a neutral party without national affiliation. As a result, when we were hired, Aeromexico pulled out of the program but this only reduced the participation from 15 down to 14. LatinPass is possibly the single most ambitious inter-airline cooperative venture in Latin America or any other airline region in the world. The marketing potential is impressive. The 14 founding airlines operate almost 1,000 daily flights to 400 destinations in Latin America. It has been called "the world's most extensive frequent flyer program" by the media which is fascinated with the program and gives it far more coverage than it deserves. While LatinPass has not yet begun to match American's AAdvan-tage program, the dominant frequent-flyer program in the market, they have the ability to do so if they will work together.

Managing LatinPass allowed us to move to better quarters located on the second floor of a three-story building, only a few minutes from Miami Airport. This location also serves as the customer service center for Latin-Pass. Eduardo Gallardo became the Program Director and managed the oper-ation until early 1997 when he decided to take a one-year sailing sabbatical. Which led to our favorite line, "Call me on channel 16" (the sailor's way of saying I am going sailing). At that time my son Guy took over the position and has been doing a great job. By 1997 LatinPass had 1.4 million members, a number of non-airline corporate partners including but not limited to AT&T,

American Express, Diners Club, Hilton, Marriott, Avis, and two major airlines from outside Latin America, K.L.M., and US Airways.

On other fronts, I feel good about the work we have done in advising governments in the privatization of their national airlines, in helping some existing and new startup airlines. I also believe that we may have been instrumental, because of the work we did earlier in Brazil and Argentina, in the developing South American originating charter market, which I believe will develop in the next few years into a major activity, creating a second-level air transport system along the lines of the highly successful European charter market, which carries more than 50% of the European originating passenger traffic.

Our ongoing five year annual Traffic Forecast has also given us a lot of exposure and it is picked up and used by a number of international organizations, including I.A.T.A. and the U.S. Federal Aviation Administration, which has invited us to speak at their annual forecast conferences.

In 1993, our efforts with Ian Bertrand, to convince the carriers domiciled in the Caribbean to work together may be about to pay off some dividends. Recently Butch Stewart of Air Jamaica, Gilles Filliatreault of BWIA, and other CEOs in the region have made noises about implementing some of our recommendations. But I am not holding my breath. Butch is one of the more fascinating entrepreneurs in the Caribbean. He has built a major hotel and resort presence not only in his native Jamaica but also elsewhere in the Caribbean, and is bringing fresh thinking into the airline business as a result of having acquired control of the Jamaican airline in 1995.

## The Harder I Work, the Luckier I Am

As a result of the newsletter, the CEO Conferences and our reputation as the single aviation consultancy which specializes in Latin American and Caribbean aviation, we receive considerable credit, some of which may have been earned, some of it because when we started out, we were the 'only game in town' and a sort of voice in the wilderness, and some of it by sheer 'dumb luck.' We also receive a lot of media coverage and are probably the most often quoted consultancy on the subject of airlines in Latin America.

I shall tell you one secret: I return telephone calls. This is something Latin American airline executives seldom do, so I end up receiving calls from *The Wall Street Journal*, and other business publications which would otherwise be answered by an airline. But do not tell anyone because it is free publicity for the company and I love doing it. I am also reasonably good at the single 'sound byte' line which is often quoted. Jokingly, some people have accused me of being the Simon Bolivar of Latin American and Caribbean aviation. I accept this as a great—if totally uncalled for—compliment. After all, he is one chap I would like to have known, personally. We both like the same things, to ride, drink, and party; and we share a passion for independence.

## Just the Beginning

The rest is, more or less, more of the same. We get up every morning and go to work and have more fun with our clothes on than seems politically correct. Between 1988 and 1997 we managed to build a real business undertaking, with more than 150 assignments of one kind or another, always related to aviation in Latin America and the Caribbean. This is something that I really never imagined could happen when I started out in 1987. I started the business in self defense because I had nothing better to do. And this is just the beginning.

The hero of "The Other U.S.A.", the novel which I still want to write, started and ran his own airline and thereby managed to inspire the political union of South America. I like to think that, in a small way, I have done a little bit of the same, but not quite. In the mid-1960s we created SATO, the South American Tourism Organization. This was 30 years ahead of its time, was a great idea, and succeeded for a short while in generating considerable interest in the entire region as a tourist destination. During my Braniff years I was involved in some very exciting events, such as the development of El Clan Braniff and a number of tourism projects which were highly successful and placed Braniff on the map in more ways than one.

I am gratified about some other projects, such as, with Eduardo Gallardo, convincing 15 Latin American airlines that they can work together and form the first multi-carrier frequent flyer program, LatinPass. I have been the mentor (of sorts) to a bunch of bright young chaps who are doing well in a number of separate situations, most of them in the airline business. I also feel the CEO Conferences have served a useful purpose, even though the potential is still barely scratched for the airlines in the region to work together.

In 1998, at the 6th International Airline CEO Conference in Orlando, we announced a strategic alliance with SH&E, the world's largest airline consultancy (see page 178) to be known as Avman–SH&E, the alliance will concentrate on Latin American aviation consulting and should give Avman a real boost. The best is yet to come.

I have tasted some measure of success and the power that goes with it, particularly as a senior corporate officer. It was satisfying and rewarding, financially and otherwise, but I always felt that being in business for myself was better. I have also had my share of failure. While that was not much fun at the time, it gave me a certain measure of strength to face the future and I believe that you learn a lot more from failure in business than the alternative. It is also useful to know, in retrospect, that you can fail, and yet recover and pick yourself up by the bootstraps. It also helps to find out who your friends are.

For you, the reader, who have stayed with this book thus far (assuming you are not one of those people who read mystery books from back to front) and in appreciation for your interest, I offer a few thoughts which might be of value in your career, whether you are self-employed or working for a corporation.

**First**—someone once told me and I've lived by that rule—"it is always darkest just before the dawn." The line has helped me weather some of the worst storms, including a live experience on *Gilead*, when Guy and I missed Bimini in the Bahamas late at night and finally navigated the difficult channel just before dawn to a safe harbor. We were out of beer and the thought of turning around and heading for Dinner Key (ten hours of sailing) without a beer on board gave us the required incentive. And the early light was just barely enough so that we could line up the little white house with the big palm tree and make the entrance to safe harbor. I did not fancy ending up on the reef just outside Bimini.

**Second**, be creative. I used to give sales people this pitch, think 'sideways.' If at first you can not get in the door to make a sale, find another way. One good approach is the third party endorsement. I learned how to exploit this through the media, thanks to Mac Seligman, probably the best p.r. (public relations—although he likes to call it "corporate communications") practitioner in the business. If you give the media a reason—and sometimes provide them with a few key words or phrases—to quote you, or your product or service, it is amazing the doors it will open. I have practiced creativity, that is to say, having an idea and working my fanny off to put it into effect, with a vengeance. Our Aviation-Latin America & Caribbean newsletter is a great example. This was Claudia's idea. When Pratt & Whitney canceled the need for our Faxnews, she turned an adversity into a positive. I think the success of the newsletter, after the creative idea, is that I write about what I love and know something about, Aviation and Latin America and the Caribbean, and I suspect it comes through. And we were the only one around for a long time so we have created a niche for the publication. In fact, for a while we had a virtual monopoly. Not a bad thing to have. The other example of creativity, I believe, is the CEO Conferences, now going in their sixth year in 1998.

**Third**, I am convinced that management is more art than science. It takes intuition, gut feel, and above all, a healthy respect for people. So much so that in my unpublished attempt at fiction, my hero started something he called "MAD", which stands for Management Arts Development, a management development program based on bringing the best out in people, an amalgam of the learning's from B.F. Skinner's Positive Reinforcement, Dalila Platero's workshops, and just plain common sense.

**Last,** "success is 5% planning and strategy, 95% execution", a variation on the old adage: "genius is one percent inspiration, 99% perspiration." Which is right back to "The harder you work, the luckier you get."

I have been extremely lucky. When we started Aviation Management Services no one was remotely interested in Latin American aviation. But things happened at the end of the 1980s and suddenly it is the hottest airline market in the world. And we were already there. I should mention Bob Crandall and American Airlines, because they became the focus for Latin American and Caribbean aviation as they expanded the airline from its 1990 take-over of Eastern Airline's Latin American routes. American is the driving force in the region, with a strategy (that we coined Divide and Conquer) which involves establishing AAlliances with a whole series of airlines. This has given it tremendous visibility and (assuming these are approved by the U.S. Department of Transportation over the objections of every other U.S. carrier) will consolidate its already dominant position in the area.

Paradoxically, without Bob Crandall and American Airlines we would not have been successful with the CEO Conferences nor with LatinPass. So thank you, Bob Crandall; who probably heads up the most finely-honed group of airline executives in the world. One of the effects of American's alliance strategy is going to be an expanding Open Skies throughout the region. This may hurt those airlines who are not prepared to compete in a deregulated environment, but it will eventually be healthy for the industry on the whole, for the individual countries, and for the consumer.

The entire Latin American region is experiencing an economic revolution. Net private capital inflows have exceeded $300 billion since 1991. While 1995 was a glitch, because of the Tequila Effect from the 1994 Mexican Peso devaluation-debacle, a record $78 billion flowed into the region in 1996. So I am optimistic about the future. Which is not new.

I believe that business is driving politics and also driving the whole idea of integration throughout the region. If I live long enough, I may yet see a political union, not necessarily Bolivar's dream of a Federation of American States, but at least a private sector-driven unity. The Europeans are already half-way there with common passports, absence of visas and customs barriers, and soon to have a common currency.

I am personally convinced that, after a century-long process of political experiment with military dictatorships, populism, socialism, even communism, in varying degrees, Latin America has finally found the right approach as it begins to embrace the free-market system. As my friend Jose Carlos Martinelli says, "It is up to the private sector to decide the structure and organization that it needs to be successful. And the governments will follow." Young people throughout Latin America are entrepreneurial and are spreading their wings and practicing what they themselves preach.

Family and friendship are by far the greatest riches. And I have been blessed with great riches in both categories: my wife, Martha; children, Valerie, Robbie, and Guy; not forgetting Patty, Fiorella, and Claudia; and, of course the four of you, Shawnpaul, Vanessa, Nana, and Gandi. And my brother Ronald's Jenny and Michael. For all of you, I hope you can find life to be as much fun as I do.

If I have one single message, it is that the glass is always half full, not half empty. Optimism will always triumph over pessimism. In essence I have truly had a fabulous life and enjoyed almost every bit of it. What goes around comes around.

# *Acknowledgments*

This book would not have been possible without tremendous support, help, advice and counsel from a number of people, too many to list here. But I cannot avoid mentioning some key individuals, without whom neither the book nor I would have made it to this point.

Martha, my wife of 45 years has naturally played a major role. Without her staunch support throughout, I just would not have survived. She has always been there, during good times and bad. And I want to acknowledge this publicly, as I rarely have privately—strange how some of us extroverts are introspective in other ways. My mother and father who somehow managed to give me some of my better qualities. The other ones (the bad ones) I suspect I picked up entirely on my own. Unfortunately, even they could not work miracles. But I have missed both of them tremendously.

John Casey, my boss at Braniff and a great friend afterwards, especially when such friendship counted all the more, was an example and a model in so many ways. I have missed him sorely during these last few years. Rex Brack, my long-time mentor at Braniff, was a terrific influence throughout my career, as was my brother Ronald, who passed away much too young. We never spent as much time together as we should have. But he was always available when I needed him. Others who stepped in and helped out financially and with friendship and support, include (but are not the only ones): in Argentina, Horacio Mazza and his partner, Eduardo Cermesoni; in Peru, Gianmarco Nizzola, Juan Pardo, Eddie Arrarte; in Colombia, Juan Ucros; in Uruguay, "Gordo" Buencristiano; in the U.S., John Phillippe, Dick Haberly, Bill Spohrer, Captain Phil Bradley, George Batchelor and a host of others. John MacDonald, who has worked with us for the past five or six years, has been a staunch friend and great associate.

Others who have given generously of their time to advise on this book are R.E.G.Davies, my publisher, and his associate copy-editor Jackie Scott-Mandeville. Ron and Jackie are responsible for whatever decent writing there may be, but not for the alternative. Without their support and enthusiasm this book would not have happened. Jim Woodman, Luis Zalamea, and Mac Seligman, all of them professional writers, were generous in their praise, and gave inspired suggestions for improving on what would otherwise be even less readable. All three of them can write a whole lot better than I can and you, the reader, would probably have been better served if I had merely told them the story and had them write it. But then it would not be my story that I so badly wanted to write. They at least are not responsible for the book's short-comings. So many others have contributed but space just will not permit mentioning them all.

Finally, without Martha having put up with me for the past 45 years, and Valerie, Robbie, and Guy, their 'better halves,' and the grandchildren, the book would never have been written. So thank you all. Claudia and Guy deserve special mention because they have been pillars of strength at Aviation Management Services and I don't know how I could have made it without them.

# Index